## Praise for *The Open-Air Life*

"Whatever you do, get outside! It's time to reclaim our mind-body health, as well as the lives of our children, from the indoor grind of always-on tech and brain-scattering media. Linda Åkeson McGurk's gentle but inspiring approach rekindles our faith in the outdoors, whether we're just sleeping on our own porch or taking a long hike in the woods. With her useful everyday tips, we're reminded how easy it can be to reconnect ourselves and our families to the instant and deep benefits of nature."

—ANU PARTANEN,
AUTHOR OF *THE NORDIC THEORY OF EVERYTHING*

"In *The Open-Air Life*, Linda Åkeson McGurk takes us on a fascinating journey to explore how nature can enhance our lives. While some of the general concepts are familiar, she adds a unique perspective by introducing us to terminology and customs rooted in strong tradition from her native country, Sweden, and the surrounding Nordic countries. Through poetic storytelling, helpful checklists, and informative illustrations sprinkled throughout the book, she educates and inspires us to step outdoors into the fresh air and bring a number of nature-connection habits into our daily lives no matter where we live, our age, or what language we use to describe them."

—SANDI SCHWARTZ,
AUTHOR OF *FINDING ECOHAPPINESS*

"Discover the Nordic secret to unplugging and connecting more deeply with nature: friluftsliv. I highly recommend *The Open-Air Life* to nature lovers everywhere."

—DR. QING LI, PROFESSOR, NIPPON MEDICAL SCHOOL,
AND AUTHOR OF *FOREST BATHING*

"Linda McGurk has given us a fine guide to caring for our true nature by connecting to the rest of nature. My hat's off (but soon to be back on, as I'm going for a hike)."

—RICHARD LOUV,
AUTHOR OF *VITAMIN N* AND *LAST CHILD IN THE WOODS*

"Reading the prose of Linda Åkeson McGurk is always a reminder to be intentional about connecting with what I know deep in my bones: that going outside is going home. *The Open-Air Life* is an invitation to claim a way of being in the world that deems time outside as essential as breathing or drinking clean water. Full of practical tips and inspiring stories, this book is an essential guide for anyone who wants to further embrace life in the open air."

—HEIDI BARR,
AUTHOR OF *COLLISIONS OF EARTH AND SKY*
AND COAUTHOR OF *12 TINY THINGS*

# THE
# Open-Air
# Life

A TARCHERPERIGEE BOOK

# THE
# Open-Air
# Life

Discover *the* Nordic Art *of* Friluftsliv
*and* Embrace Nature Every Day

## LINDA ÅKESON McGURK

*Illustrations by Heather Dent*

**tarcher**perigee

AN IMPRINT OF PENGUIN RANDOM HOUSE LLC
PENGUINRANDOMHOUSE.COM

Most TarcherPerigee books are available at special quantity discounts for bulk purchase for sales promotions, premiums, fund-raising, and educational needs. Special books or book excerpts also can be created to fit specific needs. For details, write: SpecialMarkets@penguinrandomhouse.com.

Library of Congress Cataloging-in-Publication Data
Names: McGurk, Linda Åkeson, author.
Title: The open-air life: discover the Nordic art of friluftsliv and embrace nature every day / Linda Åkeson McGurk; illustrations by Heather Dent.
Description: New York: TarcherPerigee, [2022]
Identifiers: LCCN 2022020346 (print) | LCCN 2022020347 (ebook) | ISBN 9780593420942 (hardcover) | ISBN 9780593420959 (epub)
Subjects: LCSH: Outdoor recreation—Social aspects—Scandinavia. | Nature—Social aspects—Scandinavia. | Lifestyles—Scandinavia. | Scandinavia—Social life and customs.
Classification: LCC GV191.48.S34 M34 2022 (print) | LCC GV191.48.S34 (ebook) | DDC 796.50948—dc23/eng/20220810
LC record available at https://lccn.loc.gov/2022020346
LC ebook record available at https://lccn.loc.gov/2022020347

Printed in the United States of America
1st Printing

Book design by Lorie Pagnozzi

Outdoor recreational activities are by their very nature potentially hazardous. All participants in such activities must assume the responsibility for their own actions and safety. If you have any health problems or medical conditions, consult with your physician before undertaking any outdoor activities. The information contained in this guidebook cannot replace sound judgment and good decision making, which can help reduce risk exposure, nor does the scope of this book allow for disclosure of all the potential hazards and risks involved in such activities. Learn as much as possible about the outdoor recreational activities in which you participate, prepare for the unexpected, and be cautious. The reward will be a safer and more enjoyable experience.

MOTHER NATURE, THIS ONE IS FOR YOU.

# CONTENTS

In the lonely seter-corner,


My abundant catch I take.


There's a hearth, and a table,


And friluftsliv for my thoughts.


—HENRIK IBSEN

# —INTRODUCTION—

ON ANY GIVEN WORKDAY, I spend most of my time sitting at a desk, in front of a screen, while my phone and email notifications are constantly poking me for attention. I have about fifty-six different website tabs and seventeen Word files open on my laptop while simultaneously fighting Wi-Fi issues and at least a couple of software installations gone wrong. Subconsciously my brain is also processing an incessant flow of mental clutter, from remembering to schedule dental appointments for my daughters to planning what we are going to have for dinner and wondering if I really emptied that load of laundry that I ran two days ago. By the time I wrap up work and the girls come back from school in the afternoon, I often feel like I'm spent, finished, deep-fried.

I know I'm not alone. In fact, this is the reality for many of us. We do our best to balance the demands of family life, work, and other commitments, but many of us do it in an environment that researchers have found is inherently bad for our mental and physical health—indoors, plugged into our various electronic devices, and with little daily contact with nature. For lack of a better word, an increasing number of us are what neurophysiologist and educator Carla Hannaford has dubbed "SOSOH"—stressed-out, survival-oriented humans.

Almost 80 percent of the population in the developed world lives in urban areas today, due to a mass migration to the cities that essentially started less than two hundred years ago. That makes our human experience radically different from that of our distant ancestors on the savanna, and even distinctly different from the lives our rural ancestors lived as recently as a few generations ago. But humans have evolved in nature for millennia, and even though we might like to think otherwise, our bodies and brains haven't changed that much since we lived in caves. We even have internal biological clocks that synchronize with the rhythms of nature, functions that are suppressed by our modern lifestyle. Neither urbanization nor digitalization is likely to go away, so what's a frazzled modern human being to do?

Enter the Nordic concept of *friluftsliv*. This garbled collection of syllables with Norwegian roots (roughly pronounced FREE-loofts-leeve) has been translated as "open-air life," "free-air life," and "fresh-air life," but unlike the equally tongue-twisting concept of *hygge* ("cozy" or "comfortable" in English), few people outside northern Europe seem to know what it means. And actually, not even people from the Nordic countries can agree on an exact definition. The Norwegian government defines *friluftsliv* as embracing nature and enjoying the outdoors as a way of life, a "possibility of recreation, rejuvenation and restoring balance among living things."

The Swedish Environmental Protection Agency contends that it's about "spending time outside in natural and cultural landscapes for personal wellness and to experience nature without pressure to achieve or compete." Swedish American authors and outdoor enthusiasts Roger and Sarah Isberg define it as "simple life," whereas others have described it as living in harmony with nature. Personally, I think of friluftsliv as a way of returning to our true home.

Friluftsliv, or open-air life, is where humans and nature intersect and the values that we create in those meetings. Simply put, it's a way to nurture a personal relationship with nature through direct experiences. How you do it is up to you. Friluftsliv can be as simple as an evening walk around the neighborhood or as advanced as a multiday backpacking expedition in the remote wilderness, or anything in between. It can be enjoyed solo, with a group of family or friends, or together with others through an outdoor organization. It's about knowing nature, yet it has no curriculum or classroom. Learning comes through hands-on practice and the passing of knowledge and useful skills from peer to peer and from one generation to the next. Although it sometimes involves gear, it doesn't require it.

Friluftsliv is a form of outdoor recreation, but not all types of outdoor recreation are considered friluftsliv, at least not in the traditional sense. While outdoor recreation could be any activity that is done outside for fun, including outdoor sports and motorized activities, friluftsliv is noncompetitive and nonmotorized. By those standards, foraging for wild berries, paddling a kayak, and watching birds are all different forms of friluftsliv, while snowmobiling, waterskiing, and running a 10K are not, even though they all take place outside. By the same token, friluftsliv is not the same thing as the Japanese practice of forest bathing, or *shinrin-yoku*, although both recognize and harness the restorative power of nature. While shinrin-yoku is a form of nature therapy and mindfulness practice centered on the medicinal benefits of spending time among trees, friluftsliv is a broader philosophical lifestyle that spans nature, culture, history, and personal and environmental health.

In essence, traditional friluftsliv is less a set of activities and more of a culturally learned rhythm that revolves around being outside and experiencing oneness with both nature and the cultural landscape. Just like there is slow food, slow parenting, and slow entertainment, friluftsliv is a form of slow nature. It's about embracing simplicity, resisting consumerism, and living in a way that is sustainable to both ourselves and the planet. It's the kind of life that transcends generations and connects us deeply with the land that sustains us. And it is in every respect a rich life.

When I was growing up in Sweden, friluftsliv was more or less consciously passed down to me from the adults in my life—grandparents, parents, early childhood educators, teachers and other caregivers. When I was little, they made sure I got to play outside every day, rain or shine. They taught me the names of our local plants and wildlife and passed down old stories and legends that made the forests come alive with magic. They gave me the time and space to wade in shallow creeks looking for frog spawn and fill my pockets with rocks and other special treasures. They let me nurture my sense of wonder while observing the frenzied activity of an anthill and trying to grasp the concept of infinity while gazing up at the Milky Way. Thanks to them and the culture I grew up in, the outdoors was the constant backdrop against which my childhood played out.

By the time I became a teenager, my relationship with nature changed. The woods were no longer a place for play, but somewhere my friends and I would test the boundaries for our burgeoning independence and discover ourselves. At that point, we were not in it so much for the nature experiences as for the opportunity to withdraw from the pressures of school and the prying eyes of our parents. I don't think I realized it back then, but friluftsliv was the one constant that I was always able to fall back on, a comforting routine for self-care and my antidote to stress and anxiety. And it still is.

When you are raised in a friluftsliv culture, you will forever have a little voice inside your head that cajoles you into going outside every day. I'm no exception, but interestingly enough, I became even more committed to the lifestyle after I moved to Indiana and gave birth to my two daughters, Maya and Nora. It was as if an age-old parental instinct to pass on not just my genes but also my fondness for going on rainy-day walks and making bread over the open fire suddenly kicked in and I realized that I had only a short window of opportunity to pass down the ways of my forebears to my children. If I didn't show them the way, nobody else would, and I was afraid the open-air lifestyle would be forever lost to them. Although I was neither an expert naturalist nor a hard-core adventurer dreaming of bagging big peaks, I decided to make friluftsliv the guiding light of my parenting journey. By letting my daughters whittle sticks, sleep under the stars, and build campfires, I have attempted to anchor them to a beyond-human world that is much greater than themselves. Over the years, I've seen their confidence and self-reliance grow, and no matter where in the world they will choose to live when they grow up, I know that the natural world is one they will always feel comfortable in. I like to think of friluftsliv as their secret superpower, one that will give them equal parts strength, happiness, solace, and purpose as they journey through life and love.

As my daughters grew older, my yearning to share the land of my ancestors with them grew stronger, and in 2016 I brought them to Sweden for nearly six months while researching my first book, *There's No Such Thing as Bad Weather*. After living somewhere else for most of my adult life, I saw my homeland with new eyes, and it dawned on me how much I had missed the open-air culture of my youth. Two years later, after a lot of soul-searching, we moved to Sweden permanently, and I embraced friluftsliv with greater fervor than ever. As soon as there was snow on the ground, I brought out the antique cross-country skis that my parents had given me for Christmas the year I turned sixteen, and put in more miles in the tracks that winter than I had in the twenty-five years prior. I greeted the spring by reacquainting myself with the local bird population and taking my daughters to a famous crane-dancing locale. I spent part of the summer soaking up the midnight sun in the Arctic north and savored the fall by hiking through moist evergreen forests, making pine needle tea, and scouting for edible mushrooms.

Nature also became my saving grace when my personal life slowly began to fall apart. The year after I returned to Sweden, I went through a divorce while at the same time bordering on exhaustion from a toxic work situation. While trying to navigate my new life as a single mom, I often sauntered around among the firs and the beeches near my home, with no particular goal or agenda. Under the tree crowns, it seemed like my mental burden lifted and I found space to breathe, think, and heal. I even walked when I saw my therapist, an avid hiker and outdoorswoman. Opening up about myself and my failed marriage came easy under the open skies, and we walked and talked mile after mile on tiny, rocky trails and dusty country roads.

Realigning myself with my native culture made me realize that while friluftsliv is a Nordic concept, it holds the potential to benefit all of us, regardless of your culture, religion, ethnicity, or socioeconomic background. Sure, the Nordic countries have some unique circumstances that make them an ideal region for friluftsliv. For one thing, natural areas are abundant, even in big cities. For another, a unique customary law called *allemansrätten* in Swedish (which literally translates to "every man's right" but is usually called "the right to roam") gives everybody in Norway, Sweden, and Finland more or less universal access to the land, whether it is publicly or privately owned. Moreover, friluftsliv enjoys strong cultural and political support, ensuring that the tradition not only lives on, but thrives. Having said that, friluftsliv is more about your mindset and less about a certain location or a specific activity. It's a calling that can be followed just about anywhere with some green space and a willingness to seek oneness with nature. This book will tell you how. So turn off your phone, forget about the busywork, and do as the Nordic people do—just step outside.

IF YOU'RE AT ALL FAMILIAR with Nordic culture, you may have heard the notion that the people of the North have an innate, almost mythical bond with nature, bestowed upon them by their ancestors hundreds, if not thousands, of years ago. The harsh beauty of the vast unpopulated wilderness areas and the stark contrast between the dark fold of the polar nights in the winter and the perpetual pink glow of the midnight sun in the summer provide the perfect backdrop for this Nordic self-image of a people closely connected with nature. Norse mythology abounds with gods and goddesses that embody the wind, the woods, the rain, the seasons, and the fertility of the soil, which goes to show that nature had a keenly felt presence in people's lives, not only because it sustained them with firewood, food, medicine, and other essentials, but also because it bridged their earthly existence to the spiritual world. (True to the Nordic people's penchant for winter sports, there was even a goddess for skiing and snowshoeing—Skaði.) The ancient mountains, glowing skies, and silent forests of the North have also inspired countless legends and folklore tied to the natural world, and at least part of the traditional right to roam is believed to go back to medieval times.

Even so, the idea of consciously using nature for rest and recreation in the way we today call friluftsliv is less than two hundred years old and was indirectly a consequence of the Age of Enlightenment, when the leading philosopher of the time, René Descartes, famously claimed, "Man is ruler and owner of nature." Descartes's worldview paved the way for the Industrial Revolution, which would forever change people's relationship with nature and started the downward spiral of environmental degradation that we are still living with today. The urbanization that followed alienated people from the woods, the mountains, and the farm fields that had sustained them for millennia. Like all big movements, industrialism triggered a countermovement, Romanticism. The devotees of Romanticism, typically found among artists and intellectuals in the upper echelons of society, glorified nature and saw it as the ultimate source of spiritual rejuvenation. The only problem was that these wealthy people had no natural connection to the land—they were not hunters, fishermen, or farmers—so they had to create one. They did it by escaping the cities to relax and explore nature in the countryside, where they laid the foundation of what later would be known as friluftsliv.

Later, in the 1930s, when the working class got more disposable income and time off, they, too, joined the waves of mostly wealthy men from the cities who up until then had flocked to the ocean, the mountains, the forests, and the open pastures. Maybe the blue-collar workers, just like their wealthier fellow countrymen, felt an inner craving for fresh air, relaxation, and mental restoration. But they were also the target for a deliberate government campaign to implement friluftsliv among the broad population. In 1919, the Swedish government, like the governments of many other European countries, finally responded to long-standing demands of labor unions by adopting a new law that limited the workweek to forty-eight hours, and the politicians were deeply concerned that the workers would spend all this newly granted free time the "wrong" way. What if they were consumed by junk culture and resorted to dubious activities like dancing and drinking? Or worse, simply languished when they had nothing useful with which to fill their time? Friluftsliv was cast as the antidote that would keep the country's working class physically active and healthy. The military, too, had a vested interest in a strong and healthy population that could defend the nation against threats, and it saw friluftsliv as a means to this end.

The socialization into a physically active, nature-connected lifestyle started in childhood, as friluftsliv was introduced as a mandatory part of PE classes. By the end of the 1930s, the term "free time" had essentially become synonymous with friluftsliv, and new green spaces, city parks, and nature preserves were created to accommodate the new pastime. With that, the government did with friluftsliv what IKEA later would do with upscale furniture design: democratized it by making it available to everybody.

The word *friluftsliv* was coined not by the Swedish government, however, but by famed Norwegian playwright and poet Henrik Ibsen, who first used it in his poem "On the Heights" in 1859, at a time when he struggled with depression. The poem depicts a farmer's son who is at a crossroads, trying to decide whether to take over the family farm in the village, which is what is expected of him, or to follow his inner voice and lead a life as a free hunter in the highlands. The protagonist sets out on a transformative one-year trek through the mountains and eventually chooses the freedom of the wild over the stable life as a farmer in the village, which he comes to view as a prison, both for humans and animals. Scholars believe the poem reflected Ibsen's own longing for nature and a problem-free life in the mountains, where he felt liberated from society's norms and the expectations of others. He summed up his feelings in the word *friluftsliv*—a compound of the Norwegian and Swedish words for "free," "air," and "life."

The meaning of friluftsliv has evolved since Ibsen's days and will likely continue to change as the lifestyle gains more followers. Historically speaking, open-air life was strictly associated with activities that people engaged in during their free time. Today the lines are more blurred. In the Nordic countries, friluftsliv has made its way into the preschool curriculum and workplace team-building events, as well as paved the way for various forms of nature therapy and countless new professions within the realm of ecotourism. Also, in the past decades, traditional friluftsliv activities like hiking, cross-country skiing, and bushcraft have been joined by a slew of niche outdoor pursuits like forest yoga, nature parkour, forest bathing, and gourmet campfire cooking. Simultaneously, a more sports-inspired and gear-heavy faction of friluftsliv has emerged, focusing more on individual adventures through activities like rock climbing, mountain biking, and trail running.

If you search the one million plus friluftsliv tags on Instagram, you will inevitably find droves of stunning images of lone hikers standing on cliffs overlooking the magnificent Norwegian fjords, waking up in tents amid spectacular sunrises in the mountains, or being dazzled by the otherworldly northern lights of Swedish Lapland (known by the native Sami population as Sápmi). But living an open-air life is far more profound and all-encompassing than taking the perfect selfie by an iconic destination. It's the pleasure of going for a brisk walk right before the storm, feeling the sun on your forehead on a chilly spring day, and making food over an open fire in the company of good friends. It's the joy of devouring a fistful of plump berries straight from the plant and the excitement over making the first snow angels of the season—the down-to-earth, everyday outdoor moments that may or may not make it into our social media feeds.

This book will focus on the traditional or novel forms of friluftsliv that align with its original slow nature ethos. It is for those who long to get away from the noise, stress, crowds, pollution, must-haves and must-dos, and—more recently—the incessant pinging of our smartphones. Those who strive to live simpler, more sustainable lives, deeply connected with nature.

Scholars sometimes debate whether a concept that is so closely associated with the landscape, traditions, and culture of the Nordic countries can be applied in a relevant way somewhere else. I say it's needed in the world now more than ever. The ideas behind friluftsliv are universal and timeless, even though the expression of the practice may change over time or be adapted to fit the local culture. Across the world, our lives have become increasingly removed from nature, and we lead lives that are not sustainable, neither for our own health nor for the planet. Open-air life could be our ticket to change. Or as Nils Faarlund, a Norwegian mountaineer and prominent friluftsliv guide, put it, "Our present culture is on a collision course with nature. *Friluftsliv* is one of a number of ways that could help us avoid this collision. It's a way of bringing us back to a contact with what we have already lost."

Through friluftsliv we seek to connect with something that is real and pure, the ways of our ancestors, and our most basic survival instincts. In nature, we can peel away the demands of modern life and simply focus on existing. With this simplicity comes freedom.

# THE TEN CORE PRINCIPLES
## OF FRILUFTSLIV

## 1. BE ONE WITH NATURE.

Friluftsliv stems from the notion that nature is the true home of humans, and that the natural world is for us to carefully maintain, not to exploit and destroy. By nurturing our connection with the natural and cultural landscape, we experience a spiritual oneness with the world around us and understand that what we do to the environment we ultimately do to ourselves.

## 3. USE YOUR BODY.

Friluftsliv is about feeling pleasure and contentment from using your body in the natural and cultural landscape, alone or with others. While not all open-air activities are strenuous, challenging yourself physically outside is considered key to maintaining good health, developing resilience, and achieving a harmonious state of mind. Plus, it makes the reward of resting all the sweeter.

## 2. DON'T MIND THE WEATHER (OR THE SEASON).

The open-air lifestyle challenges us to be active outdoors in all types of weather. By living life the friluftsliv way, you align yourself with the cyclical changes of the Earth rather than the linear calendar and celebrate the positives of all the seasons. Once you make getting outside a part of your daily rhythm, the seasonal changes will become an inseparable part of your inner fabric.

## 4. APPRECIATE YOUR NEARBY NATURE.

Getting a change of scenery is an important aspect of friluftsliv, but you don't have to venture deep into the wilderness to achieve a nature-connected lifestyle. Being active outside in your local community every day will help you develop a sense of place and has a much greater impact on your health than going to a wilderness area once every year. Minimizing travel also aligns with the environmental ethos of friluftsliv.

essary to protect you against inclement weather, but keeping a garage full of state-of-the-art equipment is not a requirement for friluftsliv and won't necessarily bring you closer to nature.

## 5. LEARN USEFUL SKILLS.

You don't need to be able to tie twenty-five different knots or light a fire using flint stones to fully enjoy friluftsliv. Just have a genuine curiosity about the natural world and a desire to learn useful skills through hands-on experience. Open-air life gives you an opportunity to grow confidence through greater self-reliance but also get a deeper knowledge of yourself and your role in the beyond-human world.

## 7. DO NOT COMPETE.

Open-air life is a chance for you to challenge yourself to get out of your comfort zone and experience nature in new ways, but it's not a race. The minute you introduce competition into the equation, you're shifting the focus away from your experience in the natural world, thereby changing the character of your interactions with it and losing the undemanding qualities of friluftsliv that make it so beneficial.

## 6. KEEP IT SIMPLE

Simplicity and frugality are part of the purpose of open-air life, so try to resist the temptation of over-consuming outdoor gear. Having some basic outdoor clothes and knowing how to layer them is nec-

you immerse yourself in the landscape and learn how to navigate it firsthand, whereas motorized vehicles tend to disturb wildlife and put a barrier between you and nature.

## 8. DISCONNECT TO CONNECT.

In a society that idolizes having a packed schedule and always being online and available, friluftsliv is an invitation to turn off the distractions and just be grounded in the present moment. By putting away the electronic devices and activating all our senses outside, we take the edge off the prevailing stress-inducing culture and allow ourselves to tune into nature, ourselves, and our loved ones.

## 10. NURTURE YOUR SENSE OF WONDER.

Traditional friluftsliv is about finding joy in everyday nature experiences rather than chasing temporary adrenaline rushes from extreme activities that may harm the environment. It hones your ability to feel awed by bringing out your inner child and letting you see the world through their eyes. When you feel contentment and peace from looking up at the night sky or into the glowing embers of a campfire, you know you're home.

## 9. PROPEL YOURSELF.

Getting to a nature area sometimes requires motorized transportation, but friluftsliv doesn't start until the engine is turned off. By walking, biking, skiing, skating, paddling, pedaling, swimming, or propelling yourself by other means,

# PART I

*In nature there is peace and quiet,*

*where the air is clean and*

*where fresh winds blow that can cool you down*

*and chase away tiring thoughts.*

—BOKEN OM *FRILUFTSLIF* (THE BOOK OF FRILUFTSLIV)

Of all the things we need to stay alive, air is the one we can't manage without for the shortest time. It's also the only element privileged enough to be a part of the name *friluftsliv*, or "open-air life." No surprise there, since fresh air was a prized commodity in the cities during the heyday of industrialization, when there was little control of pollution and the streets often lay heavy with smoke. Fresh air, along with rest and nourishing food, was also a common way to fight diseases like tuberculosis and the Spanish flu, at a time when medicines and doctors were scarce.

The longing for fresh air was real and people found it in the forest, by the ocean, and among quaint country pastures. But the open-air life was more than breathing in a specific mixture of oxygen, nitrogen, and other gases; it became a symbol of a lifestyle that used to be, one connected with nature, unlike the unnatural, noisy, and dirty indoor environment associated with the factories and life in the cities.

Today, pollution control has made for cleaner cities, and medical interventions have greatly improved our chances of surviving disease, but in the Nordic countries, fresh air remains a symbol of freedom, slow living, and good health. That is why parents here leave their babies outside to nap all year round, children at preschool play outside for hours every day, and adults savor every possibility to sneak outdoors, even in less than perfect weather. In Sweden, getting outside on a daily basis is considered an act of essential self-care, and in Norway, office buildings clear out after lunch on Fridays, as an afternoon hike is the near-universal way to hail the weekend.

Health care has improved significantly in the past century, but fresh air is still providing physical, mental, and spiritual rejuvenation to the people. In fact, the Nordic governments even acknowledge the open-air lifestyle as key to preventing disease. Go figure—promoting friluftsliv to improve public health is a bargain when you consider the human and financial cost of having a person on sick leave. With an open-air lifestyle, you can give yourself a dose of preventive health care all year round—virtually for free.

## The air is free

WHEN COVID-19 HIT AND TURNED life on its head in 2020, some countries implemented drastic measures to prevent the spread of the virus. The most severe restrictions even banned people from leaving their homes, except for fulfilling the most urgent needs like buying food and medicines, turning normally bustling cities into virtual ghost towns. In many places, the restrictions encompassed outdoor venues as well. From London to Louisiana, parks, playgrounds, and beaches closed, leaving few options for

*Friluftsliv gives us breathing room in a busy world. Friluftsliv gives us an experience of freedom.*

—BØRGE DAHLE, NORWEGIAN AUTHOR AND OPEN-AIR LIFE ADVOCATE

outdoor recreation. In the Nordic countries, the strategies to fight the virus varied, from a widespread lockdown in Denmark to mostly voluntary measures in Sweden, but even throughout the worst of the crisis, one space remained open: nature. Not only were parks and nature areas open, but people were encouraged to use them, as long as they didn't have an active infection and kept a safe distance from those in other households.

In Iceland, the social distancing measures that temporarily stopped people from hugging each other prompted forest rangers in the Hallormsstaður National Forest to encourage the Icelanders to come out and hug a tree instead. "We recommend that people spend time outside during these difficult times. Why not enjoy the forest and hug the trees and just soak up the energy from this area," forest ranger Bergrún Arna Þorsteinsdóttir told the local paper *RÚV* about the initiative, which ended up making international headlines.

Meanwhile in Sweden, a company developed a free app for pairing up strangers to go on walks together (no more than two people at once and safely distanced, of course). The app quickly became popular, not only among lonely retirees but also among people working from home and twenty- and thirtysomethings who substituted nature walks for their normal weekend bar crawls.

Thanks to the friluftsliv tradition, the habit of outdoor recreation was already well established when the pandemic was a fact in the Nordic countries. When gyms closed and indoor gatherings were restricted, people simply started to do more of what they were already doing, namely exercising and meeting up with family and friends outdoors. The interest in outdoor pursuits like hiking and camping also soared to new heights during the pandemic, and outdoor retailers were having a field day as new friluftsliv fans stocked up on gear. As a sign of the times, the camping stove was selected as the Christmas present of the year in Sweden in 2020.

Friluftsliv offered more than pockets of freedom to socialize safely and maintain some sense of normalcy. When the magnitude and severity of the pandemic became clear, the open-air life was there as a cultural resource to lean on for support, in part because that is what people here expect from nature, and believing is healing. This goes for global crises like a pandemic as well as personal hardships. For example, one study showed that being in nature is the third most common coping strategy for Swedes who have lost a child, after talking to others about their grief and contemplating the meaning of life in solitude. Also in Sweden, spending time in nature is one of the most important strategies for handling a cancer diagnosis.

Recognizing the importance of friluftsliv for both mental and physical health, the Nordic governments did not dissuade people from spending time outdoors, not even during the worst waves of the pandemic. Outside, it was easier to keep a safe distance, and besides, it was known from fighting anything from the common winter sniffles to the Spanish flu that the sun and the fresh air would help diffuse the spread of airborne particles. While COVID-19 was a novel and, in many ways, unpredictable virus, several studies later confirmed what common sense and previous experience already indicated: The chances of contracting COVID-19 are far greater indoors than outdoors. Just how much greater is still up for debate, but a Japanese study put the number at nineteen times greater, and a Chinese study showed that none of the people in the cohort had contracted the disease outdoors.

But as the World Health Organization has defined it in recent years, health is much more than the absence of disease, and rather a state of complete physical, mental, and social well-being. Similarly, friluftsliv is about more than being outside. It's a holistic lifestyle that revolves around the idea that nature is our true home and that by spending time in the natural and cultural landscape, we will experience harmony and develop a feeling of oneness with nature. By far the easiest way of doing that is on foot.

## Have shoes, will walk

WHEN THE CONCEPT OF FRILUFTSLIV first emerged, it was more or less synonymous with hiking and cross-country skiing. It was a pastime of the elites, with daring Norwegian adventurers like Roald Amundsen and Fridtjof Nansen as the ultimate role models. But over time, the friluftsliv tradition evolved to become more accessible to ordinary people, and today, going for a walk near one's home is by far the most common way of getting outside in the Nordic countries. It may not earn you a spot in the history books, like being the first to reach the South Pole, like Amundsen, or crossing Greenland on skis, like Nansen, but it's a whole lot easier to combine with a family and the reality of a nine-to-five job. Walking is free, it can be done practically anywhere, and it requires minimal gear and preparation.

Moving your feet, whether you're ascending a mountain, walking laps around a park, or strolling mindlessly in the forest, is a powerful antidote to many of the leading illnesses of our time and even has the potential to extend our lives.

According to the British report *Walking Works*, which includes an extensive review of research on physical activity, there is strong evidence that walking regularly reduces the risk of serious conditions like

- all-cause mortality by 20 to 35 percent
- coronary heart disease and stroke by 20 to 35 percent
- type 2 diabetes by 35 to 50 percent
- colon cancer by 30 to 50 percent
- breast cancer by 20 percent
- depression by 20 to 30 percent

There is also some evidence that walking decreases your risk of

- hip fracture by 36 to 68 percent
- Alzheimer's disease by 40 to 45 percent

And we're not talking about hard-core power walks to reap the benefits of physical activity outdoors—a study of almost 140,000 people found that even walking for less than two hours per week can lower your risk of dying, compared with those who get no activity at all. Blue Zones, an organization that promotes health and longevity by drawing lessons from the cultures with the longest life spans, puts it this way: "The world's longest-lived people don't pump iron, run marathons, or join gyms. Instead, they live in environments that constantly nudge them into moving without thinking about it . . . And they walk every single day. Almost everywhere."

The best part? Unlike pharmaceuticals, walking has no side effects.

If walking is as close to a magic bullet for good health as it gets, why have so many people in the Western world come to view it as something you only do if your car is broken down? Part of the problem is obviously that poor city planning in many places basically forces pedestrians off the streets. I also believe that part of the answer is found in the separation of humans and nature, and the separation of walking from a social, natural, and cultural context. The statistics speak for themselves, but they don't speak to our hearts. For most of us, it's no longer necessary to walk to feed ourselves, worship, entertain ourselves, or socialize. Many of us don't even need to exert much physical energy to earn a living but spend most of our days at a desk. What friluftsliv does is put mindless as well as purposeful movement back into our everyday lives and into a meaningful context. Not primarily to avoid disease, even though that is a consequence of it, but to feel joy.

Thanks to the tradition of the open-air life, nearly 90 percent of Swedes walk for leisure. In Norway, close to 93 percent walk in their neighborhood and local parks, while around 72 percent go on hikes in the forest or mountains every year. For comparison, only around 50 percent of the adults in the United States go on leisure walks, and just 19 percent say they go hiking.

August Casson, an American from Springfield, Illinois, noticed this difference in outdoor culture when he spent nine years working as a teacher in Norway. Living south of Trondheim, he would often take his students into the forest to chop wood and experience nature. In his free time, he climbed the many local mountains and learned how to ski. It was a stark contrast to what he experienced after returning home in 2014 and started practicing the friluftsliv lifestyle in the United States, and not mainly because he traded the highlands of Norway for the plains of the Midwest. "My kids are very excited about friluftsliv, and we spend a lot of time outside. My daughter likes going on night walks, so we often put our headlamps on and walk around the neighborhood after dark," Casson said. "One time, I was stopped by a car because the driver was wondering if everything was okay. You never see people here walking just for fun."

In Norway, Casson noted, there is a culture of walking, whereas if you walk for pleasure in the United States, it is most likely done in an exotic locale rather than a local neighborhood. But then it is called hiking and requires another level of preparation and commitment altogether.

Competition is a no-no in friluftsliv, but challenging yourself to get into a walking habit is a good gateway to an open-air lifestyle. My eighty-year-old father-in-law, Bo, is a prime example. Every year he walks from the southern tip of Sweden to Treriksröset at the very top, where the borders of Sweden, Norway, and Finland meet. It's a journey of nearly one thousand miles one way as the crow flies, and once he reaches his destination, he turns around and starts walking back. Yet Bo doesn't leave his small hometown to complete this feat. He just wakes up early every morning and goes for a brisk walk around his neighborhood, usually around four to five miles, then carefully plots his progress on his imaginary hike to Sweden's Arctic north manually on a map.

Bo, a retired elementary school teacher, has always liked

walking but stepped up his game after he suffered a heart attack over ten years ago. The idea to track the distance came later and added a little bit of extra motivation to keep up the habit on dreary-weather days. Now he walks all year round, experiencing the changes of the seasons with the soles of his hiking boots. Coming back from his daily walk, he always seems to have a story to tell—about an animal he has seen, some tree limbs that have fallen down because of the winds, or the first spring flowers popping up in the woods and the fields. The walks keep him keenly in touch with his community, with nature, and, not least, his own body and mind.

## The many ways of walking

A WALK IS A WALK is a walk—or is it? Actually, walks can be varied almost indefinitely. They can be utilitarian, like when you walk to the mailbox or to the store, or they may not have a specific destination or purpose at all, besides providing an infusion of fresh air. They can be brisk or leisurely. They can be a way to spend time with friends and family, or an opportunity to withdraw and contemplate. They can be short or they can be long, at which point it might be more accurately described as a hike. Either way, from a friluftsliv perspective there is no right or wrong way to walk, as long as it brings you pleasure and contentment.

Since walking and hiking are important parts of an open-air lifestyle, the Swedish language is littered with words describing the act of moving on foot. This is just a small sample of the many joyful ways to walk:

*Barfotapromenad* **(barefoot walk)**—Walking without shoes stimulates the nerve endings in your feet and grounds you in the present moment, making the barefoot walk a great option when you want to practice mindfulness.

*Barnvagnspromenad* **(stroller walk)**—A *barnvagnspromenad* indicates a walk that will go through stroller-friendly terrain, often in the company of other parents of young children.

*Kvällspromenad* **(evening walk)**—This is the most common way for full-time workers to enjoy fresh air on a daily basis, along with the *lunchpromenad* (lunchtime walk). The evening walk can take place practically anywhere, as long as it gets you outside.

*Månskenspromenad* **(moonlight walk)**—For a truly unique open-air experience, try walking after dark on a clear night around the time of the full moon, with nothing but the moon to light your way.

*Reflexpromenad* **(reflector walk/flashlight walk)**—This is a walk after dark that involves finding reflectors along a trail with the help of a flashlight or headlight and is usually organized in the wintertime, to put a positive spin on the fact that the sun sets at three in the afternoon. It's popular with children and adults with their childlike minds intact.

*Skogspromenad* **(forest walk)**—The forest walk can be done alone or with company but lends itself particularly well to quiet contemplation and taking in nature with all your senses, so be sure to leave your headphones at home.

*Snabbpromenad* **(quick walk)**—If fifteen minutes between making dinner and driving the kids to soccer practice is all you have, sneaking in a quick walk near home is your best bet.

*Strandpromenad* **(beach walk)**—Whether you enjoy the coastline from a manmade boardwalk or plot your own path through a sandy beach, the *strandpromenad* is a given near water. And for cities, having a designated beach walk is definitely a selling point.

*Tipspromenad* **(quiz walk)**—The idea of the quiz walk is to follow a marked loop, through a nature area or neighborhood, with ten to twelve questions on an optional topic or theme, such as current events, fairy-tale characters, or just random facts. The *tipspromenad* makes for a fun social activity during family get-togethers, birthday parties, and other special events.

## WHY MORNING WALKS MATTER MORE

When it comes to human biology, any walk is better than no walk at all. But to get the most bang for your walking buck, the morning walk is where it's at, especially in northern latitudes, where daylight is scarce in the wintertime. That's because daylight helps regulate a host of functions in our bodies, including the signals that tell our brains when it's time for activity and sleep, respectively. Until ten o'clock in the morning, natural daylight is about twice as intense as indoor light, which not only makes us more alert and energetic; a morning infusion of light can also boost our mood and even help prevent seasonal affective disorder (SAD). As it turns out, an hour-long walk in the morning is just what the doctor ordered for keeping the winter blues at bay.

## Management by walking

WORKPLACE MEETINGS ARE LEGION IN Sweden, a country where organizations are flat and consensus is prized. A friend of mine once complained that he had eleven meetings in one day, leaving little time for anything else. "And then we have meetings to plan more meetings!" he said, visibly exasperated at the thought of spending another day sitting around a table in a stuffy conference room, drinking bottomless cups of coffee.

Considering Swedes' deeply embedded cultures of workplace meetings and friluftsliv, it shouldn't come as a big surprise that some employers have found a way to combine the two through "walk-and-talk meetings." A walk-and-talk meeting is exactly what the name implies—a conversation while walking outside—and is typically used for less formal meetings and brainstorming sessions.

"You don't have to sit in a conference room with technical equipment to have a conversation. Humans have met up and talked around the fire for hundreds of thousands of years. You don't even need a fire; I think it's just good to get away from the office environment and fill up with a different type of energy," said Johan Ekroth, a human resource specialist who runs a recruitment company with his wife. "In my experience, most people appreciate not having to sit in a meeting room."

He may be onto something. For one, walk-and-talk meetings counteract the negative effects of sitting, which 60 percent of Swedish employees do for four to eight hours every day, according to one study. When we walk, the blood flow in the brain increases, which turns on our creative juices. Simultaneously, our body increases the production of "feel good" hormones like dopamine and serotonin, making us feel happy and positive. Walking outside is also known to provide a healthy cocktail of reducing stress, lowering blood pressure, decreasing the risk of cardiovascular disease, improving sleep, increasing insulin sensitivity, and boosting the immune system. All those physiological responses can be beneficial to your productivity and well-being at work.

Ekroth previously worked as head of communications and IT

for the Swedish Outdoor Association, and during that time he did job interviews and performance reviews as well as other individual meetings while walking in the woods around Stockholm. A colleague liked to do job interviews in a canoe. When you work for an organization that has as its core mission to promote friluftsliv, bringing meetings to the outdoors is of course great branding. But for Ekroth it was about more than that.

"Nature is an outstanding meeting room. It's more relaxed outside, and I think you get a better connection," he said. "I think people are worried about the weather and the unpredictability of the situation, but that becomes a part of the experience as well. If it starts to rain, that can spark creativity—and more so than if you'd been in an anonymous conference room."

Besides generating creativity, walking is known to improve our executive function, or our ability to organize and plan the day effectively. It changes the dynamics of formal workplace hierarchies, facilitates collaboration, and brings people closer. When you're walking side by side you feel more equal, which creates a more relaxing environment and a safe space to share potential discontent or open up about conflicts in the workplace.

Petra Sabo, head of direct-to-consumer sales at Swedish outdoor brand Didriksons, said she does walk-and-talk meetings with the members of her team at least once a month. "I love it. I've noticed that some of our more introverted employees find it easier to talk when we're walking side by side rather than sitting across from each other at a table."

Walk-and-talk meetings lend themselves particularly well to getting to know people and for generating creative ideas but are less suitable for formal meetings and discussions of a more serious nature. Meetings that require a lot of documentation can also be trickier to pull off while walking, but this could change in the future, as dictation technology continues to improve.

"I also think it's valid to question whether the documentation is really needed. It's easy to get stuck in the mindset that you have to have a PowerPoint presentation for everything. But isn't it enough to bring results?" Ekroth asked rhetorically.

According to Anna Iwarsson, a business adviser who has written several books about the future of management, documenting walk-and-talk meetings is just a matter of habit. She has practiced walking meetings for over twenty years and typically uses them for performance reviews, but also when she feels stuck at something and needs a shot of creativity. Iwarsson usually makes some short notes on her smartphone or records a few sentences as a voice memo to support her memory.

For Ekroth, meetings in nature took on a new meaning when he became temporarily unemployed a few years back. While searching for his next gig, he turned to his LinkedIn network and invited people to have coffee with him in the outdoors. The meetups did not generate any jobs at the time, but Ekroth said that you never know what kind of hidden kinetic energy networking can lead to a few years down the road. And everybody who came out for the outdoor networking meetings had a good time.

"Going to a café in town is rarely as good as brewing your own coffee in nature. You put things away and get to know each other on a deeper level."

Walk-and-talk meetings have become popular in recent years, and in 2019 they were one of the top tips listed by 844 Swedish executives when they were asked what they do to motivate their team. Sure, Christmas gifts, pay raises, and paid trips are all nice and appreciated, but motivating employees on a higher level is more about making sure they feel seen at work. As it turns out, walk-and-talk meetings do just that.

Should your employer still not be on board, try getting some coworkers to come on a lunchtime walk (*lunchpromenad*) with you instead. Any walk during the workday can improve enthusiasm, increase relaxation, and reduce nervousness at work, according to research. And if you happen to be walking in a natural area, the effect becomes even more pronounced.

## HOW TO MASTER THE WALK-AND-TALK MEETING

- Try to pick a green space with as few distractions as possible.

- Set a clear agenda for the meeting.

- Bring a notepad for taking short notes or make brief voice recordings on your phone.

- Gather together right after the walk to document what you have talked about, or send out some brief notes with concrete actions to follow up on.

- If there are more than two or three people, split up in smaller groups to get the most out of the walking meeting.

## In sickness and in health

THERE IS NO QUESTION THAT walking can prevent illness, but can hiking and other forms of nature immersion also help rehabilitate people from the ravages of disease, and specifically cancer? Annelie Dahl of Stjärnsund in the Swedish province of Dalarna certainly thinks so. When she was just twenty-six years old, Dahl was diagnosed with ovarian cancer and treated with chemotherapy. She swelled up, gained weight, and felt sick all the time.

"It was a pretty dramatic and emotional experience," Dahl said. "When you get sick, all you want to do is fight the disease, and you don't think that much about anything else in life. At that point, I didn't have any knowledge about rehabilitation or how I was going to deal with everything. I was not feeling well at all after the treatment, and I had no idea how long it would take to recover mentally."

But she knew where to find strength—outside. Six months before her cancer diagnosis, Dahl's then-boyfriend had taken her hiking in the Swedish mountains, and after two days she was sold. The trip left her longing for more time in the mountains, but it was not until her cancer diagnosis that she actually acted on it.

"Going outside used to be something that I would just squeeze in after school, and often I was too tired and didn't make it out," Dahl said. "But when I got sick, I noticed that being in nature made me feel really good, and that helped motivate me. Taking in the fresh air, the blowing wind, and the sounds of nature made me relaxed, so I decided to be outside as much as possible. Friluftsliv became my own form of rehabilitation."

Nature therapy is recognized by the health care systems in the

Nordic countries as a powerful tool to treat people who struggle with depression, stress-related mental disorders, and other mental health problems, but there is scant research about the potential of nature-based rehabilitation for cancer survivors. One review of studies found that spending time in nature can indeed be beneficial to survivors, as it may decrease fatigue and anxiety while increasing the quality of life, and another review showed that friends and family who help care for cancer patients also benefit from nature exposure. Although the sample sizes were small and more research is needed, both reviews saw great potential in using nature as a means for stress relief and self-care.

Since Dahl didn't have a prescribed nature therapy program to follow during her rehabilitation, she intuitively fell back on the open-air lifestyle that she had enjoyed during her childhood. Even though she grew up by the ocean, it was the mountains that became her gateway back to nature. Three years after her diagnosis, Dahl decided to embark on a six-week hiking and backpacking trip along the King's Trail, the longest and most renowned hiking trail in Sweden. The first five weeks she hiked together with others, but the last week she hiked solo. "That gave me a completely different feeling of freedom—it added another dimension altogether. Psychologically it was very empowering to do it on my own, and since then I've hiked more by myself."

At her five-year follow-up appointment, when Dahl was supposed to be declared cancer-free, the doctors instead discovered a new tumor. Fortunately, it was still in the early stages and she "only" had to have surgery. After once again battling the disease and the fatigue that came in its wake, Dahl doubled down on her nature-connected lifestyle and went on several longer backpacking trips in Sweden and Norway, with the ultimate goal of becoming a mountain guide. Her next venture is to help other cancer survivors rehabilitate with the help of nature.

"When I got sick, I noticed how out of sync I was with my body. Along with emotion-focused psychotherapy, being in nature has helped me connect with myself and explore who I really am. Nature is a wise guide. I honestly don't know where I would've been today without it."

## Out on a trip, never grouchy

DAHL IS FAR FROM ALONE in feeling that her spirits are lifted from being out in the fresh air. There is something about being outside that just makes you happy on the inside, and in the Nordic culture, friluftsliv is considered essential to a good life. Countless books, reports, and articles have been written about life satisfaction in the Nordic countries, and every year since the first *World Happiness Report* was published by the United Nations in 2013, Finland, Denmark, Norway, Sweden, and Iceland have all placed in the top ten. The writers of the report explain this "Nordic exceptionalism" by noting the countries' generous welfare states, low rates of corruption, well-functioning institutions, and high levels of freedom and social trust. Those are all true, but if you ask the people who live here, the report misses a few key aspects of life that bring them joy and happiness, most notably nature.

Finns, who nabbed the title of the happiest people in the world for the fourth time running in 2020, appreciate their world-class education system and low crime levels for sure. But when Visit Finland ranked five things that make Finns happy, neither one of those made the list. Rather, it's supposedly the ritual of sweating in a piping-hot sauna by a lake, then submerging yourself in the freezing water that makes Finns tick, as well as walking in the forest and foraging for wild berries. Taking in the magical light and the beauty of space and silence in nature is also on the list, or as Visit Finland puts it: "In the rush and crush of modern life, the rarities are what make us happy, such as space, quiet and time. The space to breathe, a time to dream—you can find these treasures in Finland, where the lakes are many and the people are few."

Finland is arguably the king of sauna and cold swimming, but all the Nordic countries are shaped by the perception that a rich open-air life is a prerequisite for happiness. Nothing captures this shared experience better than the old Norwegian saying *"Ut på tur, aldri sur,"* which loosely translates to "Out on a trip, never grouchy." This cheerful proposition is quintessential to the Norwegian understanding of friluftsliv and sums up the idea that it's impossible to be in the outdoors and be in a bad mood at the same time. And if you're in a bad mood when you start out, you most definitely will not still be crabby by the time you get back. But just like the equally upbeat old Scandinavian saying "There is no such thing as bad weather, only bad clothing," it's more about conveying a certain feeling about being in nature than aspiring to tell some sort of objective truth.

Like their Nordic neighbors, Norwegians are generally regarded as a reserved people who rarely engage in small talk with strangers and prefer to keep others at a safe six-foot distance, whether a pandemic forces them to or not. In nature, however, this all changes. While Norwegians rarely make eye contact with others while waiting for the bus in the city, saying hello to and even chitchatting with people you meet on the trail is not just common—

it's expected. Once you part ways, custom calls for everybody to close out the conversation with the courtesy phrase "*God tur!*" which is like saying "Have a nice trip" for people wearing Gore-Tex.

To go ut på tur is generally understood as encompassing a wide variety of outdoor activities like hiking, cross-country skiing, or going to one's cabin in the country. A tur can happen any weekday, but on Sundays, it's a more or less mandatory family activity. This tradition of spending a longer chunk of time outdoors on Sunday, the *søndagstur*, is as close to a holy institution as it gets, comparable with the Sunday church service in the United States.

To go on a tur usually involves physical activity, which, as mentioned, is well beyond proved to have a number of health benefits. But this tradition didn't come about just as a way to lose weight or keep osteoporosis at bay. That can be done at a gym or on a treadmill in your garage as well. No, it's a far more holistic venture. When you go on a tur, you build family culture, strengthen friendships, and cultivate togetherness in a noncompetitive environment. By living simply and having no other distractions around, it's easy to focus on each other and for everybody to be heard and seen. It's also a way of connecting with and appreciating the local landscape, no matter the weather.

While trips often last a whole day, they don't have to amount to a grandiose adventure. That's especially true for families with young children. "If you have kids, the focus is on them having fun," said Linn Pollard of Stavanger, on Norway's west coast, who works for the Norwegian equivalent of the US National Guard. "You might take them on anything from short trips in the neighborhood to overnight camping trips. It has to be on their terms, or you're not going to have a good time."

Like Pollard, many parents in the Nordic countries are keen on passing on the open-air lifestyle to the next generation. And they waste no time—already in infancy, babies are put outside to nap in their prams all year round to reap the health benefits of fresh air. Young children quickly adapt to playing outside every day and are taught important life skills ranging from dressing appropriately for the weather to distinguishing edible berries from poisonous ones. To let preschoolers handle knives and fire is not only considered normal but is approved as good parenting, and older children are taught how to navigate with a map and compass at school. All to make them feel safe and at home in nature.

Pollard has two children of her own who are six and eight, as well as a bonus daughter who is fourteen. They go on tur all year round, each season bringing a unique flavor and different possibilities to enjoy the outdoors. In the summertime, that usually means water play, sailing, and other water activities; wintertime offers tobogganing, snowshoeing, and cross-country skiing. In the spring and fall the family often goes camping or cozies up around a campfire, practicing scouting skills like whittling, sawing, and knot tying.

"In my opinion, friluftsliv is a lot about learning how to do things. My kids learn the basics from Scouts and from being on trips with us. I see how proud and happy they become when they master skills like handling a knife and building things. I think it makes them more confident too."

While Pollard remembers only good things from going on tur with her parents and extended family as a child, that's not the case for everybody. "*Ut på tur, aldri sur* is about keeping your spirits up on the trail and solving problems as they come up. The idea is that you can't be grouchy when you're in the outdoors," explained Kjetil

Utrimark, a fortysomething outdoor enthusiast who is usually found skiing or watching the northern lights in the mountains one day, hiking or sitting around a campfire by the ocean the next. "Of course, it's a lot of bull. There are a ton of kids who are in a terrible mood when you take them hiking."

Kids, however, can be bribed with candy. Given enough sugary treats, children, too, can be happy campers on the trail, and this is the Norwegian go-to method to keep energy levels high and the atmosphere upbeat during family outings, until the children themselves develop an innate desire to spend their weekends in nature. It seems to work. Somehow, the memories of slogging around on endless cross-country tracks in the forest or sitting in a tent in the pouring rain only get rosier with time, and even the teenagers who complain the loudest about these family outings are usually hard-wired to continue the søndagstur tradition as adults.

"I didn't like going on tur when I was a kid, but then about ten years ago, it all came back to me, and now I love it," said Johan Renè Bjørnsen, a twenty-nine-year-old Norwegian marketing manager. "I think we need this now more than ever, the temporary reprieve and disconnect from all our digital devices. I notice myself that as soon as I get back in the door, they're all there again, demanding my attention—my phone, the iPad, the computer."

To go on a tur is a way to nurture relationships with friends and family in the digital age but also to develop a connection with the plants, animals, and landscape that make each place unique. It invigorates the body, frees the mind, and slows down our lives. And it makes us happy.

# MATPAKKE

To go on a tur that lasts more than a couple of hours, you most definitely need a *matpakke,* Norwegian for "food pack," and the quintessential friluftsliv food. Unlike a picnic, which typically implies an assortment of delightful, tapas-like foods packed in a pretty woven basket and served on a blanket designated for the purpose, matpakke is pure sustenance, without any unnecessary bells and whistles. Some cheese or meat slapped on slices of whole grain bread for a couple of open-faced sandwiches, coffee for the adults, and hot chocolate for the children are the classic components of the matpakke, although some people might add a few pieces of fruit as the crowning touch. If you have kids, add some chocolate bars for bribery purposes as well. While these lunches will not win any culinary awards, they do have the great advantage of being simple to prepare, using ingredients you normally keep at home. No need to plan ahead or try to impress anybody with an elaborate meal. For variation, you can always try a different topping for the sandwiches, but don't go too crazy—the idea is just to provide energy for the hike. Despite the utilitarian presentation, sitting down and eating the matpakke is often the highlight of the outing.

## TURGLEDE

Once you start living an open-air life, chances are that you will regularly feel *turglede*, a characteristically upbeat Norwegian term for "the joy of going on a trip." The term can encompass any and all of the little moments that make the trip worthwhile—the happiness of reaching your destination after a strenuous hike, having a good conversation with a friend by the campfire, hearing your favorite bird after it has returned from winter migration, or eating a special treat from your matpakke. In any case, chocolate is key to turglede, especially if you have kids.

## Is happiness a little cabin without running water?

CABIN LIFE IS KEY TO friluftsliv in the Nordic countries, and nowhere is the obsession with this culture stronger than in Norway. To a Norwegian, a cabin in the countryside is arguably the most powerful symbol of the right

*I went to the woods because I wished to live deliberately, to front only the essential facts of life, and see if I could not learn what it had to teach, and not, when I came to die, discover that I had not lived.*

—HENRY DAVID THOREAU

to rest and recreation in nature, and the adulation of cabin life cuts across social and economic divides. To say that it's deeply imprinted in the national spirit and instrumental to the national identity is nothing short of an understatement.

Most cabins fall into one of two categories: They are either owned and operated by the Norwegian Trekking Association (DNT) or privately owned. The DNT cabins serve as strategic hubs for the country's extensive trail system and offer an affordable place to stay during overnight trips on foot or skis. Most of them are tiny huts with no running water, electricity, or modern appliances; and instead of a regular toilet, they usually come equipped with an *utedo*, which is just a more upbeat word for pit latrine. The simplicity is even implied in the Norwegian word for cabin, *hytte*, which can be traced to the German word *Hütte*, for "small, humble wooden house." There are exceptions—some of the DNT cabins are full-service facilities with staff that serve breakfast and dinner—but even at the bigger cabins the rooms are purposely spartan and furnished with bunk beds; bringing your own sleeping bag liner or linen is mandatory. When you stay in a cabin with no service, it's also customary for everybody to help out with chores like chopping wood, carrying in water, keeping the fire going, and cleaning up. The simple lifestyle is part of the experience and underlines the egalitarian ideals of the open-air life. At the cabin, everybody shares the same outhouse and is dependent on the same fireplace for warmth, regardless of your income, your education level, or the size of your house. When you're out on a skiing or hiking trip, money can only buy you so much comfort.

Of course, humble accommodations are not news for seasoned nature lovers. When you're hiking and camping, roughing it is both the means and the ends of the experience, and compared with sleeping in a tent, the cabins are definitely a step up on the comfort scale. What's more remarkable is that many of the privately owned cabins, which make up the vast majority of the cabins in Norway, have an equally modest standard. Many were built by hand during the hytte boom years following World War II, when the economy started to take off, labor reforms gave workers more time off, and the increasing availability of cars made it easier to get to cabins in remote areas. Somewhere around a quarter of the population owns a hytte, but twice as many are estimated to have regular access to one, through parents, extended family, or in-laws. Since the cabins have often been in the family for generations, they have a high sentimental value. And they get used a lot. By some accounts, Norwegians spend on average sixty days per year at their cabin.

The archetypal hytte is a small log cabin that has a sod roof and is located in a secluded area, either by a lake, in the forest, in the mountains, or even at the outskirts of farmland—as long as it's away from modern civilization. Some are used primarily for hunting, fishing, and hiking, whereas others are the given gathering point for families with children during weekends, school holidays, and summer vacations. The cabin is where Norwegians go to escape Wi-Fi-induced stress and to live out their dreams of a simple life, by fetching water from a well, heating canned food on top of a woodstove, and plodding through three feet of snow to do their business in a wooden outhouse with a heart-shaped hole in the door and yellowed pictures of the royal family on the walls. If you think that I'm exaggerating, consider that as late as 2017, only four out of ten cabins in Norway had running water.

"There's so much stress in society today, with all the electronic devices and activities, and it's easy to get carried away by it all. But at the hytte, everything is relaxed and peaceful. We can put away our phones and get more quality time together as a family," said Linn Pollard, whose extended family owns a primitive hunting cabin about an hour away from home. "At home there are always chores to do, and I become irritable more easily. At the cabin there's no time to keep. All I need is a warm meal and somewhere to sleep. It's so simple, but it's so important to my mental health."

One of the most vocal advocates for the primitive cabin life is ironically a Norwegian real estate magnate who made his multibillion-dollar fortune by developing some pretty lavish commercial property: Olav Thon. His company owns over five hundred buildings, including hotels, shopping malls, and an airport, and Thon himself has been listed on the *Forbes* list of the two hundred richest people in the world. But privately, he is known for living a modest and frugal life. In line with traditional hytte culture, his cabin in the region of Hallingdal in southeastern Norway is only 130 square feet and has neither electricity nor running water. As an avid outdoorsman, he likes it just that way. "I'm happy I don't have a hytte with 15 bedrooms. I have enough to deal with as it is," he once told the local newspaper, while urging other wealthy people to lead a simpler, more frugal life. This may seem hypocritical coming from a person who made at least part of his enormous wealth on luxury properties, and obviously it takes a certain amount of privilege to enjoy vacationing like it's 1821. But Thon's yearning for simplicity seems sincere. Born in 1923 and raised on a farm, he still remembers the times when frugality was not a choice but a necessity. By keeping his primitive family cabin rather than building a luxury second home, which he could easily afford, he nourishes a profound connection with the landscape and lifestyle of his rural past.

It should be noted that not all Norwegians are on board for the traditional hytte lifestyle, and newer cabins both are bigger and come with more conveniences than they used to. This is probably a sign that while younger hytte owners leave the cities for the same reason older generations do, they tend to define "simple living" slightly differently, namely as having all the conveniences of home but with a more scenic view. This development was exacerbated when the outbreak of COVID-19 led to a cabin boom, as scores of Norwegians saw the potential in working remotely from the countryside. For that, a hytte sans electrical outlets obviously will not do.

## GET A TASTE OF HYTTE BLISS

Most of us will never own a Norwegian nineteenth-century log cabin, or even have the opportunity to stay in one. But thanks to home-sharing sites like Airbnb, VRBO, and Glamping Hub, it's easier than ever to experience the bliss of a cabin stay close to nature. Do you prefer to sleep in a primitive off-the-grid cabin, a repurposed barn, a tiny tree house, or a romantic yurt? Online, chances are you will find some or all of the above near you.

# A brief history of
# Nordic nature worship

LONG BEFORE THE NORDIC PEOPLE built rustic cabins to go "back to nature," natural phenomena were a source of fear, awe, and worship. According to Norse mythology, we owed daylight to a horse with a shining mane, Skinfaxi, who every day pulled the sun in a chariot across the sky. Another horse, Hrímfaxi, brought nightfall by pulling the moon across the heavens. Thunder was believed to be the sound of the Norse god Thor fighting off evil giants, and every time he brandished his hammer, the skies were shattered by lightning. The pagan gods like Thor; Odin, who was the god of war and death and the most powerful of the Norse gods; and Freyr, who ruled over fertility and the planting and harvesting of crops, helped explain the inexplicable during this time. Many rituals and feasts in pre-Christian times were closely tied to natural phenomena like the sun and the changing of the seasons, with the summer and winter solstices being the natural highlights of the year.

In the old agrarian society, humans were also believed to share the woods, mountains, water, and fields with an ever-evolving motley crew of trolls, dwarves, giants, elves, gnomes, and other spirits. Some of these supernatural creatures were rather fearful and personified the dangers of nature. A far cry from the feel-good Disney sagas of today, bedtime stories a few hundred years ago might have included admonitions not to go too close to the water, or you might run into Näcken, a shape-shifting spirit whose specialty was drowning people. The forest was not considered much safer, as it was the home of Skogsrået, a beautiful woman with a hollow back who led wanderers astray. Other creatures were more benign, such as the gnome-like creature called *tomten* in Swedish. His role was to bring luck to and protect the animals at the farm, but if you didn't treat him right, he could lose his temper and pull off vicious pranks. To this day, the old folklore lives on through beloved children's books as well as names of places in nature, like the national park Jotunheimen (Home of the Giants) in Norway, the rock formation Álfaborg (City of the Elves) in East Iceland, and countless hiking paths named Trollstigen (Troll's Path) in Sweden.

The presence of the old folklore and worshipping of natural phenomena was one of the reasons why Christianity struggled to take hold in the Nordic countries. This nature worship was especially pronounced among the indigenous, seminomadic Sami people in northern Norway, Sweden, and Finland. In the traditional Sami belief system, there was little separation between humans and nature to begin with. Plants, animals, rivers, mountains, and other natural phenomena all had a personality and a soul and were seen as equal with humans. The Samis' relationship with nature was so respectful and emotional that they would always ask nature for permission before cutting down a tree or picking berries from a bush, a ritual that ensured that the resources on hand were not overexploited.

When Christianity finally pushed out the pagan religion around a thousand years ago, nature worship was demonized and banned, and established seasonal feasts like the summer and winter solstices were replaced with St. John's Day and Christmas, respectively. But fragments of the old beliefs and seasonal rituals survived and blended in with Christian customs. (In Iceland, the Norse mythology was even re-recognized by the state in 1973 and is now the fastest-growing religion.)

But then, during the Enlightenment, nature spirituality began to make a comeback. According to Swedish professor of religious studies David Thurfjell, some thinkers at this time advocated for the idea that God wrote two books—the Bible and nature—and that both of them could be a way to get to know Him. In the nineteenth century, this idea started to take hold among the public and was even picked up by theologians. This laid the foundation for the near-religious relationship with nature that Nordic people, who are among the most secular in the world, seem to have today. Some would even say that friluftsliv to a great extent has taken the place of the church and that it is among the woods, in the mountains, and by the water that people find meaning and the deeper dimensions of life. Lars Lerin, one of Scandinavia's leading artists in watercolor technique, puts it this way: "For me, nature is the foundation of everything. You go out in the wild to train your eye and try to figure out what you see. Going out in the woods is good because you're put in your place. You're a part of a context. You're not your own universe; you're a part of nature. You understand where you come from, and that you're not that special."

Christians, too, perceive nature as a place for contemplation, existential deep experiences, and spirituality. In fact, confessional Christians are four times more likely to have had strong spiritual experiences in nature than nonbelievers. Many Christians describe the feelings they have when they're alone in nature as being similar to those they experience when they are in a church, except in nature they are able to think more freely. It only makes sense then that the church uses open-air life as a way to connect parishioners with the Creation firsthand.

## TROLLSKOG

*Trollskog* is Swedish for "troll forest" and is essentially a forest that is perceived to have certain otherworldly qualities, as if taken out of a fairy tale. These forests are often rich in knotty old trees and feature moss-clad rock formations that could double as an abode for mythical creatures in general and trolls in particular. The word is often used to get young children excited about going to the woods and to add a little bit of magic to the ordinary, a remnant of the country's pagan past. According to legend, trolls can become invisible and will discover you long before you notice them. But since they rarely wash themselves, their foul smell sometimes gives them away.

## Church and friluftsliv

SUNDAYS ARE USUALLY WORK-DAYS FOR Magnus Larsson, a priest who wears a gray hoodie and a guarded smile in his official photo on the Swedish Church website. That doesn't mean his workplace is always inside the four walls of a church or parish house. When I met Larsson, he was sitting on a rock ledge by a trailhead just outside Dalsjöfors, my hometown, on a sunny late-summer day,

*It is better to go skiing and think of God, than go to church and think of sport.*

—FRIDTJOF NANSEN

surrounded by a few parishioners and waiting for more to trickle in. Telltale of the declining interest in organized religion in Sweden, it was mostly a silver-haired crowd. Some carried backpacks with coffee, sandwiches, and sweet pastries for later, and an older man who was having trouble walking had brought his hiking poles.

Instead of a regular Sunday church service, they were here to go for a walk in the local woods, and I could tell from the chitchat that anticipation for the pilgrimage, as the parish called these outings, was building. After a while, the group hit the trail single file, with Larsson in the very back to make sure nobody was left behind.

"There was a longing for these types of activities among some of the members," Larsson explained. "This is a simple means to be close to others and talk about life, outside the walls of the church, with people you wouldn't see otherwise. I think we're more prone to sharing, listening, and taking in other people's perspective in this format."

Larsson, who was wearing sturdy hiking boots and a pair of black functional hiking pants that matched his tab-collar clergy shirt, recalled the first local pilgrimage during Easter 2018, following a big snow dump. "People still turned out and soldiered on through the snow," he said and chuckled at the memory. "They've showed up when it's rained too."

Churches in Sweden have a long-standing tradition of holding some religious services outdoors, especially in the summertime and in conjunction with certain religious holidays, like Ascension Day. For generations, priests have gathered their congregations on folding chairs on grassy lawns and under the tree crowns, as an informal way to take in the word of God while simultaneously enjoying the breeze and bird twitter.

Pilgrimages in the traditional sense go back even further, since before biblical times, and exist in all the world religions. But the hikes that Larsson and his colleagues in many other Swedish congregations carry out are a modern rite that differs from the original pilgrimage in several important respects. For one, the significance of reaching a holy destination has been lost, and instead, nature, friluftsliv, and silence are the means of the spiritual experience, each person creating their own sacred space within. Also, elders in the group will often share stories and sundry facts about people and places along the trail—who used to live in the old homestead, why there is a big pile of rocks on the hill, and what types of trees are growing in the area. It was spiritual transformation through nature, with a heaping of place-based connection on the side. Add to that a sprinkling of awe, that elusive state of mind that comes to us so naturally in childhood and enables us to be fascinated even with the small things around us.

"Look!" the woman in front of me suddenly shouted and pointed to the ground. "A tiny frog. We wouldn't have seen that if we'd been in the church."

Her name was Catharina Nordh, and she had been one of the initiators of the local pilgrimage tradition. She stressed that she views the pilgrimages as a complement to the regular services at the church, not as a replacement, but said that she enjoys the mindfulness of walking slowly in nature. Out here, there is space for her to be awed over the sound of water from the creek and the soft moss growing on the trees. A space to meet and build a relationship with each other, God, and nature. "I think it's amazing to be out in nature and hike together," Nordh said as we walked slowly in the soft shadows of old beech trees and shaggy firs. "There's something holy about all this existing and giving us the means to live. We were created to live in harmony with nature. This is where we belong."

After a while, Nordh prompted the group to walk in silence and meditate on the word "freedom." The silence was usually the most appreciated part of the walk, and not just because Swedes in general have a reputation for being reserved and poor at making small talk. No, this was something else. This was daring to be in the here and now, without the mindless distraction of fiddling with our smartphones.

We kept walking slowly farther into the forest, through muddy puddles and up and down rocky slopes. The man with the hiking poles was struggling with the terrain and panted slightly as he scaled the steeper parts of the hills, but he labored on, anxious not to slow down the group even more. When we reached a small clearing, we stopped and formed a circle. For a moment, we stood there, comfortable in our silence, until Nordh finally broke it, encouraging us to share our thoughts on freedom. A grandmotherly woman wearing a baby blue sweatsuit and a backpack contrasted the freedom of living a life in peace and political stability with the oppression and chaos in Afghanistan. An older man with a mustache volunteered that he was grateful to have the freedom to walk anywhere you want in nature, granted to people here under allemansrätten. Then another woman spoke up, telling the group about a hiking trip that she had been on up north earlier in the summer.

"We hiked to the top of a mountain, and once we were up there, we sat down and had coffee," she said. "Nobody asked anything of me at that moment; there were no demands whatsoever. It was just us and the mountain. That is freedom to me."

## RITUALS IN THE OUTDOORS

Rituals are a series of symbolic acts that are repeated regularly, and they exist in all cultures. Simple outdoor rituals can help rekindle a lost connection with nature, whether you consider yourself a spiritual person or not. Try hugging a tree on your way to work, mark the transition of the moon phases with an outdoor feast, or, if you have young children, make a fairy house by decorating a tree stump with natural materials like sticks, pine cones, seedpods, grasses, and rocks, and visit it often. There is evidence that the certainty and predictability of rituals can help ease anxiety, and when done in an outdoor setting, you reap the benefits of being in the fresh air as well.

# Sleep, restored

I HADN'T TALKED TO OR seen my friend Jeanette for over a year when she suddenly sent me a message out of the blue. We had both gone through divorce in the past couple of years and were in similar phases of our lives, except I had remarried, and she was still dating. She sent me a screenshot of her latest Tinder find, a six-foot-three fireman with a camper van and—judging by his Instagram account—a bent for skinny-dipping and working out. By the way, Jeanette pondered, did I want to take her backpacking? After her divorce, she had begun to delve deeper into the open-air life by taking a class in open-water swimming in the southern part of Stockholm, where she lived, and now she wanted a new challenge. Like so many other Scandinavians, she had gone camping with her parents as a child and in adulthood before she became a mom herself, but that was years ago and mostly car camping in easy locations. Now she wanted to rekindle her skills and gain enough confidence to go backpacking in the wild on her own. With summer setting in and our children now with their respective fathers, we both had some time alone to kill—what could possibly be a better way to spend a weekend than to go hiking and camping in the primeval forests of Tyresta National Park, just outside Stockholm?

A Friday afternoon less than two weeks later, we took public transit to the outskirts of the park, with our eyes set on a small lake on the north side of it. But first, a late freeze-dried dinner out of a pouch on some warm cliffs by a lake near the bus stop. It was one of the warmest days of the summer so far, and while watching some teenagers take turns hurling themselves off the cliffs and into the cool water, we got talking about Jeanette's motivations.

"Learning how to swim freestyle in open water has given me so much confidence and a desire to challenge myself with other things," Jeanette mused. "I want to improve my outdoor skills to know that I'm okay out there, that I can do this on my own. One of the drawbacks about living in a city is that it's easy to forget how stuff works in the wild. And there is a lot of freedom in knowing how to take care of yourself off the grid."

That, and she really wanted a few good nights' sleep and nothing to worry about, except for putting one foot in front of the other and finding a good place to camp. Like me, she had an indoor, sedentary job that periodically left her more than a little stressed, and a dose of nature was just the medicine she needed.

We got a late start on our hike that evening, and as the glowing sunset gradually turned to semidarkness, we were still on the trail, zigzagging between rocks and tree roots while trying to follow the orange trail markers in the waning light. It was midnight before we reached the lake and finally could set up camp. We hung our camping hammocks on some pine trees, pulled off our sweaty hiking boots, and rolled into bed. Then we slept, through the Scandinavian midsummer night.

The next morning, I woke up with a feeling I often get while sleeping outside—whole, fulfilled, and surprisingly energetic, especially considering that we had hiked for four hours with a heavy pack the day before. When Jeanette woke up, she waxed lyrical too. "This is the best night's sleep I've ever had. It beats the best hotels I've stayed at; heck, it beats my own bed."

I was prone to agree with her; something about sleeping outside seemed to work wonders on my normal, sleep-deprived self. Some of it probably had to do with my expectations: I enjoy being outside and therefore have an expectation that it will be good for my sleep. But there is a scientific explanation why camping is a boon to our sleep as well, and it has to do with our circadian rhythms. Most living beings, from microbes to humans, respond to these innate rhythms—physical, mental, and behavioral processes that are guided by seasonal changes in the natural light-dark cycle. The circadian rhythms run on a twenty-four-hour cycle and are regulated by proteins in almost every tissue and organ of our body, where they make up natural timing devices, or our biological clocks. These biological clocks affect our hormone levels, eating habits, and body temperature, as well as feelings of alertness, wakefulness, and sleepiness. Because many important processes in the body follow a circadian rhythm, disruptions in our biological clocks are linked to a number of health problems. For example, sleep disruption is a telltale symptom of depression. As many as three-quarters of people with depression have problems with insomnia, and four out of ten depressed young people suffer from hypersomnia, or abnormal sleepiness.

The modern Western lifestyle, which keeps us stuck inside for the vast majority of the time, in artificial lighting, and in front of electronic devices, means that we're missing out on important daytime sunlight and delaying our circadian timing. We stay up later than what's good for us, especially on the weekends, and are still groggy when we wake up to go to school and work on Monday morning. The key player in this process is melatonin. The levels of this sleep-inducing hormone increase at night and gradually wane in the morning as our body prepares to get up. But when we don't get enough natural daylight, the rise and fall of our melatonin levels are delayed and our biological clocks fall out of sync, potentially harming our health. Kenneth Wright, a professor of integrative physiology at University of Colorado Boulder, who has spent many years studying circadian rhythms, calls it a form of "social jet lag." When this happens, camping can help, judging from several studies.

Wright has shown that when we spend our days and nights outside, our circadian rhythms rather quickly sync with the natural light-dark cycle, and our biological night is lengthened to align with the season. In 2013, Wright sent a group of volunteers out to camp for a week in the summer and found that on their return, the campers' melatonin levels started to rise almost two hours earlier, near sunset. They began to wane earlier too, a sign that their bodies had synced with the season. Wondering how long one needs to camp to achieve the effect, Wright repeated the study four years later, but in the winter. One group camped for a week and one group for just a weekend. The study showed that as little as two nights of camping can achieve 69 percent of the effect of the melatonin shift, even during winter camping.

Back at Tyresta National Park, Jeanette and I were going to need the extra boost from a good night's sleep. It was heating up quickly, and part of our hike would go through a large swath of forest that had been scorched by a fire some twenty years ago. The new trees were still not tall enough to provide any shade, yet they were dense enough to prevent any breeze from getting through. It was like walking inside your own personal hot-air balloon. After a particularly grueling section of the trail, where Jeanette narrowly avoided heatstroke, we reached another lake, where we pumped more water, made sandwiches for lunch, and went for a quick swim to cool down.

After the swim, Jeanette started to feel better, and we kept going to reach our campsite, a beach just outside the park, before dark.

Imagine our disappointment when, after putting in two more hours on the trail, instead of a beach we found a reed-covered, mosquito-infested bay with three scattered docks that looked like they had been through a war and then some. The only place we could find to hang our hammocks was in a cow pasture surrounded by a barbed-wire fence, and we had to climb a ladder stile to get into it. After debating whether we really wanted to stay the night in a cow pasture, we eventually entered it. Our hips were sore from the weight of the packs, and there didn't seem to be anywhere else to go. Plus, the cattle were down by the waterfront, nowhere near us. (According to allemansrätten in Sweden, the public is free to access private as well as public land with grazing stock as long as you don't disturb the animals or behave recklessly, for example by leaving gates open.) Before we entered, Jeanette snapped a picture of a sign that had the cattle owners' phone numbers on it, just in case.

Soon we found a beautiful spot under some oak trees, with a hill behind us and the ocean in front of us. Dinner consisted of another mediocre freeze-dried meal and cheap rosé wine, but that was A-okay with us. We were both filled with gratitude over everything that we had gotten out of our trip so far—a healthy dose of fresh air, an opportunity to decompress and wind down, and a chance to rekindle our friendship after our respective divorces. With the "We Can Do It!" attitude of Rosie the Riveter, hiking boots on our feet and whittling knives in hand, we felt strong and powerful, bordering on invincible. And we felt free from the stuff that normally keeps us busy in everyday life. Life was so simple on the trail. There was nothing else to do here but to eat, sleep, and take care of our immediate needs. If we had been at home, we would've had schedules to keep and a million things to deal with. Here we felt the complete and utter freedom to just be.

As we began to fill up our second glass of wine, we noticed that the herd of cows was moving toward us.

"Imagine if there was a big bull in here with the cows," I said to Jeanette jokingly, and we both laughed at the preposterous idea.

But when the herd was within a hundred feet of us, we noticed that there was one particularly large animal among them, and there was no mistaking what was dangling between his hind legs. Now feeling a little less invincible for each step the herd took toward us, we debated our next move. Jeanette started questioning the wisdom of camping in a cow pasture, but I was tired and would rather take my chances with the bull than pack everything up and start searching for a new campsite just before bedtime. Besides, what would Rosie do? Probably roll up her sleeves and take the proverbial bull by its horns.

Then the bull popped his head up and looked squarely in our direction. That was it for Jeanette. She pulled up her phone and called one of the owners of the cattle, Anette. Rather than getting annoyed with a nervous camper calling her at nine thirty on a Saturday night, Anette was all too happy to field questions about her animals.

"The cows are super friendly and social, nothing to worry about. They might come check on you because they're curious," she assured us.

"Okay, but what about the bull? Is he friendly too?" Jeanette said.

"Oh yes. He's just there to do his job with the cows this summer. If he comes up to you, give him a rub behind the ears. He loves that."

With that reassuring conversation, we stowed away our backpacks and food where the animals could not get to them, then eventually tucked in. That night I dreamed of cows. But the real-life Ferdinand down the hill never came to get his ear rub, and that was probably just as well.

The next day we bade farewell to the ocean, the oak trees, and the rocky hills in the pasture, and headed back to the city. Our bodies were sore, but our minds were at rest. In line with the friluftsliv ethos, there had been no pressure to achieve anything this weekend. Yet we felt like we had accomplished everything.

# FOUR WAYS OF SLEEPING OUTSIDE

SLEEPING OUTSIDE IS A PROFOUND way to experience frilufts-liv, and there's more than one way to do it. Practice close to home if it's your first time, and always check local regulations to make sure camping is permitted before you head out on bigger adventures.

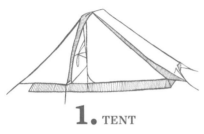

## 1. TENT

Cozying up in a tent while the rain is pouring down outside is a quintessential camping experience. Tents not only protect you and your gear effectively against wind and moisture, but they also come in many different sizes and models. If you're new at camping, a tent is a good place to start your adventures.

## 2. HAMMOCK

The camping hammock is an increasingly popular way to spend the night outside, and no wonder. Lightweight and comfortable, a hammock is a perfect option for backpacking, as long as there are trees to secure it to. Make sure to get a model with a rain fly and mosquito net for protection when needed, and put a lightweight sleeping pad on the bottom for extra insulation and support.

## 3. LEAN-TO

Some parks and preserves have simple lean-tos—wooden structures with three walls—where hikers can overnight. A lean-to is a cozy way to camp, but it's a no-frills accommodation that requires you to bring a sleeping bag and a pad to stay comfortable. Just keep in mind that since one side of the lean-to is open, you need to prepare accordingly to protect yourself against both the weather and bugs.

# 4. UNDER THE STARS

If all you can fit in your backpack is a sleeping pad and a sleeping bag, don't let that stop you from getting a good night's sleep outside. The feeling of sleeping straight under the stars is hard to beat, plus it can be done almost anywhere—in nature, in your backyard, or even on a porch or balcony. Use a good repellent if mosquitoes are an issue, and put a mosquito net over your sleeping bag if you're worried about bugs.

# Fifty-two nights of fresh air

IN THE MIDDLE OF MARCH 2017, on the opening night of the annual fair Explore Outdoor in Stockholm, thousands of people were filing through the enormous event center, shopping for kayaks and trying their hands at the indoor climbing wall. Meanwhile on the roof of the building, somebody was pitching a red-and-yellow two-person tent straight on the concrete surface, preparing to spend the night. The view from up there was not too shabby—mostly residential neighborhoods and urban parks interspersed with some industrial areas and railroad tracks. A night camping there easily met the friluftsliv definition of spending time outside to get a change of scenery. But still. It was a rooftop in the middle of a city of a million people, not exactly the most pristine environment to practice your camping skills, even though Stockholm gets high scores for its fresh air. Why would somebody voluntarily camp up there?

That somebody was Fredrik Hjort, a fiftysomething management consultant at SEB, one of the big Swedish banks, where he specializes in securities trading and uncovering money-laundering schemes. At this point, he was about two months into a challenge to sleep outside at least once a week for an entire year. To make his venture compatible with work and family life, he mostly needed to choose locations near his home, whether in parks, in the quay, or in friends' backyards. Or in this case, an urban rooftop. "I had a lot of people asking me, 'Why?' To which I responded, 'Why not?' Sleeping on rooftops turned out to be a lot of fun," Hjort said.

The run-up to the challenge was that Hjort wanted to boost his outdoor skills. He was inspired by a friend of his who had previously challenged herself to sleep outside once a month. But Hjort thought once a month would be too easy. "I think camping is like working out; if you want to get better at it, you have to do something that is slightly difficult. I decided that once a week would be reasonable and made a plan based on some ground rules. I had to sleep outside at least once a week. Spending additional nights outside was fine, but I could only count one of them," he said.

Hjort experimented with camping out on different days of the week and soon found that Sundays were the best, since the city was less busy then. Initially, he also tried to plan around the weather to avoid rain. But soon he noticed that he was longing for the feeling of lying in a tent while the drizzle trickled down the canvas. He began to long for Sunday as well, and said that it's a misconception that you can't camp out the day before work. His colleagues and manager were not only aware of the challenge but were all supportive.

"I don't think I always get as much sleep time-wise when I sleep outside, but the feeling of waking up outdoors is extremely energizing," said Hjort. "I'm completely calm and ready to meet the day. I would get up early, pack up my tent, enjoy breakfast outside, and go to work. At the office, I changed into my business suit and felt like I had completely beat the system."

Now, Hjort may be a city dweller, but he was not exactly a novice camper when he set out to sleep outside once a week for an entire year. Having grown up in Stockholm, he joined the Scouts as a young boy and is a leader within the organization today. Plus, he works as an expedition guide on the side, visiting places like Nepal, Mount Kilimanjaro, Kebnekaise, and the Pyrenees mountains. He said preparation is key, as well as risk management and a healthy dose of common sense. "Everybody knows how to do something until something goes wrong. That's when your skills come into the picture. When I started my challenge, I had quite a few backpacking nights under my belt, so I was safety-minded and did a risk analysis. I avoided the riskier parts of town and didn't camp out on Friday nights in the summer, when there were a lot of partygoers out and about."

Rooftops were not the only unusual camping spot during the year. During a ski trip to Italy, Hjort camped in a playground outside the hotel one night and was treated to hot tea by the staff the next morning. While guiding a group of fellow adventurers in Nepal, he slept several nights at sixteen thousand feet, surrounded by mooing yaks. The exotic locations were all fine and well, but Hjort contends that the greatest revelations came from exploring close to home. "I started to discover new things about my nearby nature areas, and I experienced them differently from when I walked or jogged or rode a bike. In one of them, I found an overgrown orchard and the grave of a local musician and composer, just a thirty-minute walk from where I lived at the time. Wherever I went, I was overcome with curiosity and saw nature with new eyes."

# SAMPLE PACKING LIST FOR BACKPACKING OR WILD CAMPING

Wild camping (i.e., sleeping in a place with no facilities) may take a little more advance planning than staying at a campground, but once you get the hang of it, it's no more difficult. Hiking into the campsite rather than driving is in some ways even easier, since you can bring only the bare necessities in your backpack, or it'll quickly become too heavy. Use this basic packing list as a starting point, but keep in mind that you may need to add or deduct some things depending on your unique circumstances and the size of your party.

## GENERAL

- ❑ BACKPACK WITH RAIN COVER (55 TO 75 LITERS IS USUALLY A GOOD SIZE FOR A NIGHT OR TWO)

- ❑ WATERPROOF BAGS TO ORGANIZE PACKING IN (REGULAR PLASTIC BAGS WORK JUST FINE)

- ❑ CAMPING SEAT PAD

## SLEEPING

- ❑ TENT OR HAMMOCK AND TARP

- ❑ SLEEPING PAD

- ❑ SLEEPING BAG

## TOOLS AND SURVIVAL

- ❑ CELL PHONE

- ❑ POWERBANK

- ❑ KNIFE

- ❑ HEADLAMP

- ❑ FIRE KIT (SEE INSTRUCTIONS ON PAGE 174)

- ❑ FIRST AID KIT

- ❑ MAP

- ❑ COMPASS

- ❑ REPAIR KIT (DUCT TAPE, NEEDLE AND THREAD)

## EATING AND DRINKING

- ❑ WATER FILTER
- ❑ WATER BOTTLE
- ❑ CAMPING STOVE AND FUEL
- ❑ COOKWARE
- ❑ MESS KIT
- ❑ THREE MEALS PER DAY, PLUS SOME EXTRAS
- ❑ TWO SNACKS PER DAY (DOUBLE FOR KIDS)

## CLOTHING

- ❑ DRESS IN LAYERS AND ACCORDING TO THE WEATHER (READ MORE ON PAGE 144)
- ❑ CHANGE OF CLOTHES
- ❑ HAT AND GLOVES
- ❑ RAIN GEAR
- ❑ COMFORTABLE HIKING BOOTS

## PERSONAL CARE AND CLEANING

- ❑ TROWEL
- ❑ TOILET PAPER
- ❑ WET WIPES
- ❑ HAND SANITIZER
- ❑ TOOTHBRUSH AND TOOTHPASTE
- ❑ SMALL BOTTLE OF BIODEGRADABLE DISH SOAP
- ❑ SMALL SPONGE
- ❑ DISH TOWEL/ LIGHTWEIGHT CAMPING TOWEL
- ❑ SMALL TRASH BAGS/ ZIPLOCK BAGS
- ❑ BUG SPRAY
- ❑ SUNSCREEN

# Camping adventures close to home

IF PITCHING A TENT ON your office building or in a city park sounds impractical or too risky, don't fret. Try to come up with potential wild camping spots near you, and think outside the box—you have nothing to lose by asking a landowner for permission. If you have a backyard, consider starting your outdoor nights there. Even if the scenery technically stays the same, it's a much different experience from sleeping in your bedroom. Outdoors, the sounds, the smells, and the sights are more intense, putting you in a state of alert while also giving you a sense of calm. It's while sleeping outside that the "free" in friluftsliv truly lives up to its name.

You don't even need camping gear to spend the night outside, just something to sleep on and a good bug repellent, should you be in mosquito country. When we lived in rural Indiana, my daughters and I would often sleep on our back porch, they with their duvets on the patio furniture, me on an inflatable mattress on the deck. In a state where public lands and campsites are few and far between, this was an easy way for us to sleep under the stars with zero preparations and minimal gear, even when I had to work the next day. The pasture next to us was not exactly competing with the Grand Canyon in terms of scenic views, but it was good enough. These humid summer nights on our back porch made a profound and lasting impression on all of us, and not only because we usually woke up soaked by heavy dew mixed up with dog slobber and cat hair from our beloved family pets. Gazing at the Milky Way tickled our sense of wonder as we tried to comprehend the incomprehensible and were slowly rocked to sleep by the chirping sounds of a small army of cicadas. The nights on the deck gave us pause from the everyday hustle and time to reflect—and connect.

Unlike Fredrik Hjort, we never set out to spend a certain number of nights under the open skies; it just became a regular beat of our family rhythm. It worked for us and our schedule, but something else might work for you. If you do decide to challenge yourself, make sure to match your aspirations to your current life situation and be careful not to turn your challenge into a competition with others. Friluftsliv is about being kind to yourself and the Earth, not about pushing yourself to break records or adding another "must-do" to your schedule. Just consider what might be a realistic goal for you and go for it.

## FIVE FABULOUS CAMPING HACKS

1. If you have space for it, bringing two sleeping pads—an inflatable pad and a foam pad—helps you stay warm and really boosts your comfort.

2. In the winter, fill a plastic bottle with hot water and put it in a sock for extra warmth when you go to sleep.

3. Put some clothing in your sleeping bag's stuff sack and—voilà—you've got yourself a pillow.

4. Organize your stuff by category in transparent or different-colored bags—for example, clothes, food, hygiene items. This will make it much easier to find what you need right away.

5. Bring a little something that adds a sense of luxury to your camping night, like a piece of decadent chocolate or a thermos with ready-made coffee for the morning.

# Three forms of friluftsliv

THE IDEA OF FRILUFTSLIV IS not to cram more activities into an already busy schedule. It's to make time for a lifestyle that is sustainable to you, your family, your community, and the planet. Once you start to adopt the mindset that time spent in nature is never wasted, letting go of less meaningful or even toxic habits will become a lot easier. Keep in mind that not every encounter with nature needs to be an epic adventure; open-air life spans everything from observing the birds on your street to climbing a mountaintop. In the Nordic tradition, you can in very general terms distinguish three levels of friluftsliv.

## 1. EVERYDAY FRILUFTSLIV

This is the kind of nature immersion that is accessible to you on an everyday basis. It could be things like riding your bike to work, going for a walk in a nearby park during your lunch break, or climbing some neighborhood trees with your kids after they get home from school. It relies on finding your local pockets of nature and making the most of them on a daily basis. Everyday friluftsliv requires minimal preparation, just a determination to get outside regardless of the weather.

## 2. WEEKEND FRILUFTSLIV

With the weekend comes opportunities for spending longer stretches of time outdoors, or to go *ut på tur*, as the Norwegians would say. For example, you might plan a longer *søndagstur* (Sunday trip) with friends, do a cookout over an open fire, go swimming, sleep outside, or do something else that you may find a little too time-consuming or messy for a weekday. It's a perfect time to practice new friluftsliv skills and try out gear that you're planning to use on longer trips.

# 3. VACATION FRILUFTSLIV

When you have a little more time off, you have a chance to get further away from civilization and align yourself with a more natural rhythm, away from everyday musts and stressors. Let go of your calendar, cell phone notifications, and modern conveniences like running water, and try roughing it the friluftsliv way in the wild for a few days, a week, or longer. Try to plan for at least one extended stay in a natural area every year, since these trips will help you recharge, improve your sleep, and give you an opportunity to try the simple life for real.

# The silence within

IN TELEBORG NATURE RESERVE, JUST outside the city of Växjö in southern Sweden, fifty-four-year-old Peter Lönn walked his bike through rocky, gently rolling hills covered in grass and occasional oak trees and junipers. In a pragmatic fusion of nature and culture that is a common sight here, cattle grazed the pastures to keep the vegetation down and the views in the preserve open for people to enjoy. But this was no leisurely bike ride for Lönn. He works for the city as a friluftsliv coordinator, and this day his task was to record the sound level of the preserve. He pulled out his cell phone from his backpack, and using a sound-meter app, he started to measure the soundscape, both the faint humming of the city just a few hundred yards away and the sounds of nature—the whispers of a lazy breeze, birds tweeting from a nearby fir, water trickling through a creek. The meter showed that it was well below 40 decibels, just as he had predicted.

Lönn was the man behind an initiative to map quiet places and areas near the city and put them in an app and on the web, to make them better known to the public. Using noise-data maps from 2003 and his own experience from walking and biking near the city, he narrowed down the best spots, one by one. "I sought out green spaces away from the highways and discovered that even though I was so close to the city, the sounds of nature dominated. That's important, because a good sound environment is more than freedom from noise pollution," said Lönn, whose own interest in friluftsliv was born from his orienteering days in his teens. Then, like now, the forest was his arena. That's where he had his first transformative nature experiences and learned to care for the environment. Now, connecting people with nature was a part of his job, and he saw a need for the local administration both to help the residents discover the city's quiet green spaces and to preserve them for the future.

To qualify for the list, the sound level of any given nature area must be below 45 decibels and be perceived as pleasant by at least 80 percent of the visitors. In Växjö, all the quiet places on the list fall between 35 and 40 decibels, depending on the wind, traffic, weather, season, time of the day, and other factors.

"We know from our own surveys that the most common reason why people go outside is for relaxation and mental restoration, and places with good sound environments offer the best restorative qualities. These are places where you can turn off your cell phone, let go of everyday worries, touch things, feel things, take in the atmosphere."

Lönn is not the only one seeking silence in the great outdoors. The desire to find peace and quiet, away from the noise pollution of the cities, was a major driver behind the open-air-life movement from the early days, and it's still one of the main reasons why people in the Nordic countries seek out nature. While you may be forgiven for blasting your portable smartphone speakers and being loud with fifteen of your closest friends at a busy park or beach, the tolerance for noise drops exponentially in the forest and other areas that people generally turn to in order to seek stillness. This unspoken code of conduct inadvertently sometimes leads to culture clashes.

I remember feeling slightly shocked the first time I encountered a young couple blasting electronic dance music from a speaker attached to their backpack while out for a hike in rural Illinois. Nothing personal against EDM, I enjoy it myself sometimes, but in my world, the monotonous beat from the speaker did not rhyme with a scenic wooded trail in a quiet county park. At first I dismissed it as a one-off incident. They were young and maybe this was just their way of enjoying some time together outdoors. But it would not be the last time that I encountered people playing loud music in nature, older adults too.

In the great scheme of things, people enjoying some tunes on a trail or at a campsite may not seem like a big deal, but being able to find tranquility in nature is more important than ever. The human-made noise that started to become a problem with the Industrial Revolution is now a part of our everyday lives, and our ears are constantly bombarded with stimuli. Even though we can get used to noise pollution (for example by subconsciously blocking out the sound of rumbling trains if you live close to a railroad), it can potentially damage our health in several ways. Research shows that people who live or work in loud environments are more likely to suffer from heart disease and high blood pressure, as well as a slew of health issues caused by not getting enough sleep. Noise not only affects humans, but it can also disturb wildlife and potentially disrupt entire ecosystems.

Trees and shrubs have the ability to dampen noise pollution from roads, railways, airports, and industries. That means even small urban parks can make a big difference for improving soundscapes and the opportunities for friluftsliv in cities, where it's not as easy to get away from acoustic litter. But open-air life is not just about getting away from something; it's also about training our minds to tune into nature regardless of where we are. Roger Isberg, the outdoorsman and friluftsliv author, describes how embracing tranquility from the inside and out helps us deepen our relationship with the natural world. In his book *Simple Life*, he describes how he sometimes sits in nature for hours, leaning against a fir tree and letting his mind come to peace, while quietly observing nature around him. In the beginning, his mind and senses are preoccupied with thoughts and impressions. After an hour or two, boredom sets in. Then he finds a flow. Without analyzing further, he experiences the colors of the leaves, the birdsong from the trees, and a spider that catches a fly in its web. As Isberg says, "Nature's voice is finely tuned," and hearing it takes practice. Those who are successful can find peace both in nature and in themselves.

# Five friluftsliv tips to really hear nature

1. **Seek out quiet places.** Blocking out all signs of civilization is difficult in the city, but some places are quieter than others. Hills, vegetation, and trees all absorb and deflect sound waves, and running water can help drown out less desirable sounds from traffic.

2. **Use your body.** Taking the car or riding public transit is sometimes unavoidable to get to a park or nature area, but vehicles tend to close you off from all nature sounds. Try to walk, ride a bike, or propel yourself some other way whenever you can, even if the route is not the most scenic option. With friluftsliv, the journey is an important part of the experience.

3. **Be present.** To experience a deeper connection with the land, put your cell phone and other digital devices in silent mode and use them judiciously. As long as we keep checking emails, posting social media updates, and using our phones to chat with others while outside, we mentally transport ourselves away from the people we are with and the place we are trying to experience.

4. **Take it slow.** Whether you're walking, paddling, floating, or moving yourself some other way, don't rush it. By going slowly, you have a greater chance of picking up nature sounds. Make listening stops and take in all the sounds; observe each one without judgment.

5. **Use all your senses.** Hearing is only one of our senses, and by smelling, tasting, feeling, and seeing nature, we will hear the sounds more clearly as well.

## THE FRILUFTSLIV CODE OF SILENCE

The desire to experience stillness and enjoy nature without getting disturbed runs deep within the friluftsliv culture. If you run into other people who are having a quiet moment in nature, good practice is to give them some space or try to find another spot if you're looking to make a stop.

# PART II

*Land, then, is not merely soil; it is a fountain*

*of energy flowing through a circuit of soils,*

*plants and animals.*

—ALDO LEOPOLD

F rom the craggy mountains to the soil under our feet and the green spaces that it sustains, from the old-growth forest in roadless country to the well-trodden parks in the middle of the busiest metropolitan areas, our Earth gives us so many havens of growth and life where we can experience a profound inter-connectedness with nature. How else can we explain that walking among trees can help reduce feelings of anxiety, fatigue, and depression or that living near urban green spaces literally can extend our lives? Meanwhile, digging in the dirt puts us in contact with beneficial microbes in the soil, which in turn can increase our resilience to stress and make us happier. So powerful is our evolutionary link to earth that even looking at greenery can make our bodies heal faster.

We may have migrated from the savanna to the skyscraper and invented self-driving cars and the Internet of Things, but when it comes down to it, we can't eliminate our inner craving for green space any more than we can keep a wild-caught dolphin at an aquarium from longing for the ocean.

But open-air life was never intended solely as another self-help strategy for stressed-out city dwellers who have been removed from their natural habitat. From the national park movement at the start of the twentieth century to the push to combat global climate change today, friluftsliv has always been a reaction against modernity and the damage it has wrought on nature. It's a way to strengthen the physical and mental health of the population, sure, but just as much a means to promote environmental protection through a personal attachment to nature. Regular, slow nature experiences help us become knowledgeable about the ecosystems that sustain us and help us develop an affinity with other species who walk alongside us. This strong sense of belonging to the landscape is believed to make us better environmental stewards, since we don't want to hurt the things we love. And this attachment is lifelong.

## Friluftsliv as medicine for the soul

ONE BY ONE THEY FILED into the nineteenth-century red homestead at the nature preserve Rya Ridges in Borås, six men and women in all. They came from vastly different socioeconomic and professional backgrounds but had one thing in common: They were all suffering from stress-induced mental health issues, which are now the single biggest reason for longtime sick leave in Sweden. Most were diagnosed with exhaustion disorder, a condition that is typically caused by severe stress and causes extreme fatigue, often followed by depression. Some of them had not worked for years. Here, among the towering spruces and open pastures, they would begin their healing journey, using nothing but nature and the gentle guidance of Lisbeth Lorentzon, a health coach funded by the local government.

Every day started the same way, with the group changing into work clothes and gathering around one of the tables inside the homestead. Then Lorentzon did a quick check and sometimes a guided relaxation before they all headed outside, rain or shine. "If the weather is crappy, everybody's not always too enthused about going outside, but we try to choose activities that will spark joy, regardless of the weather," Lorentzon said.

The local government handpicked Rya Ridges for this nature-therapy venture because of its unique qualities. It is far from pristine wilderness, as humans have molded the deep forests and flowering meadows here to suit their needs for centuries, adding a rock wall here, cultivating a field there, cutting down trees, and building simple farmhouses. Rather than returning it to its original feral state when it was declared a nature preserve in 2001, the government decided to retain and manage the area the same way it had been a century ago. Yet the lay of the land could not be more appealing to our inner hunter-gatherer. The solid hillside behind the farmhouse offers a sense of security, the grazed fields in front of it make it hard for enemies to sneak up undetected, and the surrounding forests and streams beckon with edibles and potential prey.

Many of the participants were high achievers before they hit the infamous wall and eventually decided to try nature therapy. Some already enjoyed walking in the woods; others were scared to death of nature. Here, they all got to explore nature on their own terms, regardless of previous experience. "Sometimes it can be a challenge for our participants to let go of their 'problem-solving brain,' but in nature, the learning happens effortlessly. We often practice being in the present moment, and it's something they can apply in their everyday lives to improve health and quality of life," Lorentzon said. To that end, the program often incorporates mindfulness in nature, for example by looking at fractal patterns. Fractals are series of patterns, or mathematical shapes, that repeat themselves over and over again at different scales, and they can be found everywhere in nature, for example in trees, snowflakes, lightning bolts, and leaves from ferns and other plants. Lorentzon picked up a fallen oak leaf and ran her finger along the protruding veins on the back. "We observe an oak leaf just as thoroughly as a scientist would; we study every detail," she said.

Sometimes they do sensory walks around the preserve, focusing on just one sense at a time—watching, listening, touching, smelling, and tasting the natural world around them. They have made a body scrub from birch bark, cooked with shoots from pine trees, and collected sap from birch trees while Lorentzon talked about the historic use of the slightly sweet liquid as a remedy for PMS, inflammation, and other ailments.

Healing did not come just from immersion in wild nature; the program leveraged the therapeutic effects of gardening as well. In a rectangular space about the size of a spacious living room and enclosed by an old-style wooden fence, carrots, cabbage, potatoes, spinach, and other vegetables were sprouting in the early-summer sun. The act of sowing the seeds, nourishing them to life, weeding out the dead parts, and then harvesting the crop became symbolic of starting over and getting a new shot at life itself. Just digging in the dirt can be particularly healing, as the soil teems with *Mycobacterium vaccae*, a group of microorganisms that are believed to have anti-inflammatory effects on the brain. This may in turn boost our mood and make the brain more resilient to stress-induced disorders.

Thirty or forty years ago, this program probably would have been dismissed as pure hocus-pocus. But while the pioneers in nature-based therapy were viewed with a mixed sense of bewilderment and suspicion, we know today that they were right. Nature-based interventions have not only been proved effective in the treatment of a host of mental disorders, but in cases of severe stress, burnout, and depression, they appear to be even more successful in getting people back to work than both pharmaceuticals and other forms of therapy. A study done by researchers at the Alnarp Rehabilitation Garden at the Swedish University of Agricultural Sciences (SLU) showed that nearly two-thirds of the people who participated in nature-based rehabilitation were able to return to work or some form of job training within a year after the start of the rehab. Not bad considering that all of them had been on 100 percent sick leave before that, most of them for over two years. The study also showed that the longer the participants had been in the program (it was available for a period of eight, twelve, or twenty-four weeks), the more likely they were to get a paid job, either full-time or part-time. The sunlight, physical activity, improved sleep, and innately destressing properties of nature areas probably all contributed to the positive results.

From being considered an experimental form of therapy accessible in just a couple of areas in Sweden, nature-based treatment is now widely available across the country. Similar programs exist in the other Nordic countries, as governments here explicitly recognize friluftsliv as a powerful antidote to a sedentary lifestyle and modern public health challenges like obesity, stress, sleeping disorders, anxiety, and depression. As these public health systems have realized, preventing and treating disease through nature exposure is good policy not just for the individuals on the receiving end of it. Since the Nordic countries have universal health care paid for through taxes, improved public health is indirectly also good for people's pocketbooks.

The program at Rya Ridges is firmly rooted in both the research coming out of SLU and other psychological interventions and theories, like acceptance and commitment therapy, attention restoration theory, the biophilia hypothesis, and psycho-evolutionary theory. For the participants, though, the science behind the nature-based therapy in the program is secondary. "A lot of people feel that nature is rehabilitating, and we talk about the research behind it, but I always say that their own perceptions about it are more important," Lorentzon said. "This program is not about presenting different theories; it's about feeling and exploring yourself. Being in nature can mean so many different things to each individual."

Like the thirtysomething man who had never spent much time in nature or even made a connection between nature and his own well-being when he got sick. By the time he came to Lorentzon at Rya Ridges, he was in bad shape, suffering from severe depression. In the beginning, he was skeptical of the treatment. But one crisp fall day, a couple of months into the program, Lorentzon found him standing completely still under a towering linden tree outside the old farmstead, looking up into the crown, visibly in awe. "'I finally get it,' he told me." The man lived in an apartment in town and didn't have much access to wilderness, but he had discovered a tree just outside his window. "'I sit under the tree outside my apartment every day now, drawing power from it. And it's magical.'"

# The special standing of trees

THE VIKINGS BELIEVED THAT TREES held magical powers and that the gods lived by the roots of a giant evergreen ash called Yggdrasil. Trees, with their roots burrowing deep into the soil and their branches sprawling high into the sky, were seen as a link between the earthly and the heavenly, the living and the deceased. An emblematic sign of trees' special standing in the agrarian society of yore was that well into the twentieth century, it was customary to build your house close to a large hardwood or, if there was none, to plant one. This was called a *vårdträd* in Swedish, or "caring tree," and supposedly protected the home against shady supernatural powers. The caring tree was a natural gathering point for special events and seasonal rites on the farm, which helped those who came in contact with it on a daily basis develop a sense of place. People typically held the caring tree in deep respect, as it represented continuity from one generation to the next, and under no circumstances was it acceptable to cut it down or even break off branches from it.

With urbanization, the significance of caring trees would eventually diminish, but today, people in the Nordic countries find other ways of connecting with trees. Tree hugging and meditating under the tree crowns are two examples of fairly new friluftsliv activities that have been inspired by the Japanese mindfulness practice *shinrin-yoku*, or forest bathing. Scientists studying forest bathing have found that it can boost the immune system, reduce stress, decrease blood pressure, and increase a general sense of well-being. A sign that trees have if not magical then at least healing powers.

## PLANT A CARING TREE

If you have a yard, consider planting your own caring tree to strengthen your sense of place and making it a part of seasonal celebrations as well as everyday life. In the Nordic countries, traditional caring trees were typically deciduous species like linden, oak, maple, ash, chestnut, and elm, but you should choose a tree that is native to and will thrive in your region. If you don't have your own yard, find a special tree in nature or a park that speaks to you and make a point to visit it often. If you feel inclined, hug it!

# OUR NEED FOR GREEN—FIVE THEORIES

## 1. THE BIOPHILIA HYPOTHESIS

The biophilia hypothesis was developed by American biologist Edward O. Wilson in the 1980s and holds that humans have an innate fondness for nature because for millennia that is where we evolved. Our brains simply gravitate toward what we know and need, and from an evolutionary perspective, that is neither five-lane highways nor advanced cloud storage solutions. Nope, deep inside we crave plants, because historically we have depended on plants as food, shelter, and a sign of water. This would also be why people in most cultures have a propensity for adding plants to human-made surroundings, for example by creating city parks or bringing in potted plants. In other words, the fiddle-leaf fig in your living room may be more than pure decor—it could be a sign of your inner caveman calling.

## 2. ATTENTION RESTORATION THEORY

If you ever wondered why you feel mentally drained after a day at work but refreshed after a walk in the woods, attention restoration theory, or ART, may offer a clue. According to ART, complex tasks like navigating through busy traffic, solving a difficult math problem, or making sense of a complicated textbook require a state of directed attention. This state makes our prefrontal cortex work really hard, which over time can lead to mental burnout. Nature, on the other hand, is free from distractions and full of stimuli that have a restorative effect. Listening to birds chirping in the backyard or watching a beautiful sunset takes up very little of our mental hard drive, instead evoking an effortless, soft fascination that provides a barrier against stress. While sleep can help us recover from the daily stressors to some extent, restoration while you're awake is far more effective. And that is why it's always worth making time for some after-work R&R in your neighborhood green space.

## 3. PSYCHO-EVOLUTIONARY THEORY

Some views and environments are not only better than others, but they also have the power to heal. That is, simply put, the premise behind psycho-evolutionary theory. The theory is the brainchild of American researcher Roger Ulrich, whose famous 1984 hospital study showed that patients recovered faster after surgery and needed fewer pain medications when their room had a window with a view of trees, rather than a window facing a brick wall. According to psycho-evolutionary theory, the explanation can be found deep down in our evolutionary past and our bodies' responses to stressful situations. While the human-made cityscapes that we normally surround ourselves with tend to induce stress, natural elements like greenery and water trigger positive emotions and feelings. In fact, simply looking at a video of nature scenes can tame stress reactions like increased blood pressure, pulse rate, and muscle activity. When the stress response is curbed, our ability to heal also improves rapidly. The moral of the story? When given a choice, go for the room with a view.

## 4. CULTURAL LEARNING THEORY

Some researchers believe that the positive effects of being in nature are not a result of biological factors but are rather a cultural construct. According to this view, we feel good in nature because we have been taught that nature is good for us and therefore expect it to have restorative properties. Cultural differences, internalized thought patterns (that would be our parents repeatedly telling us that "fresh air is good for you"), and ideals in society all come together to infuse us with a love for nature. This could help explain why the friluftsliv tradition is so strong in the Nordic countries, where the view that nature heals has been around since the Romantic era, and questioning that idea is almost on par with treason. The cultural learning theory also suggests that our experiences of certain nature types in childhood are key to how we perceive them as adults. For example, if you grew up near the forest and spent a lot of time in it as a child, you're prone to favor a similar landscape, climate, and wildlife as an adult. Don't worry, though. In line with this theory, you can always learn to appreciate something else later in life.

## 5. CALM AND CONNECTION THEORY

One of the newest theories about the restorative effects of nature revolves around the calm and connected feeling that participants in "green" rehabilitation programs all seem to share. When we feel calm and connected, our stress levels go down, and we can develop health and coping skills that help us heal. A new theory proposes that the reason why we easily find our zen in nature is that it triggers the release of oxytocin, also called the "love hormone," which promotes bonding and attachment between humans and humans and animals. We already know that our bodies release oxytocin when we breastfeed, cuddle, have sex, or even play with our dog. Now researchers believe that nature has a similar effect, especially when we visit places that we associate with positive memories. This in turn supposedly helps us develop an attachment, or "friendship," with nature that is similar to the relationships that we have with other humans or our pets. The stronger this attachment, the more relaxed we will feel when spending time in nature and the more powerful the restorative effect will be. For the full effect, bring your favorite human to the park. Or at least your dog.

# The power of parks

IT WAS THE REINDEER FOOD that ultimately would change the course of Patrik Grahn's life. Not the kind you and your kids might make out of oats, crushed pretzels, and colored sprinkles to help guide Santa's sleigh to your home on Christmas, but the real, moss-like lichen that is the primary winter food for reindeer and caribou in the wild. Reindeer husbandry is the traditional occupation of the indigenous Sami people in Sweden, Norway, and Finland, and as a research assistant at a field research station in Storuman in northern Sweden, Grahn was tasked with studying the rate at which lichen grows, to determine the limitations of the animals' winter grazing. In a "is this really what I want to do with my life?" moment, he instead decided to move south to study landscape architecture at SLU's campus at Alnarp in southern Sweden. Little did he know that he would go on to pioneer a new field of research focused on the therapeutic effects of nature and the connection between human health and urban friluftsliv.

But first, a slight detour. It was the mid-1980s, and local government officials in Lund were on a mission to make the city more compact and efficient. All parks and green spaces that were considered redundant must go to make way for new apartment buildings. And Grahn, who was just out of school, was the person holding his finger on the trigger. "My job was to go around and dole out death sentences to a number of parks, and I thought that was really strange. I wanted to know who was using the parks and why, so I turned to researchers for advice, but there were no studies on it," said Grahn, who despite having lived down south for over forty years still speaks with a distinctly northern, unhurried dialect.

With no existing research to guide him, he applied for—and received—grants to study the parks himself. He approached organizations, preschools, and elderly people at assisted-living facilities who were all using the local parks and green spaces and asked them to keep diaries of their visits. The result of Grahn's investigation came as a surprise.

"The respondents' answers puzzled me. They said they felt so good outside, and that being in the parks was beneficial to their health. Nobody talked about that back then; they might as well have been talking about electromagnetic hypersensitivity or crystals—it just wasn't in the public consciousness at all."

Professor Grahn's initial pilot study was the first of many to come, all exploring how people from different demographics used urban parks and other nature areas, and how this affected their physical and mental health. One of his most-cited studies showed that children at so-called forest schools, where the majority of the day is spent outside, had better gross motor skills, higher concentration levels, and fewer sick days than their counterparts had at traditional preschools. A few years later, he led several studies with a public health focus, involving tens of thousands of city dwellers in southern Sweden. The researchers looked at the location of people's homes in correlation to green spaces, and as they began to crunch the numbers, they made a startling discovery. The farther away people lived from a green space, the more stressed they were. They also reported being in worse health, had a higher average body mass index, and were less satisfied with their home and neighborhood. But why? Some factors behind the improved health outcomes for people who have easier access to urban green spaces were simple to explain. More daylight helps regulate cortisol and melatonin levels, which in turn improves sleep. UVB rays from the sun generate vitamin D, which is key to a host of bodily functions. People who lived closer to a green space were also more physically active, which can reduce stress by stimulating the production of endorphins, our "feel-good hormone."

But Grahn felt like there was more to uncover behind the numbers. He was particularly interested in learning what the magic distance was to a green space to facilitate urban open-air life on an everyday basis. After multiple studies involving tens of thousands of people, he eventually established that the breaking point was at three hundred meters, approximately one thousand feet. "When the distance from the home to a greenspace is greater than that, going to the park typically becomes a weekend activity, not an everyday habit. And young children and people with disabilities ideally need to have the green space right outside their door," Grahn explained.

Intrigued, Grahn and his colleagues delved ever deeper down the rabbit hole of urban friluftsliv research. They asked themselves what size a green space needs to be to have a positive health effect (ideally, at least a couple of acres), how often people need to visit and for how long (the more the better, but at least two to five hours per week), and what types of green spaces are the most restorative (it depends on the purpose of the visit—different green spaces provide different benefits). Ultimately, they defined eight different characteristics, or "sensory dimensions," of a green space that meet different human needs and therefore make it beneficial from a personal and public health perspective. For example, that it is spacious enough for wandering around in; is perceived as natural and serene; is rich in species; has space for playing and socializing with others; has areas where users feel protected; and has an open area with a view and cultural elements like flower beds and water fountains. Of all the dimensions, the people in the studies tended to rate serenity, space, and natural elements the highest.

"If we can include these eight perceived sensory dimensions of urban greenspace, parks can function as venues for friluftsliv. In those parks you get a feeling of leaving the city and entering something else. Stress goes down, you're able to organize your thoughts, and the executive function begins to recover. It makes a huge difference."

So, what happened to the parks and green spaces that Grahn was tasked with condemning all those years ago? Most of them are still there. Only a couple of big lawns were ultimately selected for development; they were the ones with the least recreational value. The political pressure to build more condensed cities remains, but at the same time, more people in power are becoming aware of the therapeutic and general public-health effects of nature. With a vast majority of the population in the Western world now living in cities and only a small percentage of our time being spent outside, it certainly seems like we need our urban parks and green spaces more than ever.

"Most people live in cities today, and I think it's important to make nature accessible to everybody," Grahn said. "Anytime you can get outside your door, it's a good thing."

## THE BEST GREEN SPACES FOR COMBATING STRESS

Do you suffer from stress or anxiety? If so, research suggests that natural green spaces that are rich in wildlife and offer secluded "hideaway" areas are your best bet for restoration. Parks that are more geared toward social activities are great for meeting people face-to-face and cultivating community but are thought to be less restorative from a stress perspective.

# Bird radio and moose TV

IN EARLY MAY 2020, NEARLY four hundred thousand people tuned in to Swedish public radio to listen to a new type of live show, one that promised to take the listeners through a "magical night" of concerts from five scenes, from north to south. The lineup for this unprecedented eight-hour event included some of the country's foremost artists, and some commentators went so far as hailing it as "the greatest cultural event of the year." But the main characters of this hyped-up marathon concert were neither rock stars nor famous opera singers. They were blackbirds, Eurasian curlews, wrens, black grouses, robins, nightingales, and many others. The idea for the show, called *A Night of Birdsong*, was simple—to draw attention to the birds' return from their annual migration south and celebrate the reawakening of nature after winter hibernation.

"[Birdsong] is something wonderful, and this gala that opens every morning is maybe a little underappreciated," the cohost Mats Ottosson said about the motivation behind the show, as he and the other cohost, Jenny Berntson Djurvall, came on the air. He did not need to worry about the turnout, however. The program was an instant hit, and the radio station was flooded with social media messages and phone calls from listeners providing commentary and asking questions.

In 2021, the program returned by popular demand, and the radio station once again placed its reporters and bird experts in five different bird locales around Sweden, from Abisko in the north to the island of Öland in the south, to air an eight-hour bonanza of birdsong.

"Are the artists fine-tuning their instruments? Have some of them already started with the first movement, or are they still silent, while waiting for dawn?" Ottosson asked, building anticipation for the avian musical numbers that were to come, before delving into a dueling pair of sedge warblers. Then he and the rest of the team treated the listeners to a cavalcade of birdcalls, bird trivia, and birdsong bingo, and carefully guided them through impromptu sessions performed by the melodious willow warbler as well as the hoarsely hacking graylag goose. Between 4:00 and 5:00 a.m., or what is sometimes called the "dawn chorus," since that is the time of the day when birds are typically the most active, the show reached its crescendo, with an hour of uninterrupted birdsong.

This time, nearly five hundred thousand people, or 5 percent of the Swedish population, forsook sleep to listen to the avian choir from around the country. When comparing numbers as a share of the population, there were more Swedes tuning into *A Night of Birdsong* than there were Americans watching the Academy Awards and the Emmy Awards combined. The concept for the show, which originated in Ireland under the name *Dawn Chorus*, clearly met an unserved need among the public.

Meanwhile on TV, some of the country's most popular celebrities are not reality stars or actors, but a herd of moose. Because around the same time as the birds start to return from their winter abodes, hundreds of moose in Ångermanland, in northern Sweden, begin their annual migration to their summer pastures, an ordinary event that is now documented by a TV production team using thirty cameras, including several night cameras, a superzoom, and a drone. For three weeks every spring, the moose are streamed around the clock, for a total of approximately five hundred hours, in a program aptly named *The Great Moose Migration*. The show breaks all the rules for today's frenzied, fragmented media logic; most of the time the cameras have little to show but an empty stand of spruces or some ice floes quietly making their way down a river. In addition to the livestream, the production team selects the daily highlights and posts them with enticing titles like "Three Moose Walk Toward the Camera," "Moose Finds the Microphone," and "Dancing Canada Geese."

Despite the excruciatingly slow pace, or maybe because of it, the program was a huge success from the first season and even won a prestigious TV award for "Most Innovative Show" in 2019. The following couple of years, the livestream of the migrating moose gave comfort, company, and predictability to scores of people working from home because of the pandemic, boosting the popularity of the show even further. Society had been shaken to its core by an invisible foe, but in front of their TVs and computer screens, people found joy while keenly awaiting the climax of the migration—the moment when the first animals would enter the river at the same place where they have crossed it for thousands of years.

Far from all the fans of this new genre of bird radio and moose TV are ornithologists or expert naturalists. Many, if not most, are just regular people seeking pause and reflection in an age when both tend to be in short supply. Just as looking at nature scenes can make our bodies heal faster, waiting for hours to hear the nightingale sing or see a moose that may or may not show up at the riverfront can be a boon to the stressed soul. Maybe more important, these types of shows give us a way to feel connected with elusive wildlife and be awed by the natural world, even when we are inside. Or as Ottosson, the *Night of Birdsong* cohost, said when he tried to describe his feelings while listening to the dawn chorus: "I became very moved; it was like listening to a live broadcast of life itself. Judging by the reactions from our listeners, many of them felt the same way."

*When the flowers appear in the meadows,*
*And the birch trees leaf in the bower,*
*The cuckoo will sing in the forest*
*At both morning and evening hour.*

*When the scythes have swept through the meadow*
*And the flowers all lie on their bier,*
*The cuckoo is mute in the forest,*
*And stays silent till spring is near.*

—AUGUST STRINDBERG,
"THE CUCKOO"

# In search of the elusive cuckoo

EVERY SPRING, USUALLY AROUND ASCENSION DAY according to the Christian calendar, the cuckoo returns to Sweden from Central Africa, where it spends the winter. So do a lot of migrating birds, of course, but the cuckoo's return is traditionally marked with a *gökotta*, which loosely translates to "cuckoo dawn." To celebrate the gökotta, you get up early in the morning—preferably before sunup—pack a picnic, and head out to the woods or a park.

Nobody knows for sure when the cuckoo received this special standing in the friluftsliv tradition, but the custom has roots in the old agrarian society. Nor is it completely clear why the Swedes decided to throw a party for the cuckoo and not for, say, the stock dove, but it probably has to do with the old folk belief that cuckoos held special powers to predict the future with their distinctive calls. During the gökotta, calls coming from the west were considered the best, whereas calls from the south were believed to be a precursor of death. Women especially paid close attention to the cuckoo, since the number of calls was believed to equal the number of years that were left until they would get married.

Today, the demand for cuckoo prophecies about life and love has declined, and so has the number of cuckoos, but nevertheless the tradition lives on. Ironically, it's not unusual for a modern gökotta to involve both choirs and troubadour music, which is a nice way to hail the spring but inevitably makes it a lot harder to hear the cuckoo, or any birds for that matter. Churches have also picked up on the tradition, and many take the opportunity to merge the gökotta with Ascension Day, celebrating both with an outdoor service. *Fika*—Swedish for the social time that typically involves coffee or tea and a sweet treat—is usually a mainstay of these events, as is venturing into the woods to listen to and identify the spring birds.

In all, the gökotta is a motley mix of pagan beliefs interlaced with Christian practices and a little bit of nature worship sprinkled on top. It's yet another way that open-air life makes something extraordinary out of the seemingly ordinary in nature. And you don't have to live in cuckoo habitat to enjoy an early-morning birding session. Although the cuckoo has one of the most distinctive sounds of all birds—the name even gives it away—plenty of other species are easy to identify once you know what to listen for. In North America, for example, the rich, throaty sound of the American robin can be heard almost everywhere and is considered a surefire sign of spring, even if most robins don't migrate in the winter.

At a time when a packed calendar has become a status symbol, there is something quaint and comforting about the idea of getting up at the crack of dawn simply to tune into the sound of birdsong. There are hidden benefits of this pastime as well. A multidisciplinary research team at the Swedish University of Agricultural Sciences has found that listening to birds can boost our well-being and make us feel more positive about living in the city. The team spent three years studying the effects of different sounds and smells on city dwellers who were subjected to stress and found that natural environments had the most soothing sounds. Most calming of all, even more so than the sound of water and rustling leaves, was the sound of birdsong. While the vocals of showier songbirds like the cuckoo and nightingale typically get the most attention in the public mind, more inconspicuous yet melodious species like the Eurasian blue tit, common blackbird, and woodpecker also had a calming effect, the study found. The more species that are in the mix, the more notable the effect.

For some, the mental benefits of birdsong can literally be a lifesaver. Joe Harkness, teacher and author of the book *Bird Therapy*, discovered birding after years of battling drug abuse and depression, eventually hitting the bottom with a failed suicide attempt. The turning point came when he was out for a walk to soothe his angst and heard a couple of common buzzards calling each other while diving up and down in the air. He was fascinated and in awe. This pivotal moment was followed by many more, as birding became a crucial part of Harkness's rehabilitation. In fact, he found birding more powerful and long-lasting than any other forms of therapy that he had previously tried. Whether he was embraced by the ecstatic whistling of a wood lark after a rough day at work or spending a day tracking down the local species with his grandfather, he gradually started to find his way out of the darkness and his will to live returned. The experience prompted Harkness to develop his own bird therapy program, "five ways to well-birding," which focuses on attachment to birds, people, and places in nature.

The beauty of birding is that it can be done everywhere, including in the city. If you don't have woods or other wild spaces nearby, pick a park or other urban green space for your early-morning birding sessions. Make it as simple as bringing a picnic and enjoying the burst of birdsong, or go all out and learn which migratory birds come through your area and what they sound like—the choice is yours. Getting to know some common bird sounds will certainly add another dimension to the experience of the gökotta, but don't get hung up on finding a specific species if it feels overwhelming. Harkness noted that going to big bird events and traveling to far-flung locations just to put a check mark on a particularly rare species may actually trigger anxiety and stress in those who are prone to it, especially when it's done under competitive forms. Competition runs counter to the friluftsliv ethos, since it shifts the focus away from communing with nature and by default puts you in a different mindset.

A gökotta could be a good starting point to get to know your local bird population, and whether or not you hear a cuckoo, you will not be sorry that you made the effort. You will most likely hear other birds, and the benefits of birdsong are real. Besides, nothing beats drinking your morning coffee under a tree at the crack of dawn.

## What to bring for a successful morning birding session

- Seat pad or blanket to sit on
- Thermos with a hot drink
- Sandwiches (and maybe some cookies)
- Binoculars
- Bird book or bird guide app
- Clothes for the weather

## BECOME AN AMATEUR BIRDER IN NO TIME

The Audubon Society is a good place to start if you want to learn more about your local bird population. And yes, there's an app for that. In fact, *The Audubon Bird Guide* is one of many bird guides that now come in the form of an app and will help you identify species by photo or sound, search for recent sightings, and learn what birds are common in your area. Other popular birding apps are eBird and Merlin Bird ID, both developed by the Cornell Lab of Ornithology. Another way to try your hand at bird-watching is to participate in the Great Backyard Bird Count, a citizen-science project that engages tens of thousands of people every year.

# Keeping your feet on the ground

AN EVEN MORE LITERAL WAY of connecting with the earth than birding is to walk barefoot. The invention of shoes about forty thousand years ago marked the beginning of the end of this habit, but in the friluftsliv culture it has experienced a revival lately, with some paths across the Nordic countries now being designated barefoot trails. Runners clamoring for a better, more natural step and fewer injuries have led the charge when it comes to ditching their shoes or switching to minimalist models, but many walkers enjoy it as well, and not just for the physical benefits. It's also a way to practice mindfulness in nature.

A barefoot trail can be a short trail where different materials have purposely been placed on the ground to offer a range of sensory experiences. But it can also be any trail where you decide to walk barefoot.

"Wearing boots removes you from the ground and limits your sensory input," said Caroline Winroth, a thirty-five-year-old mother who volunteers for the Swedish Outdoor Association. "Walking barefoot brings you closer to earth by heightening the senses. All of a sudden, you're feeling whether the ground is warm or cold, prickly or soft, or whatever it might be. Normally when you walk, you activate your smell, vision, and hearing, but when you're barefoot, you add the sense of touch as well."

Winroth decided to organize a barefoot walk in the urban forests outside Stockholm, where she lives, after hearing and reading about the benefits. Proponents of walking barefoot emphasize that treading on uneven surfaces not only promotes a more natural gait, it also stimulates pressure points on the soles of the feet. This natural foot massage improves circulation, eases tight muscles, and releases endorphins, which in turn can relieve pain and make us feel relaxed and contented. A study of nursing home residents even showed that walking barefoot on cobblestones can improve balance and reduce blood pressure. While the long-term effects of barefoot walking are under-researched, scientists seem to agree that it does result in stronger feet. That's a big deal, since your feet provide the base for the rest of your body, each containing twenty-six bones, thirty-three joints, and over one hundred small ligaments that are keeping it all together, as well as a number of nerve endings. With stronger feet comes improved stability, balance, and posture, as well as the prevention of common injuries.

Anecdotally, it's also a phenomenal way to wind down after work, and one that leaves you feeling far more refreshed than a night at the bar. That's why Winroth picked a Wednesday evening at six thirty to meet up. The area for the walk was deliberately chosen as well; this was her "home forest," a place she knew well, so she didn't need to worry about using a map to find the way and could focus solely on being mindful in nature.

In addition to Winroth, three women and a man gathered for the first walk in September. The small group headed into the woods, following a narrow trail through the spruces. Initially, some were worried about stepping on slimy mushrooms or slugs, but once their feet hit the trail, their concerns dissipated. They walked over pine needles, roots, and rocks, embracing the texture of each surface through the soles of their feet. After a while, they left the narrow trail and strolled through large swaths of electric-green moss and gangly blueberry bushes before crossing over a small creek with a muddy bottom, an inviting footbath for the brave.

"Some pinecones felt like pieces of Legos when you stepped on them, but a lot of it comes down to what pace you keep. If you walk slowly, you can spread out your weight more, so it hurts less," Winroth said.

About halfway through the walk, the group of five stopped in a small glen for fika. As they sat down on the moist ground, they ended up chest-deep in blueberry bushes. It was starting to get chilly, so they wiped off their feet and put their wool socks on for warmth while they ate. On the way back, they picked some funnel chanterelles in the quickly fading daylight. While it was Winroth's first organized barefoot walk, it most definitely won't be the last.

"The guy in the group sent me an email right after he came back from the walk," she said. "He said he had gotten home with a big smile on his face. That alone made it worthwhile."

## Six tips for your barefoot walk

1. Put your shoes, socks, and a first aid kit in a backpack and bring it on your walk, so you have footwear and Band-Aids on hand should anything unexpected happen.

2. Warm up your feet by doing some simple movements, like flexing and rolling your feet clockwise and counterclockwise, before you head out.

3. Bring a small towel to wipe moisture and debris from your feet after the walk.

4. Avoid busy areas, and pick a trail that you know well to minimize the risk of stepping in trash.

5. Try to choose an area that offers a variety of surfaces and sensory experiences, like rocks, moss, leaves, mud, grass, and water.

6. Walk slowly to let your feet get used to the ground, and make sure they don't hurt.

# Allemansrätten—the right to roam

"HI, MY NAME IS ÅKE, and this is my home. Roughly one hundred million acres of land that is all mine." Thus begins a YouTube video that, tongue in cheek and with a voice-over sporting a distinct Swedish accent, explains *allemansrätten*, a unique right to roam on public and private land that is protected by the law in Sweden, Norway, Finland, and, to some extent, Iceland. With drone footage panning over grandiose Arctic mountain vistas and picturesque lakes shrouded in fog, the film follows Åke as he touts the benefits of Swedish nature, as if narrating an ad for a holiday rental. The lakes are not just natural bodies of water; they are the "spacious relaxation area" featuring "one hundred thousand tempered infinity pools." A cliff by the ocean is the "terrace," with "panoramic floor-to-ceiling views in every direction." The bathroom is found on a moss-covered forest floor, "Swedish minimalistic style," and the open pastures billowing with wildflowers (and potentially home to a few sheep or cattle) are the bedroom, "where the magic happens." The video ends with an appeal to explore Sweden's freedom to roam, a cultural heritage enshrined into law that gives anybody the right to recreate outdoors pretty much anywhere—all free of charge.

The video was a clever PR stunt by the government organization Visit Sweden and part of a campaign that also temporarily listed the entire country on the home-rental site Airbnb in a bid to draw tourists to the region. But long before it became a marketing ploy, allemansrätten was an integral part of the friluftsliv tradition in this part of the world.

At heart, allemansrätten is a right for all people to enjoy nature regardless of whose name is on the property deed. Exactly what it entails varies from country to country, but in Sweden it means that you can walk, ski, ride a horse, bike, paddle, swim, camp out, pick flowers, or forage for berries and mushrooms pretty much anywhere except near people's homes and in places where it's explicitly forbidden to do so (which are rare). In Sweden and Norway, you're also allowed to have a small campfire, unless there is a fire ban in place. Allemansrätten became official Norwegian law as late as 1957 and didn't make it into the Swedish Constitution until 1994, but it has roots in local laws from medieval times.

Thanks to the tradition of allemansrätten, access to nature is basically seen as a birthright in the Nordic countries. The No Trespassing and Keep Out signs that are legion in many other countries are rarely seen here, and in areas where allemansrätten applies, they're even illegal. Tellingly, the Norwegian language doesn't even have a word for trespassing. Torill Christine Lindstrøm, a psychology professor at the University of Bergen, sums up the conceptual understanding of the right to roam like this: "A path in nature is created by thousands of feet, often through thousands of years. To claim a path in nature to be private is therefore ludicrous . . . We regard it as a human right to be in nature."

That doesn't mean outdoor recreation in the Nordic countries is a free-for-all. The right to move freely over other people's property comes with a responsibility to treat it and the plants and animals that live there with utmost care. It requires people to be knowledgeable about the rules, and it does come with some limitations. For example, you cannot pitch a tent in somebody's backyard (you need to be out of sight of the home or ask permission), light a fire on rocks (they will crack), walk through farm fields (crops may get trampled), leave gates open (livestock may escape), or litter (duh). Landowners have rights too, mainly not to have their property or economic interests damaged. Nor can you pick flowers that are red-listed or forage for edibles in other people's yards or farm fields. Hunting is not encompassed by the right to roam; fishing is to some extent but the regulations vary.

Allemansrätten may be distinctly Nordic, but one of its key principles applies to anybody wanting to practice friluftsliv, regardless of where you are: Do not disturb, do not destroy. This may sound like an impossibly vague instruction to follow, but it's purposely open-ended. Like most things in life, situations in nature are rarely black-and-white, and what this principle does is force us to consider the impact of our actions, on both nature and other people around us. It implores us to educate ourselves about our surroundings, since an activity that is harmless in one type of environment might be devastating in a different one just a few miles away. It also tells us to be mindful of our own limitations to avoid unnecessary risk. A reminder that while friluftsliv comes with great benefits for our personal health and well-being, it's inseparable from our responsibility to treat the Earth with respect.

## More allemansrätten for the people?

MOST COUNTRIES DON'T GRANT THEIR citizens the right to roam private property á la allemansrätten, but in some places, attitudes are changing. In England and Wales, intense campaigning resulted in new rights-of-way legislation in 2000, expanding the public's access on foot in mountains and the countryside. Three years later, Scotland went even further by enacting land-access legislation that is similar to the Nordic model, allowing for nonmotorized recreational and educational activities on most land and inland water, as long as it's done responsibly. There are currently campaigns for the rest of the UK to follow Scotland's lead.

In the United States, where private property rights are king, there has never been a similar movement to introduce a right to roam, even though it might prove to be popular with walkers. Here, liability is a hurdle, as US landowners, unlike their European counterparts, can get sued if a person were to get hurt on their property. Moreover, the Fifth Amendment warrants landowners to be compensated for any opening of their land for public use. That means a

Nordic-style allemansrätten probably would come at a steep price. Could it still be worth pursuing? Ken Ilgunas, a journalist and author of the book *Trespassing Across America*, believes a conversation about opening up land in the US countryside is at least worth having. Safer, more scenic routes to walk could help the United States shake its reputation as being one of the most sedentary countries in the world, and besides, Ilgunas writes, "Something as innocent and wholesome as a walk in the woods shouldn't be considered illegal or intrusive. Walking across the so-called freest country on earth should be every person's right."

## Nature + culture = landscape

WHEN WE TALK ABOUT NATURE, spectacular vistas in pristine wilderness are often what come to mind. After all, experiencing wild nature, away from civilization, can restore inner balance and nurture our souls, which is at the heart of the friluftsliv purpose. In the United States, the government started to set aside many of these most scenic places as national parks at the end of the nineteenth century to protect them for the education and enjoyment of the people for all future time. There's only one little problem. Everybody else wants to visit them too.

In the spring and summer of 2021, Americans flocked to national parks in record numbers, leading to bumper-to-bumper traffic, noise, pollution, and litter—essentially all the things people were going there to escape. According to *The New York Times*, hikers in Zion National Park, in Utah, had to wait for four hours to get on certain trails, and those attempting to visit Arches National

Park, in the same state, were turned away at the gate. Meanwhile at Yellowstone National Park, "the crowds were reminiscent of those at Disneyland," the newspaper noted.

There is a fine line between experiencing nature and consuming nature, and nowhere is this line crossed more often than in easily accessible nature areas with great selfie potential. The intention is good, of course. You want as many people as possible to be able to enjoy the feeling of being in a place that is largely untouched by humans. But as more people start to discover the beauty of spending time in nature, it becomes all the more important to do it in a way that respects the land. What friluftsliv does is encourage you to experience the outdoors in everyday life instead of thinking that nature is a destination to which you have to travel. It broadens our definition of "nature" and encourages us to find it closer to home, sometimes where we least expect it.

Klas Sandell, a professor emeritus at Karlstad University and one of Sweden's foremost friluftsliv scholars, goes as far as saying that the whole concept of "wilderness" is rather unusable in a day and age when no place on the planet can be considered unaffected by human activity, whether or not you protect it from development and call it a national park. Just take Sápmi (also known as Lapland), the region in northern Sweden, Norway, and Finland that is sometimes called "Europe's last wilderness." The harsh, windswept mountain region is largely uninhabited and certainly seems wild to the hikers who arrive in droves every year. But to the semi-nomadic Sami people who have tended to this land for thousands of years, it's anything but. For that reason, Nordic scholars prefer to use the term *landskap*—landscape—over "wilderness" or "nature" when discussing open-air life. Landscape is a spectrum that encompasses both nature and culture, the wild and the human-made, the uncontrolled and the controlled.

"In the landscape, nature areas, agriculture, industry, and infrastructure all interact," Sandell said. "Of course, it's easier to see nature in places with less human interference, but we can find nature in the garden, parks, and cities as well. Nature is all the forces that we can't control, even the rain that falls on your forehead when you don't have a roof over your head, the mold that starts growing on a sandwich in the fridge, or the gravitational force that pulls your pencil toward the floor when you drop it. Through open-air life, we can practice and develop our ability to notice nature everywhere."

Discovering that last week's leftovers unintentionally have turned into a science experiment may not be the stress-relieving nature therapy you dream of, but by being aware of the natural processes that are everywhere, including inside our own bodies, we are more likely to experience oneness with nature, rather than seeing it as something separate from ourselves. Because we can't detach ourselves from nature any more than we can stop the ticking of time.

"Friluftsliv is one of the few ways we, in our modern society, get to experience the relationship between nature and culture directly, concretely, and palpably with our own bodies, and not just on an intellectual level. It's very different from reading about it in books or seeing numbers and diagrams, and it helps us make an emotional connection with the natural landscape. This is important because while we can't see the carbon dioxide that causes global climate change, being in nature can affect our attitudes and behavior for the better," Sandell said.

# Responsible friluftsliv

THE MORE PEOPLE WHO ARE wanting to enjoy open-air life, the more important it is to minimize the impact on the environment.

- **Think local.** The less time you spend on traveling, the more time you have to experience the outdoors. Are there any nearby green spaces that you have yet to discover or would consider spending more time in? Although "wilder" places where nature is more palpable are generally more restorative, spending time in parks as small as a couple of acres can have substantial health benefits. If you can walk or bike there, your visit also leaves a smaller footprint on the environment.

- **Avoid peak times.** Many of the most popular parks are especially busy at certain times of the year—find out what they are and then choose a different time if at all possible. When we spread out, there is less risk of the popular places being loved to death. Besides, being stuck in long lines of traffic, jockeying for a parking space, and then elbowing yourself to the trail is no fun way to practice friluftsliv, and you will get much more out of your trip during the off-season.

- **Be prepared.** The old Scout saying is highly relevant today. The farther from civilization you go and the longer you plan to be out, the more important it is to plan ahead and research your destination. Check the weather but don't rely on the forecast alone—make sure to bring clothing and equipment that will protect you if the conditions change quickly. You don't want to be the person whose tent is not up to par or who has to get rescued off the mountain because you were in over your head.

- **Pack in, pack out.** This simple principle applies to all natural areas, so make a habit of it. And yes, food scraps are trash too. I know our parents told us it was okay to throw them out because they decompose, but unless there are pasta and banana trees growing along the trail, your leftover mac and cheese and banana skins should be packed out too.

*If you do not know the names of things, the knowledge of them also perishes.*

—CARL LINNAEUS, SWEDISH EIGHTEENTH-CENTURY SCIENTIST

# Where the wild edibles are

ON A COUNTRY ROAD NEAR Tranemo in southwestern Sweden, Stina Kullingsjö pulled over her car and retrieved her gear out of the trunk: a woven basket, some knives, and a mushroom field guide. We were surrounded by steady spruces whose tops were clamoring for the sky, but Kullingsjö's gaze was transfixed on the ground beneath them. She scanned the bright green moss with a practiced eye and began walking. This was one of Sweden's many production forests and destined to become timber, but it had not been harvested since the 1960s. Perfect conditions for fungi to thrive. Sure enough, it didn't take long before we came across a mushroom about three inches tall, with a thin stalk and brownish-red cap. Kullingsjö, a tall woman in her forties with curly, dark hair in a bun, picked it up and held it up against the light.

"It's a bleeding fairy helmet," she said assertively and pressed the edge of the knife against the gills to demonstrate how the fruit body oozes a reddish liquid when cut. "It's not edible."

Kullingsjö is one of approximately 240 official mushroom counsels in Sweden, trained to facilitate the foraging of fungi. The counsels are educated in mycology at local universities and community colleges, and their mission is simple: Spread the joy of wild foraging to the public and keep people from getting poisoned while doing so. The counsels not only organize mushrooming excursions on demand, but they also teach what species are edible and what ones you should skip, how to cook mushrooms, and where and when to find them. I had decided to call Kullingsjö since I'd had a feeling that mushrooming might be a friluftsliv activity that the entire family could get excited about, from my five-year-old bonus daughter to my own teen, Maya. We knew how to pick chanterelles and funnel chanterelles safely, but that was the extent of my mushrooming know-how, and I was anxious to learn more.

In the Nordic countries alone, there are around ten thousand species of fungi, of which around one hundred are considered delicacies and ten are very poisonous. The rest fall somewhere in between, ranging from the edible but tasteless to the mildly toxic that might give you cramps but will not cause permanent damage. In other words, foraging for mushrooms requires skills, at least if you're planning to put them on the dinner table.

According to a 2018 report, nearly half of all Swedes forage for

mushrooms or berries at least once per year, but somewhat para-
doxically, it's not the filling of the pantry with wild edibles that's
their main motivation. When asked what the reason was for their
last foraging session, "relaxation" and "being close to nature" were
the top two answers, with "foraging" only coming in third. One
woman wrote, "The nice part about picking berries is experiencing
'space in nature,' the feeling of home. How much berries or mushrooms you bring home is irrelevant." Another one stated, "Foraging for berries and mushrooms is like any other activity in nature.
The picking has no value in itself, it's the nature experience that is
important to me."

Kullingsjö had noticed the same tendencies among the people
she introduced to foraging. "I think a lot of people like hunting for
something and finding it, plus it gives them a reason to get outside
and enjoy nature. Some people don't even like or pick the mushrooms, they just enjoy looking at them. I can see why—they are
beautiful," she said.

Not even Kullingsjö used to like eating mushrooms when she
was little, but she loved picking them with her parents. As with
most avid foragers, the family had their secret spots, bulging with
delicacies like chanterelles and bolete mushrooms as well as poisonous fly agaric and deadly webcap. Guided by her parents, Kullingsjö learned to separate the proven delicacies from the ones that
will give you kidney failure, and somewhere along the way, the forest began to feel like home. Today, Kullingsjö is a biologist who
works for the local government and shares her wealth of knowledge about fungi with people like me in her free time.

All of a sudden, Kullingsjö's dark eyes lit up and she dived
down over a mushroom that was about four inches tall with a

cream-colored base and a yellow-beige hat. "Oooooh, I was hoping we would find one of these!" she blurted out and quickly cut it off with her knife. "This is a *Russula*, but there are several species, and I'm not sure which one, so we have to do the *Russula* test to see if it has a mild or bitter taste." I could tell Kullingsjö was now in the zone. She methodically inspected the mushroom from all angles, then tried to peel off a piece of the stem to see if it had a stringy consistency or broke off easily. Then, like a sommelier who had just poured herself a sample glass of vintage Domaine de la Romanée-Conti, she buried her nose where the gills of the mushroom met the stem and, finally, put it up to her mouth and bit off a small piece of the spongy cap. She let the soft, white fungi fragments roll around in her mouth for a moment, then turned her head away and spit them out on the ground. "It's mild. That means it's edible," she said and put the fungi in her basket. She quickly added, "Tasting the mushrooms is another way for us to identify them, but if there are kids around, I never show them that I do it. You don't want them to go around putting mushrooms in their mouths."

While the use of mushrooms in prehistory is poorly understood, ethnographers have established that people ate them at least ten thousand to fifteen thousand years ago. (Even the Chalcolithic Tyrolean Iceman "Ötzi" had a knack for foraging and was found carrying several types of fungi.) The Greeks fed them to warriors before battles for extra strength, the Romans hailed them as "Food of the Gods," and in countless other cultures they have been used in traditional medicine to prevent and treat disease. Nutritionally, mushrooms are low in carbs and fat but high in protein, fiber, vitamins, and minerals, on top of which they contain a range of bioactive compounds that are beneficial to human health. Then again, their nutritional makeup is not why foraging for mushrooms is so popular in the Nordic countries. It's the act of being and relaxing in nature that makes the trip worthwhile.

Since it requires certain skills, foraging is typically something you're socialized into, by family, friends, or a professional guide like Kullingsjö. I personally came to mushrooming late in life and only chanced upon it the first time thanks to my friend Linda. We were out for a fall walk when she suddenly got distracted and diverged from the trail. "Hang on a sec," she said and vanished among the spruces. When she turned back up, she had a fistful of sloppy, yellow-brown fruiting bodies in her hand. "Funnel chanterelles!" she exclaimed, excited to now have dinner plans. She kept picking until she couldn't hold on to more and vowed to come back later.

Growing up, I really didn't like mushrooms, and the only one I could identify was the iconic red-and-white fly agaric. But I felt inspired by Linda's chance discovery that day, and later, when I got a tip about a hot spot for funnel chanterelles in some nearby woods, I sold it to the kids as a treasure hunt and brought the whole family for an impromptu foraging session. It was an immediate hit, and we ended up coming back again and again.

Funnel chanterelles were my gateway species, but I eventually added more to my repertoire of known fungi. And the more I learned, the more I wanted to know—about the species of mushrooms and their role in the ecosystem, like the fact that their microscopic mycelium creates vast webs belowground that bore into tree roots and help supply the trees with water and nutrients. A "woodwide web" for trees, as German forester Peter Wohlleben calls it, as the mycelium also allows the trees to communicate information about which saplings need nutrients and sugar from older trees, for example. In return, the network helps the fungus keep its carbon levels stable. But the fungus doesn't offer its services for free; it retains about 30 percent of the sugar produced by the connected trees through photosynthesis—a toll fee of sorts that secures the growth of the fungus.

"Mushrooms can tell us a lot about the environment in which they grow," Kullingsjö said as we kept walking deeper into the woods, our eyes scanning the ground. "Take the cauliflower fungus, for example. If you see that, you know you're in a forest with high biodiversity, one that is worth protecting. It's what we call a signal species."

I felt slightly ashamed that for years I had walked right past these essential and hardworking laborers of nature without acknowledging their role in keeping the trees healthy. If I, who walked in the woods almost daily, didn't know or care, then who would? Walking around with Kullingsjö was like possessing an ultraviolet light in a world written with invisible ink, and as she shone the light over the milk-caps, deadly webcaps, and slimy spike-caps littering the moss-covered ground around us, I was able to see what had once been hidden from plain view. It was empowering and humbling all at once. I wanted to know all about these fungi, name them, evangelize about them to my children, pick them, and—except for the deadly webcap and its ilk—bring them to my kitchen.

It's true that we don't need to be expert naturalists or trained mushroom connoisseurs, like Kullingsjö, to enjoy open-air life or reap the physical and mental health benefits of it. A walk in the woods will increase the oxygen flow in our blood and improve our mood, along with a host of other health benefits, whether you can identify a portobello mushroom in the wild or not. The difference is that knowing the basics about wild edibles makes us able to use yet another sense when we are outside—our taste—which in turn can deepen our relationship with nature. It can also be a way to experience nature with children, to show them how the Earth sustained our hunter-gatherer predecessors before food came from the supermarket. And not only kids. Older generations sometimes mock children for thinking that chocolate milk comes from brown cows, but how many adults are able to point out the edibles in any given natural area today? Or even put a name to any but the most common plants and animals that surround us? While our migration to the cities has given us many things, a richer nature vocabulary is not one of them.

Author Robert Macfarlane drew attention to this phenomenon in his and Jackie Morris's 2017 book *The Lost Words*, and given its international bestseller status, it struck a nerve. The book came about when common nature words like "acorn," "fern," and "dandelion" were removed from a widely used children's dictionary because they were not being used enough. Instead, they were replaced with virtual "indoor" words like "blog," "broadband," and "voice mail." The book soon took on a life of its own and became a symbol of our disconnect from the natural world, as well as a passionate plea for rediscovering it.

Macfarlane writes, "We've got more than 50 percent of species in decline. And names, good names, well used can help us see and they help us care. We find it hard to love what we cannot give a name to. And what we do not love we will not save."

In other words, if nobody notices the signal of the cauliflower fungus, will the forest still be protected?

# Wonderful weeds

MOVING FROM ONE COUNTRY TO another is a little bit like conducting an organ transplant: you move a living organism into a foreign environment, and whether the operation is successful depends on how well the organism is received and adapts. When I moved to Indiana in my twenties, I didn't just change continents—I left behind the entire biome that I had grown up with. The damp, moss-covered pine forests I used to hike through were replaced by hot and humid cornfields; in lieu of wild lingonberries, the woods were thick with plump blackberries; and instead of the tiny blue tits that used to hop across my porch when I was a child, bright red northern cardinals gathered in my backyard. Fireflies, sassafras, American bald eagles, poison oak—species that were all well known to the locals were foreign to me, and many of the codes of nature that I had learned through friluftsliv in Sweden were completely lost on me in the new homeland. I didn't know the names of several trees that I passed every day, which berries were edible, or which plants were better left untouched. I wasn't able to tell Maya and Nora the names of the wildflowers we saw popping up in the woods behind our house every spring, or the names of some of the leaves that we saw turning colors in the fall. And it bothered me.

In Sweden, knowledge about plants and animals is a part of the national curriculum for both preschool and grade school, and what children don't learn through formal education they normally pick up through friluftsliv with their parents and grandparents. I don't even remember how old I was when I learned that tiny yellow coltsfoot is a surefire sign of spring, or that wood sorrel is an edible plant with a distinctly tart flavor. Just like my language, it seemed as if this knowledge had always been there, or at least had been acquired early enough that it had become an inextricable part of my consciousness. On the new continent, I had to learn again, or risk that my daughters would miss out on this knowledge too. I didn't want this to happen.

One spring, when Maya was six and Nora three, we went for a walk in the small woods behind our house and decided to see how many species of white wildflowers we could find. I pulled out my phone and started taking pictures of each one, six of them in total. Once we got back, I compared my photos to images of wildflowers that I found in online guides and was immediately able to identify four of the flowers. The last two I needed help with, so I posted them on social media, and it didn't take long before I had the remaining pieces of the puzzle. Of the six species that we had found, one stood out, and not only because it was the most prevalent of the bunch. The small, white flower with five sepals had always looked surprisingly familiar to me, and once I took the time to look it up, I realized that it was a false rue-anemone, a close relative of the Swedish wood anemone. Celebrated in countless Swedish songs and poems, this abundant flower dresses the ground in deciduous forests in bright white every spring, signaling the end of winter and holding a promise of the summer that is to come. In those billowing fields of white, I picked some of my first straggling wildflower bouquets, creating fleeting mementos of childhood and internalizing the landscape in the process. The discovery of the false rue-anemone in Indiana was just what I needed to begin to heal the link that had been broken somewhere over the Atlantic Ocean. By being able to put a name on it, I no longer felt lost in my own backyard.

You certainly don't have to be able to name all the wildflowers and plants that you see during a walk to enjoy friluftsliv, but the more you know, and the better you become at "reading" the natural world around you, the more deeply you will be able to connect with the land. You will even be able to taste it—and not just prized edibles like mushrooms and berries. Each spring, nature explodes with wild foods of a different kind—yarrow, lamb's-quarter, stinging nettles, ground elder, clover, dandelions, broadleaf plantain—or weeds, in plain English. Far more weeds still perish by way of herbicide than end up on the dinner table, and that's a shame, considering the nutritional, and sometimes medicinal, benefits of many wild plants. The best part about foraging for wild weeds is that they grow just about everywhere and are easy to cook with (if in doubt, just use it like spinach). Poisoning from eating wild weeds is unusual, but obviously the same rule applies here as with the mushrooms: Eat only what you know, and avoid picking plants growing by the roadside because, well, cars and dogs . . .

# THREE EDIBLE WEEDS THAT GROW
# ALMOST EVERYWHERE

## NETTLES

Stinging nettles may not be the friendliest plants on the planet, but then again, they have a lot of nutrients to defend. In the Nordics, they are prized for their crisp, peppery flavor and high content of vitamins A, C, and K as well as folic acid, calcium, magnesium, iron, and potassium. Nettles taste best early in the season but can be picked throughout the summer; just avoid the bigger leaves and go for the smaller ones on the top of the stalk. Don't forget to wear rubber gloves to protect yourself from pesky stings while picking. Once you cook, grind, or process the nettles in some other way, they will lose their ability to sting. Nettles are an extremely versatile weed that can be dried and consumed as tea, ground into a powder and added to smoothies, parboiled and used in cold dips and hummus, sautéed in stews, and much more. If you've never cooked with nettles before, I highly recommend starting with a classic soup.

## *Stinging Nettle Soup*

Serves 4

### INGREDIENTS:

1 pound tender nettle leaves

1 yellow onion

6 green onions

2 tablespoons olive oil

3 to 4 potatoes

1 tablespoon or 1 cube vegetable bouillon

Pinch of nutmeg (optional)

1 cup heavy whipping cream or plant-based alternative

Herbal salt and pepper, to taste

Garlic-butter toast, for serving

### DIRECTIONS:

Rinse the nettles and remove the thick stalks and debris. In a large pot of water over high heat, bring the nettles to a boil, remove from the heat, and let them stand for a minute. Drain the nettles but reserve 3 to 4 cups of the water to use as the base for the soup. Chop the yellow onion and green onions, then sauté them in a pot with the olive oil over medium heat until they're translucent. Cut the potatoes into 1/2-inch cubes and add them to the pot, along with the reserved nettle water, the bouillon, and the nutmeg, if using. Bring to a boil and then let simmer on low heat for 15 to 20 minutes, until the potatoes are soft. Add the nettles to the pot and bring to a boil. Remove from the heat and add the cream. Use a stick blender to mix the soup to the desired consistency and add herbal salt and pepper to taste. Serve with garlic-butter toast.

## DANDELIONS

It's virtually impossible to exterminate dandelions, so instead of trying to fight them, eat them! Since it is rich in nutrients and grows almost everywhere, this amazing plant is one of fourteen wild edibles that are prioritized in a survival situation by the Swedish Army. If you're lost and in desperate need of energy, the roots will provide the most calories for your buck: twenty to thirty roots will cover your carb intake for a day. Dandelions are also rich in antioxidants like beta-carotene and polyphenols, vitamins A, C, and K, and calcium and iron. The roots are not the tastiest part of this plant, however, and you need to soak them for an hour and boil them in new water for fifteen minutes to get rid of the bitter taste. If foraging dandelions for pleasure, go for the first small leaves or the flowers. Cut them into a salad, blend them into a smoothie, or substitute dandelion leaves for basil leaves in your favorite pesto recipe. You can also make tea out of dried or fresh leaves.

### *Sautéed Dandelions*

Dandelion flowers can be eaten raw, both as buds and after they bloom, but they are even better when sautéed for a few minutes with a little bit of garlic, olive oil, and sea salt. Eat as a side or toss them in a salad.

## BROADLEAF PLANTAIN

Broadleaf plantain is a common weed that grows particularly well in compacted soil in lawns, as well as along roadsides and other areas with human activity. This little plant is a powerhouse of nutrients, containing calcium, iron, and other minerals and vitamins. Eat the young, tender leaves as they are and use the older leaves in casseroles as a substitute for spinach. Aside from being edible, plantain has been used in traditional medicine at least since the Middle Ages to help heal wounds. Modern research has confirmed what the folk healers of yore already knew: Plantain does in fact contain bioactive compounds that speed up cell growth. Simply wrap fresh leaves over the wound or crush them and apply as a poultice.

## *Broadleaf Plantain Tea*

Dried plantain leaves make for a tasty herbal tea—just grind them into a powder, and add a couple of teaspoons of it to a cup of hot water. Add a few drops of freshly squeezed lemon juice and a little bit of maple syrup for extra flavor.

## FORAGING BASICS

- Make sure you have permission. In countries where allemansrätten does not apply, the right to forage is usually restricted and may vary from place to place.

- Try to go with an experienced picker initially and bring a field guide or download an app that can help you identify your finds.

- If you're foraging for food, focus on just one or two edible species that are easy to identify, then add more once you know those species well.

- Do a rough cleaning of the mushrooms or plants as you pick them to avoid bringing home bugs.

- Join a foraging group online. The members of these forums are usually very quick to respond to questions about identifying mushrooms and plants.

- Finally, this may go without saying, but don't eat anything that you cannot positively identify, whether mushrooms, berries, plants, or other wild edibles.

## BERRY KEBABS

A playful way to introduce wild foraging to children is to invite them to thread berries on a strand of straw, like a kebab. This common friluftsliv activity is a beloved mainstay of summer in the Nordic countries and super easy to do. While mainly associated with wild strawberries, just about any soft berry can be threaded on a straw, for example blueberries and raspberries, so mix and match as you wish. Oh, and threading berries on a straw is not just for kids—plenty of adults enjoy this pastime in the summertime as well.

1. Pick your berries of choice.

2. Find a straw with a spike that is sturdy enough to hold the berries.

3. Using the bottom of the straw as your "needle," puncture the berries in the end where they used to be attached to the stalk and thread them on the straw. Leave about an inch of space at the bottom of the straw.

4. Eat the berries immediately off the straw or give it to somebody you like.

## SMULTRONSTÄLLE

*Smultronställe* literally means "place of wild strawberries" in Swedish and is a special spot, often in nature, that you go to for comfort, relaxation, and relief from everyday stress. In short, a lovely but lesser-known place that you have discovered and enjoy returning to over and over again. You may want to think twice about posting about your smultronställe on social media, since overcrowding could potentially cause the place to lose its appeal.

# The friluftsliv way of aging

FRILUFTSLIV IS BASED ON PHYSICAL activity outdoors, but unlike competitive sports it's not just for the young and physically strong. On the contrary, it's a practice that can bring joy and health through all seasons of life, not the least to the elderly. As a result, many nursing homes and assisted-living facilities in the Nordic countries feature gardens, nature-inspired courtyards, and outdoor activities to help residents maintain the open-air lifestyle that they're used to.

*But it is not only young people who need an open air life. It is often just as necessary for older people. Tired, overworked and edgy, they will regain health and strength much more easily through regular outdoor activities than through hundreds of different kinds of medicines.*

—BOKEN OM FRILUFTSLIF
(THE BOOK OF FRILUFTSLIV)

Take the long-term-care facility for the elderly with dementia in Svenljunga County, Sweden, for example. Here, the smell of grilled meat and vegetables infuses the courtyard when the staff puts on barbecue evenings in the summertime. The courtyard is also where the residents grow potatoes, flowers, and herbs in raised beds and have afternoon fika at the tables, weather permitting. During the colder months, the staff takes turns going for walks with the residents, so that everybody who wants to get outside on a regular basis can do so. My Magnusson, who is an activity coordinator at the care home, said she sometimes walks residents downtown to look at the murals on the buildings or just do a bit of sightseeing.

"Almost all our residents have been active in life, with everything from advanced skiing to foraging for mushrooms. My role is to tune into what they've done previously in life and what they're interested in now," she said.

For some of the residents, that is fishing. One fall day, the staff took a group of residents down to the local river. Equipped with walkers, fishing poles, fika, and memories of a life lived outdoors, the elderly men and women began to cast their lines among the faded water lilies, their bobbers hitting the dark water one by one. Soon, one of the women, who had spent a lot of time fishing in this particular river with her husband when they were younger, caught a small roach. She might as well have won the lottery jackpot, and her joy quickly spread to the rest of the group.

"Whether you've been into fishing before or not, this moment is incredibly valuable," said Magnusson. "It gives the residents something to talk about and helps them remember things from back in the day. This moment may not look like much to an outsider, but it brings a lot of joy."

Many other care facilities and nursing homes use simple outdoor activities as a way to boost the well-being of the elderly, changing up the old bingo nights with waffle making over an open fire, harvest parties in a greenhouse, and wheelchair and walker "races" around the neighborhood. Keeping the elderly connected with nature through friluftsliv lights a spark in their eyes and is a boon to their quality of life. There are other, measurable benefits as well. Studies suggest that green spaces for gardening and wandering can make residents with dementia less aggressive and reduce symptoms of stress, depression, and anxiety, in turn reducing the need for medication. Sleep quality and cognition can improve as well, while the risk of falling and getting severely hurt decreases.

A town that has taken the research to heart is Hällefors, in northern Sweden, boasting the largest park in the country devoted specifically to meeting the sensory and cognitive needs of the elderly, especially those admitted to an assisted-living facility or nursing home. Created by a publicly owned housing association in partnership with the county health care board, the park has many distinct spaces, or "rooms," designed to stimulate different senses. One garden is restorative, featuring places for reflection and solitude as well as social areas with seating for picnics and parties. The other garden prompts activity, with a greenhouse, a pavilion, an outdoor spa bath, and a creek near an adjoining forest, where blueberries and wildflowers abound. Arguably, one of the most interesting parts of the park is the one dedicated to memories. This is where the meadow is still mowed with scythes and the hay is hung up to dry on a rack, the old-fashioned way, and visitors can pick apples, pears, and berries from a fruit orchard filled with heirloom species. In the seventeenth-century homestead that has been moved to the park, the old woodstove is still fit for baking bread, and in the shed next to it, you can pick up and feel tools that go back to the time when everything was made by hand. There is even an open-air rotunda where old-time dance nights are re-created, complete with darts, chocolate wheels, and hot-dog stands.

"In this park, the residents can re-create a relationship with nature and feel safe, which is very important to them," said Barbro Beck-Friis, a pioneer and professor of geriatrics, in conjunction with the opening of the park. Beck-Friis, who has spent a great deal of her career advocating for improved end-of-life care, noted that elderly people who enjoy life and feel better require less medicine and care, which in the end saves the public health care system money. Then again, that is not the main point, according to Beck-Friis. "The most important part is that the quality of life improves for the elderly if they get to be outside a lot and feel the joy and well-being of experiences in nature."

## From the cradle to the grave

WHEN VISITORS ENTER THE FOREST Cemetery in Stockholm, death is strangely enough not the first thing that comes to mind. On the contrary, this is a place that is teeming with life—wildflowers, pollinators, birch and pine trees, rare mushrooms, deer, squirrels, birds, and the occasional fox all call this home. The graves are not even visible from the entrance; they are located in the forested areas farther in. It's exactly how the architects behind the cemetery wanted it. Because just as friluftsliv permeates all aspects and phases of life in the Nordic countries, it also influences the realm of death.

When the Forest Cemetery was created at the start of the twentieth century, the idea was to create a space centered on the Nordic forest, a place where nature and architecture would flow in seamless confluence. Every feature of the cemetery is carefully planned out to allow the visitors to be supported by nature, wherever they are in their mourning process. When they walk down the path to one of the chapels to say their final goodbyes, they are shouldered by tall firs on both sides. The closer they get to the chapel, the thicker the stands of fir become, encouraging the mourners to delve deep into their grief. After the funeral ceremony is over, they exit through a different door, leading to a brighter, open landscape that serves to lift them up and help them let go of their sorrows. Not too far from the chapel, near the entrance to the cemetery, visitors can meditate over their loss among a stand of elm trees on top of a grassy knoll. And the tombstones, typically the focal point of a cemetery, are discreetly nestled, all the same size, among stands of gangly pine trees to highlight that in death, everybody is equal.

Rather than a manifesto for the deceased, the Forest Cemetery is a celebration of life and the inseparable union of humans and Earth. Here, just like in the forest or mountains or by the ocean or on the open plains, the grandeur of nature makes us feel small and puts our lives in perspective.

# PART III

*I am most at home in open landscapes*

*Near the sea, I want to stay*

—ULF LUNDELL, SWEDISH SINGER-SONGWRITER

In the opening lines of his ballad "Open Landscapes," Ulf Lundell beautifully captures his yearning for the sea, where he purportedly goes a few months every year to rest his soul. And judging by the massive popularity of the song—it's even called Sweden's unofficial national anthem—he's onto something. Maybe you, too, have found yourself entering a meditative state from walking by the roaring waves of the ocean or marveling over the sounds of a trickling creek. Many people find water in its many forms—lakes, creeks, oceans, rivers, waterfalls, snowfields—relaxing and calming. This should not come as a huge surprise. Water makes up 75 percent of Earth's surface and almost as much of our own bodies. It's the foundation of all life and crucial to our survival; in fact, we couldn't go more than a few days without water. It simply seems to make a lot of evolutionary sense that we gravitate toward "blue space," even though our most basic need for water now can be met by just turning on the faucet.

Water has also been used as a source of healing throughout history. Hippocrates, widely regarded as the founder of medicine, believed hot- or cold-water therapy could cure everything from pneumonia to herpes. While water may not be the panacea he and other ancient Greeks dreamed of, several studies show that the perceived restorative powers of water are real. The EU project Blue-

Health found that all else being equal, people who live within a kilometer from the coast score higher on mental health than those who don't, and the difference is more pronounced among low-income earners than those with a higher income. Other studies have showed that people are happier in general when they are in nature than in urban environments, but especially happy when they are near water. Obviously, happiness is subjective and can be affected by many things, but if in doubt, just take a look at real estate prices. In Sweden, a house with a view of a lake or ocean is valued 21 to 33 percent higher than one without, depending on whom you ask. This isn't unique to Sweden. Across the globe, the question isn't so much *if* proximity to water increases the value of a property, but rather by *how much*. For the same reason, hotel rooms with a view of the ocean are typically more expensive than those without.

Given the prized qualities of blue space—and its winter equivalent, white space—it's no wonder that spending time on and near water is a cornerstone of friluftsliv. Whether kayaking or skinny-dipping in the ocean, skiing in the mountains, ice-skating on a frozen lake, or listening to the magical sound of ice singing, water in different forms is a constant source of awe and life that inspires our minds and soothes our souls.

# Cold water, calm mind

YEARS AGO, WHEN MY THEN husband, an American from rural Indiana, visited Sweden with me, my dad vowed to introduce him to the finest cultural pastime he could think of: the Friday-night sauna. The sauna, although historically mostly associated with Finland, is a common way to enjoy swimming outdoors all year round in all the Nordic countries. In my dad's case, the weekly sauna session with the neighbors was sacred. Not so much because of the purported health benefits of shocking your system by throwing yourself into a hole in the ice after sitting in a 200-degree sauna, but because of the camaraderie and relaxation that it brought. (The amount of whiskey that this particular group of middle-aged men consumed in the sauna during any given Friday most definitely would've erased any positive health effects anyway.) My husband, however, was struggling to understand my father's unbridled enthusiasm over this part of our cultural heritage. He didn't really mind the sauna, but the idea of immersing himself in water that was cold enough to make the skin feel like it's being stabbed by thousands of tiny needles didn't appeal to him on any level. And the thought of doing it in the company of a half dozen unknown, butt-naked middle-aged men, one of whom was his father-in-law, left him feeling more than a little awkward. Eager not to disappoint my dad, he eventually went along with it, and my dad, blissfully unaware of my husband's qualms, was proud to have given a foreigner a proper introduction to Swedish sauna culture. My husband would visit Sweden many times over the next twenty years, but somewhat sadly, he never asked to go back to the Friday-night sauna.

No doubt, cold swimming can be an acquired taste. I was not too crazy about it myself until recent years, when I discovered that if I could just get past the initial discomfort, immersing myself in cold water gives my body and mind a natural high. In Scandinavia, cold swimming was part of the friluftsliv tradition long before Dutchman Wim "the Iceman" Hof popularized exposure to cold temperatures by doing spectacular stunts like climbing Mount Kilimanjaro in shorts and plunging into large barrels of ice water. Many cities in Sweden have so-called *kallbadhus*, facilities by a local lake or the ocean where clothing is typically optional and the public can enjoy a sauna and swim all year round. In Finland, every self-respecting municipality cuts up holes in the ice and puts up portable changing rooms as a service for residents craving a midwinter dip. For many, cold swimming is just a feel-good pastime. For others, like my neighbor Anna, it's a matter of self-preservation.

I was still new in the neighborhood when I first saw Anna walking across her yard, right below my living room window, with her hair in a messy bun and wearing nothing but a bikini, a white bathrobe, and some plastic clogs. She was by herself and moved resolutely across the yard, then onto the trail that went down to the lake. When she came back—and she was not gone long, ten minutes tops—I could tell from the wet edges of her hair that she had been in the water. Normally, I wouldn't have thought twice about it. After all, the vicinity to the water was why most of us had moved here in the first place. But it was in the middle of winter and there was no sauna by the lake. I didn't know it at the time, but what I was witnessing was part of Anna's new mental health regimen.

Earlier that year, Anna, who works as an elementary school teacher, had been diagnosed with exhaustion disorder ("burnout" in everyday speech), a stress-induced condition that can cause a loss of cognitive functions, anxiety, depression, and severe fatigue. "I was stressed, I couldn't concentrate or remember things at work, and I was always tired, no matter how much I slept. It was scary, because I lost control over my body. The hardest part was that I felt so indifferent, everything was just gray," Anna said, looking back at that dark time of her life.

The doctor ordered sick leave and prescribed a course of powerful antidepressants.

"I said yes, but I already knew when I sat in the doctor's office that I wasn't going to take the pills. I wanted to have full control over my body, and I wanted some sort of natural treatment."

Anna had been on sick leave for about six months when she watched a TV show about a woman who suffered from exhaustion and depression and was persuaded by a researcher to treat her symptoms by going winter swimming. The idea was not as far-fetched as it may sound. Research has shown that depression is linked to a dysfunction in the production of the stress hormone noradrenaline. Being immersed in cold water triggers the production of noradrenaline, which in turn makes us more resilient to stress—a little bit like how a vaccination can protect us against disease by triggering the body's immune response. Case studies are promising. In 2018, a twenty-four-year-old woman who suffered from severe depression and anxiety and had been unsuccessfully treated with antidepressants for seven years was prescribed cold-water swimming on a weekly basis. Her mood improved immediately, and the symptoms of depression gradually decreased. A year after beginning the treatment she was free of both symptoms and medications. Another study showed that cold swimming can improve your mood, memory, and general well-being, while decreasing tension and fatigue. After four months, the cold swimmers felt more energetic and active than those in the control group.

In addition to being a great mood booster, cold baths can enhance your memory and energy levels and increase circulation, while reducing fatigue, pain, and inflammation from conditions like rheumatism, fibromyalgia, and asthma. And forget your parents' dire warnings not to swim in cold water because it would make you sick—short-term exposure to cold water actually makes you less likely to come down with airway infections.

With the lake nearby and plenty of time to kill, Anna figured she had nothing to lose. She picked a time when the neighborhood would be empty—for some reason this felt too private to share—then she bundled up with clothes over her swimsuit and went down to the lake. Once by the lake, she undressed and, while holding on to the ladder hanging on the wooden dock, quickly immersed herself in the freezing water. "The first time was a shock; I didn't breathe, I just forced myself to do it," Anna said. "Then I started timing myself. I'm a competitive person, so the first few months it was all about trying to stay in longer. But then I did some more research and I realized that it was important to breathe right and be present in the moment, so then I started doing this deep breathing through my nose that I've learned in yoga class."

Soon, Anna developed a complete ritual for her cold baths. First, she prepares mentally for taking the plunge, then she walks down to the lake and slowly immerses herself in the water while doing her deep breathing. While holding on to the ladder on the dock, she lies down in the water with water up to her ears and her toes pointing toward the horizon. Then she takes ten deep breaths, allowing herself to be in her "bubble," a completely relaxed and calm state of mind. When she's done, she gets back up on the dock and takes a few more breaths while looking out over the lake before slowly putting her clothes back on.

A few weeks after Anna started her winter swimming routine, she started noticing results. She slept better and felt calmer and more energetic. Her new regimen also relieved the symptoms of her osteoarthritis and endometriosis, two inflammatory diseases that cause chronic pain. "The exposure to the cold triggered some sort of primeval power inside of me. I became healthier and my immune system improved. Now I'm rarely sick, even when the rest of the family comes down with something."

Today, Anna is back to work and keeps exhaustion disorder at bay by combining cold swimming with yoga and strength training several times per week. She never did take the antidepressants. "I'm glad I found a natural way to treat my exhaustion syndrome. I read up on the side effects of the medications, and they scared me. Cold swimming is natural—it's something I can keep doing until I'm at least eighty."

## Tips for aspiring cold swimmers

- Decide to believe in it and be confident in your body's ability to cope with the cold.

- Be patient and don't expect miracles the first time; you may feel an immediate effect, but it can also take a few weeks before you notice a difference.

- Set reasonable goals but don't turn it into a competition; you're doing this for you, nobody else.

- If possible, start in the summer to acclimatize gradually to the sinking temperature of the water.

- Immerse yourself slowly into the water and observe closely how your body reacts to the cold.

- Breathe slowly through your nose, all the way to your stomach, and resist the impulse to hold your breath.

- Keep your movements slow and controlled and try to be present in the moment.
- Repeat it two or three times per week in the beginning to make it a habit.

Please note: Cold swimming is generally not recommended for people with heart disease or chronic high blood pressure, so be sure to check with your doctor if you suspect that you have a pre-existing condition.

## COLD BATHING AT HOME

If you don't have easy access to a lake or other natural water source, a small tub in the backyard can get the job done. Galvanized water tanks for farm animals are just the right size for cold baths and often come with a drain hole and plug that makes them easy to empty and clean. An aerator will help prevent the water from freezing solid in the winter and keep algae from building up in the summer. In warmer weather, adding ice to the water will keep the temperature down.

### No one ever steps in the same lake twice

WATER CAN OF COURSE BE key to experiencing nature even if you're not in dire need of mental or emotional healing. For some, the act of walking slowly by the ocean or sitting quietly by a creek in the woods offers a much-needed sense of calm and relaxation. Others prefer water activities that involve physical exertion, like paddling a kayak, canoe, or stand-up paddleboard. Then there is Martin Johansson of Uppsala, Sweden. A psychologist and father of four, he is on a mission to swim in every body of water in his home county in northern Sweden, simply out of curiosity. At least that's how it started when he leaned over a county map at his parents' house in Ludvika when he was home for Christmas in 2014. Astonished by how many lakes there were—he counted 581 in all, even though some were no more than tiny tarns—he wondered what they looked like in real life and decided to find out. As of fall 2021, he had swum in 144 of them.

"I made it a project to make it easier for me to get outside. If I'd only said to myself, 'Sometime I'd like to wander around the county with some friends and go for a dip in a lake,' it probably would never happen, because I tend to procrastinate. Now I have to keep myself accountable, and that works well for me."

Johansson's venture is far from an ordinary beach crawl—and not only because he swims all year round. Many, if not most, of the lakes on the map are hidden away, far from any regular hiking trails, and require him to navigate with map and compass along overgrown logging roads, through thick fir forests, and across soggy bogs. Once he finds what he is looking for, the next challenge is getting into the water. Many of the tarns are surrounded by floating mats—a thick layer of mosses and plants that grow from the shore into the water—that he needs to navigate across, treading carefully in order not to sink down. Then he immerses himself in the water, sometimes holding on to a small surfboard for extra support or to slide farther out in case the bottom is sludgy.

"I always hesitate a little bit before taking the plunge, but I've gotten pretty good at telling myself that that moment is the worst part and that it'll feel a lot better once I get in," Johansson said. "So I try to think a few minutes ahead and focus on what is to come. I always have a really positive feeling afterward."

To somebody who is not accustomed to wild swimming à la friluftsliv, hiking for hours into the middle of nowhere to swim in something that is little more than a mudhole, sometimes in freezing temperatures, may sound like complete insanity. But to Johansson, the outings are a welcome break from his busy city life with four kids under the age of nine, as well as a chance to connect in a very tangible way with the landscape where he was raised. When planning his outings, he often checks the map for historic sites that he might pass on the way, like a clearance cairn from the time his distant ancestors plowed and cultivated the rocky soil. He also sees the trips as an opportunity to bond with his friends, both new and old. And he never has any trouble finding partners in crime. Usually, they make a day of it and hit three, four, five, or even six lakes along the way. Sometimes they camp in the forest and make a weekend of it. "It's more fun going together with others. There's also the safety aspect of having somebody with me to make sure I don't drown or in case I hurt myself where there's no cell phone coverage," he said.

With 437 lakes to go, Johansson's project will probably keep him busy for years to come. That doesn't bother him. In fact, he is in no rush at all, since completing the project is secondary to just doing it. What started as a personal challenge has turned into something bigger, where history, nature, landscape, and friendship flow together seamlessly, the friluftsliv way. "In the beginning I thought I wanted to do as many lakes as possible, as quickly as possible," Johansson said. "Then I realized that the swim itself is only one part of the experience."

## THE WATER NEAR YOU

If cold swimming, or even swimming in warm weather, is not for you, there are plenty of other ways to enjoy water. Just sitting by a small creek and listening to the water trickle through is a relaxing way to experience nature. For a full sensory experience, take off your shoes, roll up your pants, and stick your feet in the water. Not sure where to go? Start by looking at a map of your local area and try to find your local water holes, then check which ones are accessible to the public. Trying to explore them all can be a fun challenge to engage in with a friend or your family.

## Finding flow

MY SISTER, SUSANNE, AND I have an ongoing, albeit friendly, argument about her canoe. Every time I want to borrow it, she suggests that I take the electric motor as well. "It saves you from all the paddling, and you move faster, so you can get farther," she likes to argue. Susanne is a wise person who enjoys friluftsliv as much as the next person. We often go for walks in the woods together, and being a yoga teacher, she has opened my eyes to a number of mindfulness exercises in nature, including tree hugging. But this is a point where I stick to my guns. Susanne is factually correct about the motor speeding up the trip, of course, but she misses the point that going fast is not my objective. Nor do I want to be "saved" from paddling. That's the meditative part for me, just like doing yoga by the ocean is for her. Even though the electric motor in question is neither large nor loud, it would fundamentally change something about my paddling trip if I strapped it to the canoe. Rather than being a part of the friluftsliv experience, the canoe would simply become a means of transportation. The quiet humming of the motor certainly would not make the canoe the most intrusive boat on the lake, and the environmental impact would probably be minimal, but it would still be a reminder of the civilization that I was trying to leave behind, even if only for a few hours.

To propel yourself is a key ideal of traditional friluftsliv for several reasons. Motorboats, Jet Skis, snowmobiles, four-wheelers, and other recreational vehicles can be fun and all, but in nature, one person's idea of fun can easily turn into another person's nuisance. The noise factor is just one reason motorized vehicles often cause controversy in natural areas. The propeller movement, turbulence, noise, and emissions caused by Jet Skis and other, bigger boats can also disturb aquatic life and impair water quality where they are used. Likewise, snowmobiles and four-wheelers cause exhaust pollution and may disturb wildlife in areas where animals are otherwise sheltered from traffic.

An occasional motorboat on the water is probably not going to tip the scales, but motorized outdoor recreation is booming, with sales of new powerboats in the United States increasing by 12 percent in 2020 from the year before. With travel restrictions in place and more people vacationing close to home, the Nordic countries saw a similar development. For example, the registration of new boats grew by 19 percent in Finland, with smaller motorboats and

Jet Skis making up the greatest share of the increase. Many people undoubtedly found a welcome relief from pandemic stress on the water. But could there be another downside to racing through nature on a motor-powered vessel, aside from the environmental cost? Hans Gelter, an associate professor of biology at Luleå University of Technology and a prominent friluftsliv writer, thinks so. In the anthology *Nature First: Outdoor Life the Friluftsliv Way*, he puts it this way: "In addition to being flooded by information, speed has become the icon of our time, determining both our behaviours and consumption patterns. All our technological development is oriented towards increasing speed and 'saving time,' resulting in an ever increasing quickening of the pace of life."

In his writings, Gelter often contrasts the traditional, or what he calls "genuine," friluftsliv with newer forms of motorized outdoor recreation and concludes that where the speed goes in, the deeper connection with nature—and our inner selves—usually goes out. Having water-skied and wakeboarded plenty myself when I was younger, I can relate. Riding behind a boat is intoxicating, and the sense of freedom beyond belief. But when I water-skied, my attention was always squarely focused on me and my personal achievement. The water was just a playground, the means to an end, and I paid little attention to what else might be going on underneath or above the surface.

These days, I prefer quietly gliding down the lake with my daughters in a canoe or on a stand-up paddleboard. Then the relationship with the water is present in every paddle stroke. As we float through shallow waters, we often see schools of young perch or spot a great crested grebe dive for prey. Gentle ripples travel across the water as the wind strokes the surface, and we steer through clouds of insects dancing up and down as if they were jumping on tiny, invisible trampolines. Above us in the sky, flocks of geese lazily pass by. Every time the sun peeks out from behind the clouds, our bodies revel in the warming light and we reminisce about the many times we have gone ice-skating on this same water in the wintertime. Back at the put-in, we go for a swim in the cool water before we pull the canoe up on shore. I place my feet carefully on the seaweed- and rock-covered bottom to avoid slipping. As I begin to submerge myself in the deep blue, I'm filled with joy and gratitude.

What I'm often feeling on the lake while paddling is what I—and many others—would call a natural high, the feeling of being so immersed in what you're doing that you forget about time and space. Other experts on open-air living call it "flow." In his book *Simple Life*, Roger Isberg, the Swedish American author and outdoorsman, describes entering this state after paddling for several hours. In the flow state, paddling happens intuitively, and Isberg is seemingly gliding across the water almost effortlessly. He writes, "The water pressing on the paddle and the canoe gives direct information to my body, which causes me to put more or less muscle into the next paddle stroke. I feel how much power is needed without 'knowing' it." He compares the feeling of flow to being in harmony with oneself and nature, and to be happy with just "being." But as soon as he becomes conscious of and starts to analyze the feeling, it disappears, like a sudden summer rain immediately evaporating from hot asphalt.

To experience a feeling of flow, whether you're paddling, cross-country skiing, or walking, is common when practicing friluftsliv, and you find yourself at the sweet confluence of mastering a skill and experiencing complete oneness with nature. To acquire a skill in this context is different from practicing to become the best at something, like you would practice competitive sports or an outdoor activity like waterskiing. It's acquiring a skill—whether using the most efficient paddle strokes, lighting a fire in the rain, or identifying a bird by its calls—while at the same time developing a relationship with nature. It's learning the way of friluftsliv so that you can learn to find yourself.

## MÅNGATA

If you spend time near water on a moonlit night, you may see a golden, glimmering pathway on the surface of the water. This reflection of the moon is called *mångata* in Swedish, a word that lacks an English equivalent and literally means "moon street." Sitting by the water and watching the reflection of the moon is a relaxing friluftsliv activity that is particularly fit for still, clear nights around the time of the full moon.

## Paddling along Foggy Mountain

ON CALM, SUNNY DAYS, THE nutrient-poor water of Sweden's second biggest lake, Vättern, is so clear that you can see its rocky bottom from sixty feet above. If you for a moment ignore the surrounding wheat fields and pine forests, the sometimes turquoise, sometimes cobalt blue water might fool you into believing that you're in the Greek archipelago or somewhere off the coast of Croatia. Lake Vättern was created by a fault in southern Sweden six hundred million years ago and has been central to life in these parts of the country since it was settled after the last Ice Age. The most dramatic coastline is found along the eastern side of the lake, where a forest-covered ridge rises from the water and licks the shore for six miles. The ridge, called Omberg, or Foggy Mountain in Old Swedish, boasts remnants from no less than three ancient forts and is dotted with more than a dozen caves along the water.

Legend has it that a giant once rode his horse across the ice on the lake one late-winter day to propose to the love of his life, Queen Omma, who lived in one of the forts on the ridge. But when the giant approached land, something went terribly wrong and his horse slammed into the mountain with his hoof by one of the caves, setting off a rockslide that cracked the thin ice. Both the horse and the giant were swallowed by the cold, deep water, never to be seen again. When Queen Omma discovered what had happened, she was so devastated that she could not stop crying, and the vapor from her tears blanketed the entire ridge in a heavy fog. To this day, the mark from the horse's hoof can be seen on the rock wall by the cave, and whenever Omberg is veiled in fog, Queen Omma is said to be crying.

The story about Queen Omma and the giant is one of many legends about Omberg that date back to pre-Christian times. Local entrepreneur and friluftsliv guide Linda Staaf probably knows most of them, and she enjoys sharing them with anybody who joins her on a tour. Omberg is the hub for her ecotourism business Woods & Water, which offers everything from kayak and mountain bike rentals to guided friluftsliv activities on and by the lake. Until recently, when she hired a kayak guide, she has basically lived on the water during peak season, and it speaks to her on a primeval level.

"Humans have always been drawn to water—it's a deep-seated survival instinct for us. Sure, in the forest you can feel the wind in your hair and the tickling of the grass against your skin, but nothing can embrace you like water. When you step into the water, it's like you're immersed by life itself," Staaf said as she took me on a walk along the edge of the choppy lake one late-summer day. "I like being under the water as well. Many people are afraid of tipping with the kayak, but I think it's harmonious under the surface. Above the surface, there can be a storm raging and lots of noise and impressions, but underneath, everything is still."

Staaf has been active with the Swedish Outdoor Association for nearly twenty years and has run her own nature guiding business since 2009. Having grown up on a farm not too far north of here, she is passionate about sharing the local landscape and natural features with others through friluftsliv.

"I talk a lot about enjoyment when we are on the water—that's the message I want to convey. We're here to enjoy ourselves, not to achieve something or become pros at paddling," she said.

"Do you ever get into a flow state when you paddle?" I asked, even though I had a pretty good idea what the answer would be.

"Every time," she said and chuckled. "My clients often tell me that: 'Now you're there, in the zone.' And that's why a lot of people want to experience nature with me. I don't talk constantly, I let everybody sink into their own thoughts."

Although Staaf is operating a commercial business in the tourism realm, her outings are a far cry from the adrenaline-boosting pursuits that Norwegian friluftsliv author Børge Dahle deems part of the "international leisure activity culture." As opposed to traditional open-air life, these types of outdoor experiences revolve entirely around personal thrills and entertainment, with little or no attention paid to the natural environment in which they take place. Staaf, on the other hand, has made it her mission to promote the holistic, down-to-earth kind of nature experiences that are the hallmark of traditional friluftsliv. The ones that are nonmotorized, purposely slow, and focused on connecting people with nature. For Staaf, that means offering mostly kayaking, mountain biking, and guided hikes.

"To me, friluftsliv begins when the motor is turned off. That's when you activate all your senses and really tune into a place. Some people don't think riding a mountain bike is friluftsliv, but it depends on how you ride. If you jump on the bike with the intention of breaking some sort of personal record, then no. But we ride slowly, look around, and take in all the different environments."

Staaf said she has always been passionate about traveling and exploring new natural and cultural environments, and professionally she has spent twenty-five years in the tourism sector, with a primary focus on nature-based tours in the past twelve years. But in 2018, her career choice triggered a life crisis. The launch of the image-sharing app Instagram in 2008 had reshaped the tourism landscape, and with hundreds of thousands of hashtags to their names, scenic spots in Norway, Spain, Italy, and the Greek archipelago had landed themselves on the bucket lists of travelers from all over the world. Now they were struggling to keep up with massive flows of visitors and the traffic, noise, and environmental destruction that came in their wake. Some of Norway's iconic natural features were among the worst hit. At Trolltunga, a cliff formation that got its name from its resemblance to a troll's tongue and hovers 2,300 feet over a gorgeous mountain lake, visitor numbers surged from one thousand to one hundred thousand in the ten years since the launch of Instagram.

Elsewhere, local communities were starting to push back, and Staaf realized that she hadn't reflected over the influence of tourism, even the nature-based kind, on the environment in general and the local communities in particular. She started to question her own role in promoting an already popular natural area to people traveling from far away who had no desire to develop a relationship with the landscape beyond the opportunity to snap a chill selfie. "Omberg means a lot to us who live here. I'd say that it's sacred," she said. "Sometimes I meet people who are just here to see a specific place that they've seen on Instagram, and that makes me a bit sad. There's so much else to do and experience here, and if you just come to a place to check it off your list, you're missing the full picture."

As somebody who had always had a keen interest in friluftsliv, Staaf saw herself as a person who cared about the environment. But when she scrutinized her lifestyle, she felt as if her values and actions didn't match up. As a result of her crisis, she made radical changes in both her personal life and the way she operates her business. Today she targets mainly Swedish tourists in her marketing, since she could not in good conscience continue to urge people to fly to Omberg. She serves mostly plant-based food in her business, encourages people to carpool to her tours, and has become a vocal driving force behind sustainable nature tourism in Sweden. On a personal level, she recently sold her car and started riding her mountain bike to work, about twelve miles one way. "I always cared about nature and enjoyed friluftsliv, so I automatically thought I was environmentally conscious. Then I realized that I was clueless about my footprint on the climate. I think a lot of people are in the same boat," Staaf said. "When you start buying a bunch of gear to practice friluftsliv, then need a bigger car and a bigger house just to store and transport all the gear, and you start flying places to spend time in nature . . . At some point you've got to ask yourself if it's really environmentally sustainable."

## There is no such thing as bad weather

I'M NOT SURE WHERE BILLY Connolly shops for raincoats, but regardless, he's onto something when he questions our attitudes about the weather by paraphrasing the old Nordic saying "There is no such thing as bad weather, only bad clothing." When exactly this mildly lecturing proverb originated is clouded in mystery, but it has guided the Nordic attitudes toward weather and facilitated friluftsliv in all types of weather for generations. Today it's usually accompanied by calls to "dress for the weather," which is just a more subtle way of saying that if it's pouring down rain and you're planning to be outside for any amount of time, you're better off wearing rain boots than stilettos. It's also code for letting people know that an outdoor event will

> *I hate all those weathermen, too, who tell you that rain is bad weather. There's no such thing as bad weather, just the wrong clothing, so get yourself a sexy raincoat and live a little.*
>
> —BILLY CONNOLLY, SCOTTISH COMEDIAN AND ARTIST

happen regardless of the weather, so be prepared to brave some rain, cold, snow, and wind, or all of the above.

For children at preschool, dressing for the weather is a necessity, since they spend hours outside every day, year-round, and the group is only as weatherproof as the child without proper gear. If you grew up in the Nordic countries, you probably heard the calls to dress for the weather from your preschool teacher first. It's a life skill that children practice long before they attempt to read, write, or do math, and it's one that plays well into a lifestyle that revolves around being outside.

Nordic parents encourage outdoor play in all types of weather because they believe it's healthy and fosters resilience. As my friend Nicolette Sowder, founder of the nature-based Wildschooling movement, so aptly observed, it also saves children from "merely tolerating the 'bad' days in favor of a handful of 'good' ones—a life of endless expectations and conditions where happiness hinges on sunshine."

Once children reach their teen years, many love to hate on their parents' insistence on getting outside in inclement weather, but eventually they tend to internalize the attitude. And so the calls to dress for the weather and head outside are passed on from one generation to the next. That's a good thing. In modern, urban society, the weather is one of the few things that we cannot control, and being exposed to different—and sometimes difficult—conditions can be humbling. But while you can't rule over the weather, you can be the master of your own mindset. By accepting the weather for what it is and finding something to appreciate in all seasons, we open our minds and rid ourselves of our own prejudices and limitations. When we subject ourselves to the harsher, less comfortable side of nature, we are able to uncover more layers of the landscape and gain a deeper understanding of it, just as our relationships with other humans deepen when we start digging past the facade of their carefully curated LinkedIn profiles. By experiencing the slight discomfort of inclement weather, our senses are heightened, and we feel more alive. The beauty lies in the contrasts, and it's important to recognize that sometimes the greatest reward of being outside is actually coming back inside to the comforts of home. So why let the rain clouds stand in the way of a good time?

## WHY YOU SHOULD GO FOR A WALK IN THE RAIN

Rain gets a lot of flak for ruining picnics and getting people wet, but there is more than one reason why you should embrace it.

- **Cleaner air**—A single raindrop can attract tens to hundreds of tiny particles on its way to the ground, effectively cleaning the air of pollutants like soot and sulfates as well as allergens like pollen. All else being equal, that means your best shot at breathing the freshest air is usually during or right after a rainfall, when pollutants have washed away.

- **Exercise**—We need physical activity outside to stay healthy, no matter the weather. By embracing the rain, you simply give yourself more options to get outside, especially if you live in a wet climate.

- **Gratitude**—Finding something to appreciate even on "bad" weather days can be a great way to practice gratitude. This is a big deal, because gratitude, along with mindfulness, can in turn lead to greater happiness, according to research.

- **Petrichor**—When rain falls on a surface, whether plants and trees or concrete and asphalt, aromatic molecules and bacteria on that surface are released into the air and start drifting with the wind. This is called "petrichor" and is a delight for the human olfactory system. In some places, aromatic soil bacteria are even used as a perfume ingredient. But why get the canned version when you can experience it live outside?

## Facing the heat

FRILUFTSLIV EMERGED FROM A COOL, wet northern climate with four distinct seasons, but it's a lifestyle that can be practiced anywhere. Regardless of where you live, the key to enjoying open-air living year-round is to adapt to the unique climate and conditions at hand. In the Nordic countries, the friluftsliv lifestyle is typically the most intense during summer as people take advantage of the long days and the (at least occasionally) balmy temperatures, but in a desert or more tropical climate, summer days can be anything but conducive to outdoor activity. This calls for different preparations—and a different seasonal rhythm. Try these tips to enjoy the outdoors in a warmer climate and during the dog days of summer:

- Keep a more leisurely pace on very hot days—lounging in a hammock with a good book can be friluftsliv too.

- Seek out shade and protect yourself with a sun hat, sunglasses, and even UV-protective clothing.

- Wear loose-fitting clothing, preferably white or light-colored to reflect the rays of the sun.

- Choose clothes made of breathable, quick-drying materials like polyester, nylon, or plant-based fibers like lyocell and bamboo viscose. Cotton and linen are also breathable and can be decent choices on hot days too, although they absorb a lot of moisture and are slow-drying, which can lead to chafing.

- Keep well hydrated and choose activities near or on the water whenever possible. If you can't get to a lake or the ocean, intermittently sticking your hands and feet in a bucket of cold water can help cool you down.

- On very hot days, try soaking your clothes in cold water before putting them on to take advantage of the cooling effect from evaporation.

- Avoid going outside during the hottest time of the day, usually between 10:00 a.m. and 3:00 p.m., instead savoring early mornings and late evenings.

- Sneak out to gaze at the stars before bedtime or even sleep outside—few things can fill us with awe and inspire contemplation like watching the night sky.

- Learn to recognize signs of heatstroke and dehydration (fever, confusion, nausea, rapid breathing, racing heart rate, headache) and how to treat them.

- Babies are more vulnerable to extreme temperatures than older children and adults, so don't leave them to nap unattended outside in very hot weather.

There are days in the winter when I get out for only half an hour given the extreme cold. In a warm climate, the same can be true for extremely hot days. That's perfectly okay. Pushing your comfort zone to get outside every day, regardless of the weather, is a normal part of friluftsliv. But so is knowing when it's time to call it quits.

....................................................................................................

## THREE WAYS TO CLEAN WATER ON THE GO

Water is calming and relaxing, but even more important, it's hydrating. Every day an adult needs around ten cups of water, but in hot weather or during intense physical activity, you will need more. During simple, everyday friluftsliv pursuits, it's usually easiest to bring enough water in a bottle, hydration pack, or canister, but if you're going on a longer trip with limited access to drinking water, you will need a means to collect water from natural sources and clean it yourself. As a general rule, flowing water is better than stagnant water, and you will want to avoid water sources that may be contaminated by agricultural fertilizers or chemicals from industries. These are a few of the most common water-purification methods:

- **Boiling**—Boiling water is simple and effective against bacteria, viruses, and protozoa (single-cell parasites)—all you need is a pot and a source of heat. If there are a lot of particulates in the water, let it settle and filter it through a clean cloth or coffee filter before boiling it for at least one minute. At altitudes above five thousand feet, boil it for at least three minutes, since the lower oxygen level and atmospheric pressure in the air make water boil at a lower temperature.

- **Portable water purifier**—A portable water purifier provides reliable protection against bacteria, viruses, and protozoa, and is the go-to filtration system for many campers and backpackers. Some are even capable of removing heavy metals, microplastics, and other contaminants. These purifiers come in many shapes and forms, for example as a gravity bag, pump, or straw, each with some pros and cons—choose the model that suits your needs.

- **Chemical treatment**—Chlorine tablets and iodine drops are the most common chemical water treatments, but it's also possible to disinfect water using unscented household bleach. Just add eight drops of 6 percent bleach to one gallon of prefiltered water and wait for thirty minutes. Chemical treatments are very portable and effective against bacteria and viruses but not all parasites.

## A word about gear

ONCE YOU EMBRACE THE IDEA of being outside in all types of weather, you inevitably arrive at the question of what kind of clothes and equipment you need. If you ask Are Kalvø, a Norwegian

comedian who has written a satirical book about friluftsliv, it's exactly everything that you already own, but with the prefix "hiking" or "camping." Hiking boots, hiking socks, hiking jacket, camping stove, camping cookware, camping hammock, camping chair, et cetera. And just like pretty much all products that start with "baby," those prefixes come at a premium. In his book *Hyttebok frå helvete* (The cabin book from hell; my translation), Kalvø describes how he reluctantly goes on a shopping spree to gear up for a weeklong camping trip to the mountains, a friluftsliv vacation that ultimately sets him back roughly 40,000 Norwegian crowns, the equivalent of $4,500. What else can you do for that kind of money in this day and age? Kalvø has run the numbers on that too: He could fly to New York and back twelve times, take thirteen weekend trips to Iceland—including hotel—or eat forty-four three-course dinners with a decent glass of wine at a very good French restaurant down the street. With dry wit, he concludes, "It's not cheap to live primitively."

Kalvø is wisecracking; he's a comedian after all. But satire is not funny unless it contains a grain of truth, and in some circles, friluftsliv has become associated with the need for a bottomless pit of expensive clothes and equipment. This is likely a result of both the commercialization and "sportification" of open-air life that has occurred in recent years—with a greater focus on technical performance comes a perceived need for more specialized gear. Not to mention social media, where it's easy to get the impression that no fun is to be had outdoors unless you purchase the newest super mega ultralight down jacket from the latest hyped-up gear brand. Rest assured that there are many ways of enjoying the outdoors without making massive investments in expensive, high-tech gear, though. The equipment mania is actually a relatively new phenomenon in the friluftsliv world. In its traditional, simplest form, open-air life involved very little in terms of specialized equipment. There was no other option. At the start of the twentieth century, portable espresso makers, smartwatches with GPS navigation, and mountain bikes with remote-controlled electronic gear shifting (and yes, for around $400 anybody can buy the convenience of pushing a button instead of pressing the trigger to shift gears) were yet to be invented. Not only that, but at the very heart of the friluftsliv tradition is the notion that the experience is more important than the gear and the ideal that it should be accessible to everybody, not just a privilege for the wealthiest few.

My grandparents' generation knew nothing about breathable, waterproof membranes or lightweight hiking boots. They hiked the same mountains I do in clunky rubber boots, denim jeans, cotton sweatshirts, and non-breathable polyurethane rain jackets. Having lived through both the Great Depression and World War II, they probably would have found the idea of spending a small fortune on technical outdoor clothing and equipment absurd. My grandparents made do with what they had, and even though they made the cardinal sin of wearing jeans in the mountains (cotton does not regulate temperature very well, takes forever to dry once it gets wet, and can in a worst-case scenario put you at risk for hypothermia), it never stopped them from having a deep and genuine connection with nature.

So, back to the initial question—what gear do you really need to enjoy the outdoors? Of course, that depends on your climate and what type of open-air living you engage in, but in my experience, you can get pretty far with a few key garments.

The main three factors affecting what type of gear you need are the activity, duration, and weather. As a general rule, the more specialized the activity, the higher the likelihood that you need specialized gear and equipment. Also, activities with higher intensity call for more technical clothing with features like breathable and moisture-wicking materials to keep you comfortable. The duration of the activity naturally matters too. There's a big difference between preparing to be outside for half an hour versus an entire day, or even several days. Obviously, another important factor affecting your outdoor clothing choices is the weather.

## Dressing for the weather—the basics

AS KALVØ FOUND OUT THE hard way, equipping yourself for the outdoors can add up fast, especially if you're faced with buying everything at the same time. But it doesn't have to be that way. Just as you can't buy somebody's affection, buying the most expensive and technically advanced gear won't buy you the knowledge that you need to handle a survival situation in the outdoors, or grant you a stronger feeling of oneness with nature. If you want to adhere to the friluftsliv ethos of going outside in all types of weather, you will need to adapt your wardrobe accordingly, though.

Personally, I recommend investing in a few key pieces of clothing that will keep you warm and dry and then adding more as needed. Go for high quality if you can, since garments that last longer leave a smaller footprint on the environment and are more economical over time. That doesn't mean that the most expensive garments are always the best ones; they may just be equipped with extra functions that you don't even need or care for, and a less pricey alternative may be just as durable.

The secret to getting the most out of your outdoor wardrobe is to use a layering system and choose multifunctional clothes that work in a lot of situations. This is some basic gear that is easy to mix and match to suit different weather conditions:

**Hiking boots**—There are several types of hiking boots, ranging from lightweight, low-cut shoes for easier terrain to tall, sturdy backpacking boots for heavy loads. You don't need a whole arsenal of boots for everyday friluftsliv; an all-round, mid-cut model with some ankle support and a waterproof membrane can be used for both walking the dog in the rain and hiking in the mountains.

**Hiking pants**—If you're not an avid hiker, getting a pair of hiking pants may seem like overkill, but a durable, multifunctional model can be used for much more than hiking, like gardening, bike riding, doing house projects, or taking the kids to the park. Hiking pants are often made of a water-resistant polyester-cotton mix with stretch panels in areas where you might need a little extra flexibility. If you prefer hiking pants that feel like your favorite joggers, go for a lighter-weight, full-stretch model instead. Some hiking pants have legs that can be zippered off to make shorts, essentially giving you two garments in one.

**Winter boots**—If you live in a cold climate and you're at all prone to cold feet, you will probably need a pair of insulated boots to get outside in the winter. Make sure they have deep-enough treading to keep you on your feet on icy roads and trails, as well as a waterproof membrane to keep out snow, slush, and rain.

**Insulated jacket**—The classic puffer jacket is the chameleon of the outdoor-clothing world. The best models are so versatile that you can use them for pretty much any cold-weather activity as well as for work or meeting up with friends in town. Many puffer jackets are water resistant, and some are even waterproof.

**Insulated pants**—Snow pants are not just for children and hard-core skiers. When the polar vortex hits, these pants are your ticket to outdoor bliss. Just pull them over your regular pants for a short walk or wear them together with a proper base layer if you're planning to engage in more intense physical activity or stay out longer. Higher-quality insulated pants usually have a waterproof and breathable membrane.

**Shell jacket and pants**—A thin shell jacket can be combined with an insulated jacket to make an effective outer layer in cold weather, and with a fleece or another, thinner mid-layer on milder days. The pants should be spacious enough to fit over a base layer or another pair of pants, depending on the temperature. Bonus if the pants can be unzipped on the sides to make it easier to put them on when you're on the go. Both the shell jacket and pants should be wind- and waterproof for best protection against the elements.

**Base layer**—The purpose of a base layer, a.k.a. a thermal underwear set, is mainly to keep you comfortable by transporting moisture away from your body, and it should fit snugly. Base layers come in synthetic, natural, and blended materials, each with some pros and cons, although I'm partial to natural materials. Synthetics like polyester generally have the best wicking ability and durability, whereas merino wool offers the greatest warmth and superior odor control. Choose wool or microfleece for lower-intensity activities in very cold weather, and thinner base layers made of materials like lyocell (wood cellulose), polyester, nylon, or bamboo viscose for higher-intensity activities and cool days.

**Functional T-shirt**—Just like a base layer, a T-shirt transports moisture away from your body during more intense activity. Once again, rather than buying specific T-shirts for hiking and other outdoor activities, I choose styles that I like wearing anytime. Merino wool, bamboo, and lyocell work well on their own or with some cotton mixed in.

**Shorts or hiking skirt**—In warmer weather, shorts or a hiking skirt will keep you from getting too hot. If you choose garments made of synthetic, quick-drying materials, they can double as swimwear.

**Hiking sandals**—On warm days, a pair of ergonomic hiking sandals are your feet's best friend. A well-cushioned pair can be used for both day hikes and camping, and just about any other friluftsliv activity.

**Accessories**—Sometimes the smallest garments can make or break an outing, especially in cold weather. Keep your feet toasty from the inside and out with a pair of wool socks, and if your hands tend to run cold, go for mittens rather than gloves. On very cold days, you may want to wear thin wool gloves as a liner in the mittens for extra warmth. While it's a myth that we lose more heat through our head than through other body parts, wearing a hat in cold weather is good policy. Likewise, in hot weather, a brimmed hat will keep the sun out of your eyes.


Does this still seem overwhelming? Start with the pieces that you have the most urgent need for. For a short walk around the neighborhood in fair weather, the only thing that you really need to be concerned about is to wear flexible clothes and a pair of comfortable shoes. On the other end of the spectrum, a multiday cross-country skiing trip in the mountains requires a smart layering system to make sure that you will stay warm and safe in quickly changing weather conditions.

Learning what type of clothing you need is another friluftsliv skill that gets easier to master the more time you spend outside.

## FIVE TIPS FOR A SMART OUTDOOR WARDROBE

1. **Take an inventory.** What do you already have in your wardrobe that works well for an active outdoor life, and what is missing?

2. **Do your research.** Take the time to read some reviews and consumer tests before making a bigger purchase and you will be more likely to end up with a garment that you'll love for years to come.

3. **Choose multifunctional clothes.** The more uses you can get out of a garment, the fewer garments you need.

4. **Fix it—don't toss it.** Tears, holes, and bad zippers can all be fixed, and many gear producers are happy to help. By repairing your clothes instead of buying new ones as soon as something breaks, you save money and do less harm to the environment.

5. **Buy used.** Clothing companies are slowly starting to catch up on the need for a more sustainable industry, and several outdoor brands and retailers now offer used gear for sale.

# Pushing your boundaries

THE GIRLS AND I WERE about a third into our hike up Mount Helags, the tallest peak in Sweden south of the Arctic Circle, when we stopped for a quick water and snack break. It was a tough trail, no doubt, and they were both already showing signs of fatigue. It was not so much physical as it was mental. They had been on many strenuous trips with me before, and I knew what they were capable of. Often they just went through a phase of not wanting to expend the energy. I knew the signs all too well. First, one of them would start dragging their feet. Then there would be calls for food and the unleashing of a litany of other complaints: "Do we have to go?" "How much farther is it?" "I'm tired!" And, of course, all parents' nightmare: "I want to go home!" A generous serving of hot chocolate and some sandwiches would take care of the problem nine times out of ten, but during longer jaunts, they would sometimes keep struggling—and straggling.

This time, Nora was the one who was ridden with resignation and theatrically threw herself on the ground. While I began to pull a water bottle from my pack, I noticed that a man and his wife, who looked like they were in their sixties, were observing us from a rock nearby. "Isn't it a bit cruel to bring the kids up here?" the man finally asked. I could tell from his teasing voice and the dancing crow's-feet at the corners of his eyes that he said it tongue in cheek. "I guess I'm just a sucker for punishment," I joked back, then added, "Nah, I just like vacations that challenge them a bit. Taking the path of least resistance isn't really my thing." He nodded in agreement, squinting with his whole face against the faint late-summer light. "Of course. These are the best kinds of trips. They'll remember this for the rest of their lives." We chitchatted for a while and then the

*When you take the helicopter to the summit of a mountain, the view looks like a postcard, and, if there's a restaurant on the top, you will complain that the food is not properly made. Whereas if you struggle up from the bottom, you have this deep feeling of satisfaction, and even sandwiches mixed with ski wax and sand taste fantastic.*

—ARNE NAESS,
NORWEGIAN FRILUFTSLIV
PIONEER

girls and I picked up our backpacks and got ready to move on. "See you at the top!" the man hollered as we got on our way.

The night before, the north side of our tent had been plastered to my sleeping bag as a storm swept through and pounded us with rain. Fully decked out in all the clothes we had brought, we had crawled into our sleeping bags and wolfed down our camping meals half sitting, half lying down like worms in a cocoon, then played some cards. The kids snored away that night, but I had slept lightly and on edge, as I tend to do when I'm reminded of my own insignificance in the face of the powers of nature. The next day, the storm had subsided, but our tent and the entire valley where we had camped were draped in heavy, wet fog. Once we hit the trail, the fog lifted and, as if on cue, the sun peeked out from behind the clouds. Now, as we were getting closer to the peak, I noticed how the girls began to pick up the pace. We scrambled up the last few hundred yards with the pointy wooden tower marking the peak beckoning in the distance.

At the top, the girls' spirits immediately lifted, and they rushed to write their names in the logbook where countless other hikers had put their small mark on the history of the mountain before them. Then we walked slowly along the edge of the massif, which is formed like a huge semicircle cradling a glacier below, feeling both a sense of accomplishment and relief over having completed the most difficult part of the journey. (Add a little bit of stress as the girls got a kick out of walking just a tad too close to the edge for my comfort.) The trip wasn't over yet, but we had already achieved the most important part—getting from an "I can't do it" mindset to "I did it!" I knew it from the way the girls were now semi-running down the mountain, chatting and laughing, and from the way they plunged down a large snowfield on their bottoms, sliding slowly across the crusty surface until rolling off the edge and onto the grass at the end. I knew it from the way they fawned over a herd of reindeer that sauntered past us and the way they were already telling each other stories about being on the top of the mountain, as if climbing the peak were something that had happened sometime in the distant past rather than an hour ago.

Any parent who has ever pried an electronic device out of their child's stiff, *Fortnite*-playing hands after they have been stuck on the couch for hours knows that physical activity outdoors doesn't always come naturally to children. Add some rainy or cold weather to the mix, and getting out the door may seem like an impossible challenge. But there are good reasons to make open-air living a part of children's lives, not the least because it's a way to foster resilience and grit. Kids can obviously get both exercise and mental strength from playing sports as well, and the two are not mutually exclusive. The difference is that friluftsliv makes space for families to be active outdoors together, and it can be practiced all throughout life, not just through high school or possibly college, which is usually the case with sports. And in friluftsliv, the only competition is with your own perceived limitations.

The objective to foster resilience by pushing yourself physically outdoors has been embedded within the friluftsliv culture since long before excessive screen time became a parenting conundrum, but it has evolved over time. In the beginning, open-air life in general and cross-country skiing in particular were seen as crucial to the national defense and used by the military as a means to strengthen the vitality of the population in Sweden and Norway. Daring Norwegian explorers like Fridtjof Nansen, whose stunts included attempting to reach the North Pole on skis, were the role models of the time and helped cast the friluftsliv tradition as an adventurous pursuit that was often associated with physical exertion and risks.

"Historically speaking, a common view has been that friluftsliv was supposed to be hard—it wasn't supposed to be for everybody. My father was a mountain guide, and he was old-school like that. You were supposed to carry a heavy pack and hurt a little, or it didn't count as friluftsliv," said Cajsa Rännar, spokesperson for the Swedish Outdoor Association.

She is careful to point out that modern-day open-air life is much more diverse and inclusive than this. In fact the most important raison d'être of the association is to provide a space for everybody who wants to participate—novices, experts, and everyone in between. She also emphasizes that the organization has been careful not to classify one type of friluftsliv as the "right" way. "Our members run the gamut, from the free riders who know exactly how tight they want their boots to those who think the fika is the most important part of the trip. But for us as an organization, the everyday, local friluftsliv is closest to heart."

The notion of friluftsliv as a means to strengthen physical health and mental resilience is alive and well in the public mind, however. While being a mountain guide like Rännar's father is a very literal way of challenging yourself physically and mentally, friluftsliv also fosters resilience in more subtle ways. It's about growing personally by pushing the boundaries of your comfort zone and not being deterred in the face of discomfort—mental or physical—in the outdoors. It's about daring to try new things, taking pride in the effort, and feeling joy over the accomplishment.

It's intangible—and highly individual. To the mother of three young children who often feels overwhelmed in her day-to-day life as a parent, resilience may be as ordinary as getting the entire family bundled up to go outside and have a picnic in the snow, even though it would be a lot easier to eat inside at the table as usual. To the middle-aged immigrant from Syria who has never seen the ocean, it may be learning how to swim. To the eighty-five-year-old who is desperately resisting a move to the nursing home, it may be staying fit with a daily one-hour walk.

Personally, I have many reasons for raising my children with an open-air lifestyle, helping them develop resilience against stress and adversity being one of them. I don't want them to be afraid of trying hard things or to miss out on experiences because they lacked confidence. I also want them to have the knowledge and good judgment to know when something is too risky or it's time to call it quits, and those are skills that need to be practiced in the field. More than anything, I want my girls to know that happiness can come from within and that the biggest joy can be found in the simplest things. I imagine that by feeling the discomfort of hauling a heavy backpack long distances, living without normal sanitary facilities for a few days, or working really hard to reach a peak, they become more appreciative of the comforts that they normally have at their fingertips.

Considering how widespread the association between open-air life and mental resilience is in the public mind, research on the subject is surprisingly scarce. However, a pilot study on German college students participating in an outdoor adventure program in Norway suggests that there is indeed such a link. The students spent eight days surviving in comparatively wild nature in the

Hardangervidda region, miles away from civilization. During the excursion, the students hiked long distances through rough terrain every day; slept in small tents; ate simple, strictly rationed food; and had no access to showers, toilets, or—maybe most challenging of all—the internet. After the trip, the students were surveyed, and the study concluded that being away from the distractions of modern life and going into "slow-down mode" had indeed "foster[ed] those psychological factors which are associated with resilience, well-being and good health." One of the parameters that the researchers measured was perceived self-efficacy, which is essentially the feeling of mastering something that you initially find challenging. After their friluftsliv adventure, the students' self-efficacy scores increased, as did their feelings of life satisfaction, happiness, and mindfulness. Feelings of stress, meanwhile, decreased.

I had seen this many times with my own children as well. They would start out apprehensive about a slightly difficult task, then grow with it. Once they mastered it, the joy was pure and intense. Often it seemed like the experiences that made the deepest imprint on them were not the ones that had gone completely smoothly, but the ones in which they had to work hard for the reward. And it was not unusual for feelings to become more intense when we were outside, especially on longer trips. In nature, there was no room for selfishness; we must all pull in the same direction and contribute to the greater good of the group. We pushed one another's buttons on the trail for sure, maybe even more than normal. But we also seemed more tuned into each other. We worked harder, played more, and laughed often.

When Nora was eight, I took her on a trip to Abisko, in northern Sweden, just like I had done with her sister three years prior.

The trip started out rough, and we were hit with an epic rainstorm during the first leg of our hike into the mountains. I could tell that Nora was struggling through some of the toughest parts of the trail and cheered her on as best I could, while trying to make sure that she stayed dry. Reaching a destination has never felt as sweet as then. For a couple of hours we soaked up the warmth of the mountain cabin on the top, before heading back outside to find a place to pitch our tent in the storm. The next day I woke up early and all was calm. After a picture-book sunrise, we got going and were treated with amazing views on our way to the next mountain cabin. When Nora tells others about our trip today, she doesn't talk about the views, though. To be perfectly honest, I'm not so sure she would remember them without looking at the photos in her phone. No, using her most dramatic voice, she recounts the story of us having to pitch our tent on a soggy, moss-covered cliff, how the winds almost swept her off said cliff (don't worry, it wasn't that high), and how we, when attempting to sleep through the howling storm, kept rolling to one side of the tent because the cliff was leaning. But she also remembers the feeling of being embraced by the warm interior of the cabin at our destination, and drying up after hiking for hours in cold rain, and the taste of the crispy waffles that she devoured. It's a story of trials and perseverance, and it's as old as human history.

## GETTING OUT OF YOUR COMFORT ZONE

Open-air life challenges us to get out of our comfort zone and helps us gain physical strength, mental resilience, and confidence, but you don't need to climb a mountain to get there. Ask yourself where your boundaries are and what you can do to push them.

# Know thy nature

IN 2018, WHEN I MOVED back to Sweden after living in the United States for fifteen years, I returned to my original biome, settling down in a rural area by a lake only a ten-minute drive from the small town where I'd grown up. The sights, the smells, and the sounds all came back to me as if I had never left. Still, I noticed that my neighbors knew things that I didn't, simply because I had spent most of my adult life somewhere else, whereas they had watched the seasonal cycles of the nearby woods and lake for years. The first time I realized this was when the lake froze over in the wintertime, and I found myself debating if or when it would be safe for my daughters and me to go ice-skating on it. I decided the wisest thing to do would be to follow the lead of the locals. Not only was the thickness of the ice a constant topic of conversation in Facebook groups and meetings face-to-face, but there already seemed to be some sort of informal system in place.

The first people on the ice, just after the lake had caught its first cover, were typically the daredevil outdoor enthusiasts who went wild ice-skating, or Nordic skating. Every year, they chased after the holy grail of wild ice-skating: the virgin black ice that is just thick enough to bear you, which can be as thin as two inches (or sometimes even thinner close to shore). They did it to experience the smoothest ice, before it was ruined by snowfall, and to surround themselves with the otherworldly symphony of sounds emanating from the ice as they bore down on it with their skates. They were also equipped with ice chisels, ice picks, and rescue lines, and fully prepared to take a plunge. After the Nordic skaters, once the ice reached about three inches, came the ice fishers, with their massive ice augers, fishing lines, folding chairs, and thermoses filled with scalding hot coffee. When the ice was four inches thick, most families felt safe enough to venture out as well, ice hockey sticks, pucks, and hot chocolate in tow. Thicker than that, and it was not unusual to see four-wheelers on the ice.

As I began talking to the locals, at least three or four people told me of a treacherous strait between the mainland and a small island. "There's a current there, and the ice is always thinner and more irregular there than elsewhere on the lake," they warned. The general consensus was to avoid it altogether unless the ice was really thick and you had all the equipment and experience necessary to get out of a hole. I heeded their advice but made a point to observe the area from land. As cold spells came and went that winter, I noticed that the strait was always the last spot on the lake to freeze, and the first spot to thaw. The fact that the ice is thinner where the water is moving is not exactly rocket science. Still, it takes a certain connectedness with the natural world to not just *look* at a lake, but to actually *see* the intricate character of the water and make predictions based on those clues. The locals who had watched the ice for years all knew about the hazards, and even those who had not observed the ice close-up in person knew because somebody else had told them about it. When you live an open-air life, this type of knowledge is passed down from generation to generation and becomes part of the story of a particular place. But what happens when you don't know these stories?

The same winter that my daughters and I set our skates on an ice-covered lake in the southern part of the country, a tragedy unfurled farther north near the small town of Långsand. A family of five had walked out on the ice and were about six hundred feet from shore when the ice cracked wide open under the feet of the mother and the fifteen-year-old son. They quickly succumbed to the freezing water while the father and two other children helplessly watched. The family had recently moved to Sweden from another country; I don't know where, but some media outlets noted that they were Spanish-speaking. "They were fascinated by the wintry landscape and went out on the ice to film it," local police officer Kjell-Åke Ederyd said when interviewed by the radio station P4. "Then they fell in." Chances are that the family had moved from a warmer climate and were unfamiliar with winter the way we knew it in Sweden. They had been on a video call when they fell in, probably sharing the beauty of the snowy landscape with loved ones back home when the disastrous accident happened. To the locals, it was unfathomable that anybody would have walked out that far on the treacherous ice—police officer Ederyd noted that the search and rescue crew had difficulties reaching the hole safely because of the many fragile spots—but the family had been oblivious to it. Just like I had done many years ago, they had switched biomes, and they were not able to read the signals of their new surroundings.

You don't have to immigrate to a different country to become alienated from nature; growing up in a city with little access to nature can essentially have the same effect. With nearly 80 percent of the people in the West now living in urban areas, healing this broken link through friluftsliv becomes even more important.

## Ice Safety 101

MANY PEOPLE ARE SCARED OF going out on frozen bodies of water, and while it's healthy to have respect for ice, it's possible to stay safe with the right preparations and some common sense. The strongest ice is typically the new, clear ice that appears on freshwater lakes after a period of subfreezing temperatures. As a general rule, clear ice can easily carry the weight of an average person at four inches; just remember that ice usually doesn't freeze uniformly across a lake and that the thickness may vary. If you're new to ice-skating in the wild and unsure of how to judge ice, it's a good idea to stay where the water is shallow or where others are already skating. Additionally, the Swedish Ice Safety Association advises those who want to venture out on frozen bodies of water to always bring along three things:

**Knowledge**—Get to know your local waters and how they act when they freeze. Where are the weak spots and how are they affected by changes in the weather? For example, snowfall and fluctuating temperatures can weaken ice considerably. If you're going someplace new, check with some knowledgeable locals. Also know what to do if somebody falls through the ice.

**Equipment**—Carry an ice chisel, or ice spud, to test the ice and discover potential weak spots before you go on it. A lifeline and a pair of ice claws or ice picks will help you get back on the ice if you fall through and should be part of your standard equipment when wild skating. Keep a change of clothes in a backpack—if you put them in a plastic bag, it will double as a floating device as well.

**Company**—Having company increases your chances of getting out of a hole in the ice exponentially and is your most important safety measure, regardless of how well you know the area.

## From high heels to rain boots

WHEN YUSRA MOSHTAT ARRIVED IN a cold and dark Gothenburg from her native desert city of Baghdad in 2006, she didn't just change biomes. She moved to a place with a profoundly different culture and religion, a place where everybody was a stranger and smiles seemed hard to come by. Like so many other immigrants who arrive in Sweden every year from desperate corners across the world, Moshtat was simultaneously dealing with traumas from the past while trying to learn the ways of her new country. She wanted to put down roots but didn't know where to find the most fertile soil for her burgeoning seed to grow. As she would soon discover, the key to cracking the Swedish cultural codes was understanding the locals' relationship with nature.

"I noticed that everybody was talking about the weather all the time, whether it was going to be sunny or rainy, and what they were going to do in nature," said Moshtat, who now works as an environmental inspector for the city of Gothenburg. "It almost seemed like nature was like a deity to them. And I thought to myself, 'Don't they have anything better to do than to talk about the weather? Have they never experienced war?' Because when you have, you don't think about things like the weather."

It was Moshtat's first Swedish friend, Lotta, who eventually introduced her to friluftsliv by taking her on a hike in the forest. Moshtat was on the fence about it at first. Back in Iraq, outdoor recreation wasn't really a thing, and besides, she remembered the dead fish she had seen floating around in the Tigris River, poisoned by all the chemicals in the water. Why would anybody want to see that? Plus, she was used to people looking down on women who were out and about on their own.

Despite being skeptical about Swedish nature she decided to accept the invite and dressed for the occasion just like she would have in Baghdad, in her very best clothes: a dress suit, fancy hat, and high heels. Cue the surprise when her friend came to pick her up, all decked out in rain gear and rubber boots. "I secretly thought, 'Wow, those are some ugly clothes,' and Lotta was equally horrified when she saw my outfit. She was especially worried about me walking around in those high heels, but she was too tactful to say anything."

The outing turned out to be the first of many to come. Moshtat, who had never seen a forest before she came to Sweden, knew that if she could see the scraggy firs and rocky ravines through the eyes of her new countrymen, she would be on the path to understanding their cultural identity and making it part of her own. Still, it took her ten years before she was ready to adopt the Nordic way of dressing for the weather. "I was ashamed, because in my culture, only children wear rain boots, and women are supposed to wear high heels. We dress up to go outside."

In nature, Moshtat started to realize the potential of friluftsliv to act as a means for integration, bridging the experiences of immigrants and ethnic Swedes by finding common ground in nature. For many immigrants living in segregated suburbs around the city, the ocean was less than an hour away with the tram, yet they had never seen it, let alone dipped their toes in the salty water or watched seagulls skimming the surface for prey. "I think many immigrants don't know how to get to the ocean. If you live in one of these suburbs, you feel comfortable there, and unless you know somebody who can tell you about the ocean and show you how to get there, it's not going to happen," she said.

Moshtat's job as an environmental inspector eventually gave her a chance to introduce immigrants from a wide range of countries—Iran, Iraq, Somalia, Chile, Russia, Afghanistan, Lebanon, and others—to the ocean and other nearby nature areas, as the leader of a government-funded integration project. The purpose of the project was not only to sell immigrants on the Nordic tradition of friluftsliv but also to learn more about their views of nature and, based on that information, inspire them to use their local, easily accessible green spaces and blue spaces.

The government has several underlying motives for running these types of nature-based integration projects. Studies repeatedly show that immigrants as a demographic group have worse health outcomes than ethnic Swedes, especially women and especially when it comes to mental health. Isolation, unemployment, the language barrier, and the stress of adapting to a new culture all contribute to this health gap. Immigrants in poor suburbs are often less physically active than ethnic Swedes in wealthier parts of town, even though many of them are located within walking distance of an urban forest. Plus, the great wave of migrants and refugees seeking asylum in the Nordic countries in recent years has put strain on the system and exacerbated the need for integration. By introducing immigrants to friluftsliv, the government hopes to fill three needs with one deed in these underprivileged neighborhoods: improve public health and the quality of life, facilitate integration into Swedish society, and increase awareness of environmental sustainability among immigrants.

"We knew that there was a huge need for information about environmental issues and saw nature as a potential meeting place for immigrants and Swedes. We wanted to make the Swedish forests, lakes, mountains, and ocean a platform for understanding and finding common ground," Moshtat said.

Moshtat knew from her own experience that the project would face some challenges. For one, people from poor and war-torn countries often have a completely different attitude toward nature than ethnic Swedes. For many of them, the woods are not perceived as relaxing havens of mental restoration but as a place littered with mines, where you risk getting raped or robbed. For those who don't know how to swim—and they are far more numerous among immigrants than ethnic Swedes—the soft, frothy waves of the Swedish west coast are seen not as an irresistible invitation to dive in but as a drowning hazard. Not to mention the challenge posed by the cold, wet climate in Sweden, which is not always the most inviting for outdoor experiences. Still, finding willing participants among immigrant organizations and schools in Gothenburg was not difficult.

During a period of a year and a half, immigrants of all ages were introduced to different friluftsliv activities, from fishing and canoeing to picnicking by the ocean and going on nature walks in the forest. In general, the activities focused less on textbook knowledge about plants and wildlife and more on creating an emotional bond with nature. "The way to awareness is through emotion," Moshtat said. "The emotion will create space for new knowledge to thrive."

The project in Gothenburg was one of the first in the country to document the role of friluftsliv in integration, but it has been followed by many more, not just in Sweden but in Finland, Norway, and Denmark as well. A 2016 report on nature-based integration in the Nordic countries from the Nordic Council of Ministers stated, "In the middle of a foreign culture, nature and green spaces can provide comfort, safety, a place to get together, and a platform for meaningful activities and intercultural communication and cooperation." The report also mentioned that, just like learning the language, getting to know and being active in the Nordic nature could hold the key to immigrants' connecting with the native-born population and have a positive impact on their physical and mental health.

While immigrants in Sweden still face a number of challenges when it comes to integration, Moshtat hopes and believes that her efforts made a difference.

"After the project was over, I ran into one of the participants from Syria at the railway station. She gave me a hug and told me that she was going to have relatives visit her in Sweden. You know what they were going to do? She wasn't going to take them shopping for clothes like they normally do. She wanted to show them the nature in Sweden," she said. "I think that's what I'm the proudest of—that people have made nature a part of their lives. It used to be rare to see a woman in hijab out on the islands. Today there are many."

There is another reason why friluftsliv still has a special place in Moshtat's heart. In 2003, during the second Gulf War, Moshtat and her son Mimo had been hiding in a shelter during an air raid when their hiding place was struck and destroyed by a bomb made of depleted uranium. Mimo soon developed an unusual form of blood cancer from the exposure to the chemicals, and Moshtat got chronic asthma. Being around traffic in the city became increasingly difficult because of the fumes, and after moving to Sweden, they found respite in the forests around Gothenburg. There they both found it easier to breathe and to live, Mimo in his wheelchair and Moshtat always by his side, describing the sights and the smells. But Mimo's health kept getting worse, and at the age of twelve, he lost his battle against cancer.

"When Mimo passed away, I kept returning to our places in the forest. It was a way for me to process my grief and get comfort. I'm not religious, but I developed a relationship to God out there," Moshtat said.

# "Ice singing" from another world

IF YOU SPEND ENOUGH TIME near a frozen lake, especially around the time when it begins to freeze or thaw, chances are you will hear a haunting, cosmic *pow-pow* sound intermittently break through the silence. This is neither whale song nor echoes from an armed intergalactic battle, but rather the soothing tunes of tensions in the ice as it contracts or expands. In the Nordic countries, this is called "ice singing" and is enjoyed on a seasonal basis not only by wild skaters but also people who find the sound relaxing and comforting. Jonna Jinton, a Swedish blogger and photographer who left behind a busy city life in Gothenburg to live in a village of ten people in Sweden's Arctic north, is one of them. Every year, she spends hours on the ice, preferably on the coldest nights, and loses herself in the primal thunder emerging from the depths below her feet. On her blog, she describes it as a powerful, almost other-worldly experience. "It really feels like an ancient creature has woken from its sleep and is howling in the night, telling its story in songs. And sometimes, when the ice is calmer, you can put your head against the ice and listen. Then it sounds just like you're lying in Mother Earth's womb."

A few years ago, she started to bring a recording device to capture the sounds so that she would be able to bring them home and listen to them anytime. She was having trouble going to sleep at night at the time and figured that the soothing sounds of the ice might help. She was right. The mighty but mysterious tunes of the ice cracking helped her breathe deeper and go to sleep easier. When she posted the recording, a one-hour symphony of ice songs accompanied by sweeping imagery of the black ice, on YouTube, it struck a nerve with her followers, and the comment field quickly filled up. A woman who was struggling with mood swings and her mental health said listening to the sounds made her feel grounded and calm. A fellow insomniac professed to being helped and filled with a sense of well-being. Another follower described the sounds as a bridge to something beyond this world, like eavesdropping on the spirits of the ancestors as they tell their stories. Even people who lived in tropical climates and had never seen ice, let alone heard it, attested to the healing power of the eerie sound.

When Jinton posted her second ice video, it got over eight million views. Clearly, the dark sounds of the ice reach somewhere deep within and nurture a universal feeling of belonging to something greater than ourselves.

# The serenity of snow

FOR A COMPLETELY DIFFERENT SOUND experience in the winter landscape, make a point to go outside when it snows. If the world seems a bit quieter than normal, there's a scientific reason for that. Because if water makes haunting sounds when it freezes, it does the opposite in snow form. Snow is porous and absorbs sound—and it does it well. In fact, it's equivalent to many commercial sound-absorbing fibers and foams. The ice crystals in snowflakes usually consist of six sides, or "branches," which capture sound waves on their way down toward the ground.

No rule without exceptions. New, fluffy snow consists of ice needles and air, and on really cold days, it typically makes a creaking sound when you walk on it. That would be the sound of the ice needles breaking and the air being squeezed out. The snow also loses its sound-absorbing qualities when it becomes wet or dirty, so the best way to get a serene snow experience is to head out when the snow is still fresh.

## HUNDSLAPPADRÍFA

In Icelandic, *hundslappadrífa* is a special word to define the kind of snowfall that brings big, fluffy snowflakes that slowly come gliding to the ground. It literally translates to "dog's-paw flakes"—a reference to the sheer size of the flakes—and is just one of many Icelandic words describing different variations of snow and snowfall.

PART IV

*The small sparks and dynamic crackles of*

*burning wood are probably the most hyggelige*

*sounds there are.*

—MEIK WIKING, *THE LITTLE BOOK OF HYGGE*

Scientists are still debating when exactly early humans learned to master fire and which of our ancestors were first on the ball, but recent findings suggest our predecessors *Homo erectus* might have acquired the skills as many as a million years ago. Regardless, we can all agree on one thing: Fire revolutionized humanity forever and made our existence a whole lot sweeter.

Fire gave our predecessors the comfort of heat and made it possible to survive and thrive in colder climates. It offered the convenience of light after sundown and a way to scare off predatory animals like lions and leopards. New and more advanced hunting tools were fashioned over the flames, and some researchers believe that since cooking food over the fire made it more digestible, it contributed to expanding our brains. So powerful was the impact of controlling fire that Charles Darwin considered it the greatest discovery of humanity, except for language. And as it turned out, fire had a hand in that too, as sitting around the hearth was a social custom that helped the development of language and our ability to tell stories.

Today we might occasionally light a campfire to grill hot dogs or gooey, golden-toasted marshmallows and to keep mosquitoes at bay. But the open flames can also be a way to connect us with our primal selves, the humans we used to be long before the advent of radiant floor heating and induction cooktops, back when fire helped us survive and thrive as a species. The historic link to survival and self-preservation is probably why we still feel calm and relaxed when we sit around a campfire and look at the dancing flames and glowing embers, in a way we never would by staring at a light bulb. And whereas "soothing" is not exactly a term we associate with the sound of a forced-air furnace, the crackling and snapping of burning wood is considered so relaxing that recordings of it are used as background music for yoga and meditation and to alleviate insomnia. Fire exists in the realm where hygge and friluftsliv intersect, and it's the perfect antidote to the stressors of modern life. A campfire can instantly make us feel cozy and at home in the outdoors, no matter where we are, and help us feel a certain togetherness with the people around us. So in order to fully understand and enjoy friluftsliv, we need to master fire.

## Baby, light my fire

LIGHTING A FIRE IS NOT exactly rocket science, with modern tools like matches and lighters, and for years I patted myself on the back for being pretty decent at it. It was not until my oldest daughter, Maya, joined the Scouts in third grade and learned how to make fire according to their protocol that I realized that my one-trick tepee didn't exactly qualify me as an expert. Plus, my daughter lectured me, using newspaper for tinder is most definitely cheating. What could I say? Nothing eliminates hubris more quickly and effectively than getting outdone by a ten-year-old. Now I know that making a good fire, especially in the wilderness, is something that takes practice. Even if you don't see yourself spending much time in the backwoods or aspire to become an outdoor expert, the ability to light a fire is a basic life skill that is also essential to open-air life. Knowing a few tricks will make the process much easier.

There are any number of ways to start a fire, but regardless of how you do it, you need at least three things to be successful: oxygen, flammable materials, and a source of heat. First, make sure you have all your materials gathered before you attempt to start the fire. You basically need three types of flammable materials:

> **Tinder**—This (long before it was an app that would let you connect with random strangers by swiping right) is the dry stuff that you use to light a fire. Newspaper is probably the most commonly used tinder but, as my daughter pointed out, setting yesterday's sports section on fire is not really the friluftsliv way. Instead, try using only natural materials. Dead grass, dry leaves, tinder fungus, pinecones, pine needles, cattails, dandelion fluff, tree sap, dead moss, small twigs, and certain types of bark (for example, birch) all make for great tinder. If you can't find any of the above, or you're in a place where picking natural objects is not allowed, you can also make your own tinder by cutting very thin wood shavings from a piece of firewood. The pieces shouldn't be thicker than the tip of a pencil. Tinder has to be dry to catch fire, so if it's wet outside and the only thing you can find that is flammable enough is a leftover napkin or some old receipts, that's quite all right too.

> **Kindling**—Tinder starts the fire, but kindling is what keeps it going. Kindling typically consists of thin, dry sticks that are no thicker than a thumb. You can use any type of wood for kindling, but softwood like fir, pine, and cedar dries fast and catches on fire easily.

> **Fuel**—The fuel is simply bigger pieces of firewood that sustain the fire over time. Just about any wood will burn, but hardwood like oak, maple, walnut, and hickory generally burns slower and longer than softwood. Most wood needs to dry for a year or

more before it's suitable for burning, since the moisture in fresh wood makes it smolder and burn poorly. If you can't find seasoned wood, hardwoods like ash and birch, and most softwoods, will still burn when they're green, just not quite as well. You can usually tell that a piece of firewood is green if it has the same color on the outside as it has on the inside, whereas the sides of a seasoned log will have more of a gray surface.

Once you have gathered your materials, you need a source of heat to light the fire, and using a matchstick or lighter is obviously the easiest way. It never hurts to carry both; make sure to put them in a plastic bag to keep them dry. If you want to challenge yourself, try using a fire steel (sometimes called a ferro rod) instead. Originally developed by the Swedish Army, a fire steel is a metal rod covered with an alloy that will create hot sparks when you scrape it with a sharp object. A fire steel can be used to start a fire in just about any weather, but it takes a while to learn the technique. Bring it with you even if you're just car camping or grilling out at a park, and practice using it along with very thin shavings of dried birch bark or dry wood shavings for tinder (or if that doesn't work, some cotton balls or fluffed-up tampons will usually do the trick). Place the fire steel and tinder on a flat surface (for example a piece of bark) and keep the fire steel at a 45-degree angle from the tinder so that the sparks will land on it. Use the metal scraper that comes with the fire steel, or the back side of a knife, to slowly scrape the fire steel in slow downward movements and with enough pressure to generate a rain of sparks. The scraper should be held at a 30-to-45-degree angle from the fire steel. Once the sparks ignite the tinder, you may need to blow on the fledgling fire a little bit to keep it alive, then carefully add kindling. Being able to start a fire with a fire steel and keep the fire going for a longer period of time are requirements to earn the Fire badge in the Swedish Scout organization. Can you do it?

Learning how to use a fire steel takes practice and patience, but even if you don't succeed on your first try (and chances are you won't), the simple act of focusing on this one rudimentary friluftsliv skill will help ease your stress load. Once you master it, rejoice in the fact that you're now more self-reliant and better prepared than before.

## How to make a fire kit

YOU NEVER KNOW WHEN THE ability to make a fire will come in handy, and the more ways you have of getting one started, the better. By keeping a fire kit in your backpack, you're always prepared for the unexpected and able to light a fire, whether you have plunged through the ice or been caught in a rainstorm. You can buy premade fire kits from outdoor retailers, but making your own is both cheaper and more fun, especially if you're looking for a way to involve the kids. The internet abounds with ideas for making homemade fire starters, from pinecones dipped in wax to empty toilet paper rolls stuffed with dryer lint, so there are practically infinite ways of customizing your fire kit. These are some ideas of what to include:

- ☐ WATERPROOF CONTAINER, LIKE A LIGHTWEIGHT METAL BOX OR A ZIPLOCK BAG
- ☐ FIRE STEEL
- ☐ LIGHTER
- ☐ STORMPROOF MATCHES
- ☐ BIRCH BARK
- ☐ THIN WOOD SHAVINGS
- ☐ TEA LIGHT
- ☐ CANDLE STUMPS
- ☐ TINDER-ON-A-ROPE
- ☐ TAMPONS

## Mindfulness by chopping wood

THERE WAS A PERIOD BEGINNING in my teens when I was spiritually seeking, trying meditation and reading the works of a sundry collection of more or less homespun gurus. But neither the teachings nor the meditation, at least in its traditional form, stuck with me beyond my early twenties. For one, I sit all day long while I work. Sitting even more to meditate did not bring me mindfulness; it only gave me restless legs syndrome. (This is not to knock traditional meditation—if it works for you, then you're all good.) I needed something more physical yet mindless enough not to demand my full attention. It took me years to realize that this "something" had been right in front of me all along—it was outside that I was able to still my mind and come out calmer, more focused, and creative on the other side, and not just with obviously enjoyable activities. Quite the contrary, I found that the everyday, monotonous activities, like weeding my garden, raking leaves, and chopping wood, often had the greatest potential to simultaneously quiet the mind and bring clarity, which in turn often helped me solve problems that I had dwelled on for some time.

As anyone who has spent a few days camping knows, monotonous tasks are an integral part of friluftsliv. You are not only constantly packing and unpacking your belongings, but you are also usually spending more time than normal taking care of your basic needs. Rather than being deterred by the labor involved with camping, think of the simple chores of collecting water, chopping wood, starting a fire, and cooking outdoors as a way to practice mindfulness. This is bound to make even the most tedious task, like chopping and splitting wood, more gratifying.

# SIX WAYS TO BUILD A CAMPFIRE

## 1. TEPEE

When you think of a campfire, chances are that the cone-shaped tepee is the first that comes to mind. This classic style burns hot and is great for beginners, since it's easy to build and maintain. Use it for bigger groups, when you need to warm up quickly, or to grill hot dogs.

*How to make it:* Start out by leaning pieces of kindling against one another in a circle shape to form a tepee-like structure. Leave a small opening where you add dry pieces of tinder to the middle of the tepee. Light the tinder and add bigger pieces of wood as the kindling burns up. The tepee typically burns quickly, so you need to feed it often.

## 2. LOG HOME

The log home burns slower and longer than the tepee and is a good choice when you want a fire for warmth that doesn't require a lot of maintenance. Kids love helping to make this fire, since it's sturdy and makes for an easy building project.

*How to make it*: Place a couple of big logs parallel to one another with some space in between, then add two more on top, perpendicular to the first two. The result should look something like a three-dimensional hashtag. Keep building this way with smaller and smaller logs until the fire is as big as you want it, then place the tinder and kindling in a tepee shape in the middle and light it.

## 3. UPSIDE-DOWN OR PLATFORM FIRE

The upside-down or platform fire is similar to the log home in structure, except the logs are placed closer together and start burning from the top instead of the bottom. This fire is perfect for cooking, since it can burn for a long time and the flat structure makes a sturdy base for pots and pans.

*How to make it*: Start with three or four sturdy logs and place them next to one another on the ground. Add at least two more layers of smaller logs that are placed perpendicular to the previous layer, and then place the tinder and kindling in a small tepee shape on the top of the logs. Light the fire and let it burn down to embers before you start cooking.

# 4. STAR

This campfire style was favored by Native Americans and is the best type of fire if you're low on wood or in a survival situation, since it can burn for hours with very little fuel. Because it burns sparsely, the star-shaped campfire is not the best for warmth, though.

*How to make it:* Make a small tepee with tinder and kindling and place five to seven logs in a star-shaped pattern on the ground around it. Light the tepee and move the logs into the flames bit by bit as needed.

# 5. SWEDISH TORCH

The Swedish torch was developed by the Swedish Army in the seventeenth century and is both stylish and practical. This self-contained, self-feeding fire burns efficiently and has a flat surface, which, combined with the directional flame, makes it optimal for cooking. Since it burns off the ground, it's also ideal for winter camping or wet campsites.

*How to make it:* If you have a chainsaw, you can make the Swedish torch from a single large log with flat ends. Stand the log upright and cut slits into it, either in quarters or sixths, but don't cut all the way down, so that the log will hold together while burning. Stuff kindling and tinder into the middle and light it. If you don't have a chainsaw, you can use an ax to split a log and then reassemble it, placing a metal wire around the base to hold the pieces together. Or assemble a whole log from pre-split pieces of wood that are similar in height and have flat ends, then secure them with a metal wire.

## 6. LEAN-TO

The biggest perk of the lean-to is that its design gives it natural protection against the elements. It may not burn as strongly as other types of campfire, but it should be your go-to campfire style for windy days.

*How to make it:* Use one thick log as a wind blocker and place some tinder next to it. Form a lean-to by leaning kindling on the wind-blocker log, over the tinder, then light the tinder. Once the kindling is burning reliably, put fuel-size pieces of wood on top of it.

# How to celebrate the seasons like the Nordics

AN INTEGRAL PART OF LIVING an open-air life is to align yourself with the cyclical rhythms of nature rather than the linear structure of your calendar. That's not to say you should ditch your calendar and rely on a sundial to keep track of your dentist appointments, the kids' Scout meets, and important anniversaries. Rather, it means being aware of the changes in nature that each season brings and celebrating them.

My paternal grandmother (*farmor*) combined the best of both worlds. In her pocket calendar, she made daily notes of what was going on outside with the weather, daylight, garden, and wildlife. If a woodlark showed up at the feeder, she knew spring was probably around the corner, and when she harvested the first new potatoes from her garden, it was a surefire sign of summer. In the fall she would duly note the first frost, and during the winter months she always described the vanishing daylight and treated each brisk, sunny day as if it were a gift from above. I will never know for sure, but I imagine that the notes gave her a sense of security and predictability at a time when change seemed to be the only constant in life. During her lifetime, she had lived through the ravages of World War II, been a part of the massive migration from rural farms to the cities, and seen the revolutionizing effects of digitalization (even though she never learned how to use a computer, let alone a cell phone, bless her heart). If there was one thing she was certain of, it was that although tomorrow was always a step into the unknown, the winter solstice would occur every year no matter what, bringing quiet joy to our lives as we knew the days were once again getting longer. Rain was as sure as death and taxes. And the migratory birds would show up on her back porch every spring, reminding her that the show of nature will go on, even if our own lives won't.

A keen interest in observations of the weather is not unusual at these latitudes, where *gråväder*, which is Swedish for "gray weather," and exactly what it sounds like, dominates the weather scene. The dramatic difference in daylight from the polar nights in the winter, when the sun doesn't rise above the horizon in the north, to the midnight sun in the summer, when the sun doesn't set, means that the cyclical changes of nature are woven deep into the culture. People in the Nordic countries spend a lot of time talking about these changes and since prehistoric times there have been elaborate rituals for celebrating them. Unsurprisingly, given the importance of light and warmth on the northern latitudes, these seasonal celebrations often involve sun worshipping and setting things on fire.

# Summer

THE SUMMER SOLSTICE MARKS THE longest day and the
shortest night of the year and usually falls around June 21 in the
Northern Hemisphere. It has likely been a highlight in the Nordic
culture since prehistoric times, but aside from involving ritual beer
drinking, little is known about the earliest solstice celebrations.
When the Nordic countries were christened, the pagan summer
solstice celebrations were eventually replaced by St. John's Day,
except in Sweden, where the celebration is still called Midsummer.
Folklore has it that the time around the solstice was filled with
magic, when normal laws of nature or divinity did not apply and
supernatural creatures could cross over into the human world.
Plants, especially, were thought to be endowed with magical powers, and likewise, humans were not bound by their normal limitations. Many of the Midsummer practices of yore are still around
today, and the holiday is closely associated with retreating to nature and the countryside.

These are some of the ways people in the Nordic countries celebrate the longest day today:

> **Sweden**—In Sweden, Midsummer's Eve is an official holiday,
> which pragmatically enough always falls on the Friday closest to
> the solstice to facilitate a good party. Key to the tradition here is
> to wear homemade flower garlands while playing games,
> dancing in a ring around a maypole clad in greenery and
> flowers, and singing traditional songs. Girls who pick seven
> kinds of wildflowers and put them under their pillow on
> Midsummer's Eve are said to dream of their future husband.

> **Norway and Denmark**—In pagan times, people here lit and
> jumped over bonfires to ward off witches and evil spirits. Today,
> people mostly have them for the ambience, and they often build
> them big.

**Finland**—If it doesn't involve sauna and skinny-dipping, it's not a holiday in Finland, and this is true for Midsummer too. Finns generally celebrate the holiday partying with friends and family in the countryside, and yes, it does involve the lighting of huge bonfires.

**Iceland**—In Iceland, Midsummer is still to some extent a superstitious affair. Among the more noteworthy traditions is to roll around naked in the morning dew, which is believed to bring good luck.

Of course, you can celebrate the longest day of the year even if you live in latitudes where the difference in daylight between summer and winter is less dramatic. Just invite some friends over and recognize the solstice by playing outdoor games, eating good food, singing songs, and telling stories around the fire.

# Fall

IN THE OLD AGRARIAN SOCIETY, the fall equinox was a turning point, as it signaled the end of the harvest. Falling on September 22 or 23, when the North Pole tilts away from the sun and the days and nights are approximately the same length, the fall equinox is still an important cue for life to take on a quieter pace as people get mentally prepared for the darker days that lie ahead.

In Finland, the brief period around the equinox when the leaves turn colors is so revered that it has its own name—*ruska*. This beautiful show of color before the leaves blanket the ground lasts only for a few weeks and is almost considered its own season. Thanks to the cooler temperatures, crisp air, and lack of mosquitoes, ruska is a great time for weekend hikes with friends and family to enjoy the fall foliage or lone foraging sessions in the woods (serious foragers never reveal their best spots to others, whether they are next of kin or not). If you happen to be at northern latitudes, it's now once again dark enough to see the northern lights, the other-worldly glow of green, purple, and pink shades dancing across the night sky. The time around the fall equinox is also perfect for visiting local farms or outdoor harvest festivals and feasting on the abundance of local crops. And, of course, for having bonfires.

## Winter

THE WINTER SOLSTICE FALLS SOMEWHERE between December 21 and 22 in the Northern Hemisphere and is the shortest day of the year. In many cultures, it's an important celebration of the return of the light, since the days start to get longer after the winter solstice, albeit slowly in the beginning. In the Nordic countries, there are few formal celebrations of this day, but mentally it represents an important turning point. Despite the darkness during this time, people in the Nordic countries venture out on a daily basis, donning headlamps and reflective vests to find their way and stay visible to traffic.

One of the most wondrous ways to embrace the darkness during this time is to tune into the rhythm of the lunar cycle. The moon has fascinated people since the beginning of time, and to this day, many people find it extra special to be outside during the full moon, not the least in rural areas with less light pollution. In the dark, your pupils will dilate almost immediately, and within ten minutes your eyes will have adapted to the dim light fairly well. It will take several hours for your vision to be fully adapted, however, which means that your other senses will be heightened and you will have a much different experience when you go outside in the dark than during the day. Nature behaves differently at night too, giving you a chance to peek into another world. Make the moon walk extra special by ending it with an outdoor potluck dinner and stargazing with friends.

## Spring

ON MARCH 20 OR 21 every year, halfway between the winter and summer solstices, the day and night are once again briefly equally long, with daylight gaining ground every day until its peak at the summer solstice. This astronomical event is called the spring equinox and has traditionally marked the first day of spring as well as the beginning of the busy growing season. Back in the old agrarian society, young people would run barefoot around the farm to greet the arrival of spring and toughen the soles of their feet for summer. That particular tradition has all but died out, but in the public mind, spring is still a time to celebrate the rebirth of life, as plants and trees start to bud and animals emerge from their hibernation. A popular friluftsliv pastime in early spring is looking for emerging wildflowers and trying to spot birds that have returned from their winter migration. It's a beautiful time to observe water as well, as melted snow gushes down from the highlands.

In Sweden and Finland, however, the most popular celebration of spring actually occurs over a month after the equinox, on April 30, or Walpurgis Night. On this night, people gather to watch huge bonfires and enjoy choral singing in parks, neighborhoods, or their own backyard. Like so many other old traditions from pre-Christian times, the Walpurgis bonfire used to be a way to ward off evil spirits, but over time it has morphed into a party for spring while getting rid of yard waste at the same time.

## SÓLARHRINGUR

"Sun circle" is the literal English translation of *sólarhringur*, an Icelandic word for the twenty-four hours that go in a day and night. Although the term is not an accurate description of this phenomenon from an astronomical point of view, it's practical and less ambiguous than the English "day." Plus, it's beautiful.

# Campfire storytelling— the original social network

IN THE OLD DAYS, WHEN the Sami people prepared to make a fire with steel and flint stones, they would sing their traditional *joiks* or *yoiks*, wordless, chanting songs that are used to express relationships with people and nature. Yoiking put them in a state of happiness, and this was important, since they believed that a happy person would have better luck making fire. The fire itself brought joy and happiness too. According to Yngve Ryd, author of the book *Eld*, about the Sami fire culture, the elderly always wanted fire, whether they needed it for warmth or cooking or not, and they could sit and observe it for hours. According to one of the Samis whom Ryd interviews, the fire was considered "the energy of life," to some even synonymous with life itself.

The Samis are far from alone in their reverence of fire; it played a central role to our human ancestors ever since they learned to control it, initially because it made food more digestible and provided warmth, light, and protection against predators. Fire also extended the daylight and freed up time for socializing that had not been available before, leading researchers to hypothesize that controlling fire was closely linked to the development of another uniquely human trait: language. We may not know exactly what transpired around the fireplaces of our ancestors, but we have a pretty good idea, thanks to extensive research involving the Ju/'hoan, an isolated hunter-gatherer society in southern Africa. During the day, conversations typically revolved around practical matters like foraging and what in the typical modern office would be categorized as gossip, water-cooler griping, and jokes that may or may not be safe for work. But by night, around the campfire, the focus of the conversations changed drastically. Among these hunter-gatherers, the vast majority of the time around the fire was spent telling stories, often amusing or exciting endeavors involving people both in the camp and outside of it, living or dead. The stories were a way to pass on myths and folklore, and nighttime fire was often tied to dancing, healing, spiritual celebrations, and cultural rites. Campfire storytelling was also crucial to maintaining kinships within their own band and to forming ties with other communities during larger gatherings. In other words, fire was the original social network.

Modern civilization killed the campfire culture slowly, and by the time President Franklin D. Roosevelt delivered his "fireside chats" to the nation in the 1930s and 1940s, the art of telling stories around the fire was largely forgotten. (Not even FDR actually sat by a fireplace when delivering his famous radio addresses, but behind a desk at the White House. The phrase was just meant to underscore the informal nature of the chats and evoke feelings of comfort and confidence in a nation struggling through depression and war.) Today, an entertainment binge fest is never farther away than the smartphone in your pocket, and the days of watching logs burn to charcoal for fun seem but a quaint memory. But as the hygge craze has proved, deep down we're still craving the togetherness brought by the campfires of yore. While hygge typically involves cozying up around the fireplace and lighting strategically placed candles to create a pleasant atmosphere, friluftsliv brings the ambience of the fire back to its origins—the outdoors. Although we live in a completely different kind of society than our hunter-gatherer forebears did, we can still use campfire storytelling to deepen our relationships and tickle our sense of wonder and awe. With many of us scrolling our way deeper down the rabbit hole of social media on a daily basis, you could even argue that we need real-life fireside chats more than ever.

I first discovered the power of storytelling around the campfire during a camping trip to the Chattahoochee National Forest in Georgia when Maya and Nora were still little. We had been out for a hike and had then come back to the campsite to grill some banana boats (see recipe on page 202) for dessert. The girls happily helped build a fire and spent a good hour making torches out of sticks, dry leaves, grass, and some twine, but as the flames started to subside and turn to ember, I could tell that they were getting a bit restless. I suggested that we all sit down around the fire and tell each other stories. The girls' eyes lit up with excitement, whereupon I immediately started to second-guess my idea. I have never considered myself a great on-the-spot storyteller, and my imagination is not what it used to be, but it was too late to back out now. To make it easy on myself, I started out by telling them stories from my childhood that I knew well—about the time one of my rabbits ran away, about the boy I had a crush on in second grade, and about the time my cousins and I got lost while wandering around the woods behind our house. Most of the stories were short and unremarkable by most standards, no more than snapshots from my childhood, but that didn't matter. The girls were thrilled and begged for more. They could have listened all night if I had not exhausted my storytelling repertoire around midnight, when we instead turned to watching the night sky before tuckering out in the tent. Since that night, storytelling has become just as fundamental to fire as s'mores in our family, which is not a small feat considering how much my kids love marshmallows.

Now that the girls are eleven and fourteen years old, and I have gained two bonus daughters ages five and nine through marriage, gathering around the fire has become one of the things that we do to cultivate a new family dynamic. With the girls covering such a large age span, it's sometimes difficult to spend time outdoors in a way that suits everybody, but what we have found is that activities that involve fire of some sort generally have the best chances of success. Somehow, playing with fire never gets old. When we cook over the open fire and eat together outside, it's as if we transcend age and time, and the stories we tell now become part of our shared family history. Some of the anecdotes the girls never seem to get tired of, even though I tell the same ones over and over again. Sometimes the girls share their own stories, often about things that have not come up before, feeling safe around the comforting flames of the campfire. Through storytelling, we have made the fire something more than a source of heat, light, and cooked food. It's now a place for contemplation, conversation, and bonding with each other and nature, the friluftsliv way.

# THREE GAMES FOR THE CAMPFIRE

Along with stories, playing games is one of our favorite ways to entertain ourselves around the campfire. These games require no or very simple props and are fun for both young and old. Try them on your next camp-out!

## 1. ANIMAL-SOUND CHARADES

When the Norwegian comedic duo Ylvis went viral with their song "The Fox (What Does the Fox Say?)," they had the entire world musing about the sounds of this shy, bushy-tailed mammal. (The answer is a haunting, almost scream-like howl or barking sound.) But have you ever pondered what a turtle sounds like? Or a giraffe? If not, this twist on the classic game charades will give you a chance to share your interpretation with the world.

*How to do it:* Designate a game leader who tries to think of animals whose sounds are shrouded in mystery. Cat, dog, cow, and the like are obviously out. Think penguin, moose, groundhog, walrus, beaver, praying mantis, buffalo, prairie dog, and so forth. The game leader writes down the animals on small pieces of paper, then mixes them together. The players take turns drawing a note from the pile and making the sound of the animal on the note, without talking or making gestures, while the rest of the group guesses out loud. If the guessing game gets stuck, add gestures or give some clues. The first person to guess the right animal gets one point. Continue on as long as you wish, but at least until everybody has interpreted one animal. If you don't have paper and a pen, or if the group is too small to have a game leader, each player comes up with their own animal.

## 2. THE TELEPHONE GAME

Kids are usually familiar with this simple game and like to play it over and over again. It's perfect for the campfire since you're already sitting in a circle, and as far as games go, they don't come much simpler than this.

*How to do it:* The person who starts chooses a phrase and whispers it to the person sitting next to them. This person whispers it to the next and so on, until you have gone all the way around the circle. The last person in the circle says the phrase out loud, after which the player who started the game reveals the original phrase. The final version is typically quite different from the first version, often with humorous results.

# 3. ZIP AND THREE

So you've eaten your outdoor meal and it's time to chill in front of the fire. But somebody has to take care of the dishes first. What better way to settle the age-old question of who gets to clean up than with this game?

*How to do it*: Before starting the game, everybody gets three toothpicks, matchsticks, or short sticks (they must be small enough to fit in your closed hand). Without showing the rest of the group, each player selects a number of sticks to put forward in their closed hand—none, all, or anything in between. Going clockwise around the circle, everybody makes a guess at how many sticks there are in the closed hands in total. You're not allowed to pick the same number as somebody else. Whoever guesses the right number gets to put away one of their sticks ahead of the next round. The player who gets rid of all their sticks first wins.

# The joy of missing out

IF OUR ANCESTORS REVERED AND centered their social interactions on the fire, our electronic devices are receiving much of that same love today. But rather than being limited to a few hours after sundown, our news and social media notifications are pinging all day long and sometimes (at least for a lot of sleep-deprived teens) way past bedtime. Social media apps and news sites are constantly vying for our attention and prompting us to respond with a comment, a virtual thumbs-up, or at least a few more minutes of our precious time. Perfectly honed to our brain's penchant for attention and instant gratification, they provide our central nervous system with a steady diet of dopamine that quickly can turn addictive. Before you know it, you have 179 pickups and six and a half hours of screen time on your phone alone in a day. This anxiety over potentially missing some sensational news or important events in our friends' social media feeds goes under the internet acronym FOMO, or fear of missing out. FOMO is not an actual diagnosis, of course, but it describes a real psychological dilemma that can cause unwanted stress and unhappiness with our own lives. Research links FOMO to excessive social media use, and adolescents are especially susceptible. Considering that the amount of data on the internet at any given time is so enormous that we're guaranteed to miss out no matter how fervently we scroll, it's a cause we can't win.

Fortunately, high-quality family relationships can reduce the risk of FOMO. And getting rid of it is fairly easy if you're aware of the situations that trigger it and try to avoid them. It's also important to focus on what you do have instead of what you don't, and to make time for meaningful meetings with people in real life, rather than just socializing online. If you can do that, you may find what some psychologists call JOMO—the joy of missing out. JOMO is a state of mind, and it's typically achieved when we intentionally let go of the images projected by other people's social media feeds and choose to live a more connected, less competitive life with less screen time and more face time. In a *Psychology Today* article, Kristen Fuller, a physician and clinical mental health writer, describes JOMO as "the emotionally intelligent antidote to FOMO." She elaborates: "JOMO allows us to live life in the slow lane, to appreciate human connections, to be intentional with our time, to practice saying 'no,' to give ourselves 'tech-free breaks,' and to give us permission to acknowledge where we are and to feel emotions, whether they are positive or negative."

If Scandinavian politicians a hundred years ago promoted open-air life as a healthy alternative to dancing and drinking, parents today use it to get their kids away from their screens. I'm no exception. The screen use in our family escalated when the girls got smartphones and hit their tween years, and I wasn't much better myself, often spending time glued to my laptop on the weekend, working even though I was supposed to be off. A couple of years ago, bolstered by Fuller's words and convinced that the road to JOMO went through open-air living, I decided that our family needed to try something new: a once-weekly digital fast. For one year, we would turn off all digital devices once a week and restore the campfire—figuratively and literally. Since Sunday was the traditional day of rest from work, it seemed like the most logical candidate for a day to rest the mind and escape the noise from the outside world. I dubbed our new venture Screen-Free Sundays and vowed to swear off TV, computer, tablet, and cell phone, aside from making phone calls and taking pictures. Instead, we would do something as a family outside, a Norwegian-style søndagstur, sans technology. I just had to convince the kids first.

Unsurprisingly, Maya and Nora were anything but enthused. There was whining. There were eyerolls. There were not-so-subtle threats of nonparticipation. To win them over, I challenged them to come up with suggestions for activities (within reason—we needed to stick with friluftsliv ideals like exploring locally with simple means to make this work on a weekly basis). We wrote down our ideas on little notes, then put them in a jar. The ideas were adapted for the seasons and covered everything from "going on a long walk and bringing fika" and "paddling with fika" to "building a snowman and having fika" and "cooking a meal over the fire, followed by fika." And yes, fika was included an estimated 100 percent of the time. That is typically how you create a buy-in for tweens.

Trying to go on a once-weekly screen fast quickly made me keenly aware of how deeply intertwined our lives are with tech, for better or worse. Keeping the TV turned off wasn't very difficult, but getting by without using smartphones proved to be a tall order, especially when advance planning is not your forte and the internet is your savior for everything from booking ski rentals to finding the best brownie recipe. Not to mention my dependence on navigation apps to get to our location of choice. Some exceptions to the screen-free part of Screen-Free Sunday had to be made, lest we were prepared to get lost before even getting started, that much was clear from day one.

Tech withdrawal symptoms marred the first few weekends, but once we got into a rhythm of more consciously spending longer chunks of time outside as a family—ice-skating, skiing, sledding, hiking, swimming, playing outdoor games, cooking over the open fire, and exploring some local cultural and historical sites that I didn't even know existed or had forgotten all about—we automatically spent less mindless time on our screens. The kids' initial skepticism started to peel away, and anticipation for our søndagstur was building each week.

What I learned during our yearlong experiment was that in this brave new tech world, finding a healthy level of screen time is something that takes conscious effort and practice. Having a dedicated day of heavily reduced tech use gave me permission to be offline and focus on myself, my family, and the natural world—and it was liberating. To this day, the søndagstur is a habit we stick with. As it turned out, it was the perfect antidote to FOMO and my personal gateway to JOMO.

## THE CAMPFIRE AT HOME

If you have a backyard, you can enjoy the calming power of fire right at home, by building a fire pit. A backyard fire pit can be as simple or as elaborate as you want it to be, but remember why you're doing it—to create a space where you and your loved ones can hang out and tell stories, play games, and cook meals. Bigger is not necessarily better and there are no extra points for impressing the neighbors.

1. Find a good spot, away from trees, shrubs, and tall grass that may catch on fire.

2. Build an elevated base using rocks, gravel, or sand, approximately five to seven inches high. (This is to prevent roots from catching on fire from the heat spreading through the ground.) If you can't get ahold of natural rocks, repurpose some leftover pavers or bricks.

3. Place larger rocks around the base to prevent the fire from spreading sideways.

4. Clear leaves and other flammable debris from a four-to-five-foot diameter around the fire pit.

5. Bring out some seat pads and cozy up!

# Friluftsliv for your belly—the art of cooking and eating outside

EVERY TIME I EAT NEWLY harvested potatoes, gently scrubbed and boiled with fresh dill, and served with a generous helping of butter and herbal salt, I'm transported back to the summers of my childhood in Sweden. We would sit and eat on the patio behind our house, while flies buzzed lazily in the still air, and the radio played cheesy songs about hot summer days that never seemed to last long enough. For dessert, we would have strawberries, freshly picked from a farm nearby, and vanilla ice cream, the old-fashioned recipe. I remember going into the damp, shady pine forests and foraging for wild blueberries that I ate with abandon, like a starved brown bear that had just emerged from hibernation, my fingers and hands turning bright purple in the process. And then there were the chocolate wafers that my *farmor*—paternal grandmother—would always keep in the cabinet of her house. Even though I haven't eaten them for at least twenty years, I remember exactly what they taste like and how I ate them (by carefully lifting off the top layer of the wafer with my teeth, then licking off the chocolate; repeat for the next layer) as I sat down on the dock by the lake, wrapped in a towel with teeth clattering from swimming in the chilly water. If you think about it, you probably have a lot of these food memories too.

The reason we remember and cherish certain foods doesn't have that much to do with the specific makeup or ingredients of the food, but is a result of sensory input in combination with the context, according to psychologists. Taste is a powerful sense that is prone to leave strong memories, good or bad (cherry-flavored cough medicine, anyone?), and when we're surrounded by the people we love, in a place where we feel at home, the food naturally makes a greater impression on us. It may seem like we just eat with our mouths and taste buds, but what we see, hear, feel, and smell also affects our perception of the food. In the outdoors, part of our brain relaxes and our senses are heightened, which is why cooking and eating under the open sky becomes an even more powerful experience than normal. That would explain why the cheap hot dogs that tasted like heaven when you grilled them over the campfire after a day in the woods probably won't be quite the same if you cook them in a pan at home. Plus, prepping and cooking food without the conveniences of a kitchen means that every step takes a little more advance planning and dedication. Since we must work harder for the food outside, the end result naturally feels more rewarding.

In the Nordic countries, an opportunity to cook and eat outside is never wasted, whether in the forest or the backyard. According to the friluftsliv tradition, meals are usually kept simple yet nourishing. Serving up a fancy multicourse meal with all the bells and whistles doesn't generate any bonus points under the open skies. The purpose of friluftsliv is to find inner peace while communing with nature, and if you work too hard to impress the Instagram gods, you won't be doing either. If a cheese sandwich is all you have time to make for a picnic, so be it. Eaten in the right surroundings, chances are it will taste like it cost a million bucks.

## Four ways of cooking outside

THERE ARE MANY WAYS TO prepare food in the outdoors, and generally you can cook just about anything outside that you would normally cook inside. Is one way better than the other? That mostly comes down to personal preference and the situation at hand. Few things are more quintessentially hygge than cooking over an open fire, but if you're backpacking, a portable camp stove might be more convenient, especially since open fires are often prohibited in environmentally sensitive areas. Likewise, if there's a seasonal fire ban in place, having a campfire is not even an option.

Regardless of what method you choose, a good rule of thumb to make it easy on yourself is to chop up the ingredients at home and to bring some finger foods to snack on while you're waiting for the food to cook, especially if you have kids in tow.

# 1. NO OR MINIMAL EQUIPMENT

Sometimes, simple is best, and if hot dogs or stick bread (see recipe on page 199) are on the menu, all you need is a fire and a pointy stick or a skewer. Another way of cooking over an open fire without pots or pans and with a tad more flair is to make campfire foil packs. Just wrap some of your favorite veggies with a generous heaping of olive oil and some spices in tinfoil, making sure to put the opening on the top. Then place it on the hot coals of the campfire or a grill grate, and let it simmer until the vegetables are tender, approximately thirty to forty minutes. The tricky part about cooking over an open fire is that it can be difficult to regulate the temperature, but if you can resist the temptation to start cooking too soon and wait until the fire has turned the wood into hot embers, you're in a good place.

# 2. SKILLET OR MUURIKKA PAN

If you have a cast-iron skillet, it works just as well over an open fire as on your cooktop. Skillets heat up evenly and are great for braising and sautéing—just be sure to bring oven mitts, since they do get very hot. (Also, cast-iron pans with wood handles are not suitable for open-fire cooking, for obvious reasons.) If you cook often outdoors, it might be worth investing in a Nordic-style pan made specifically for cooking over the fire. Invented in the 1970s in Finland, where it was fashioned from the inspection hatch of a steel container, this type of pan is known generically as a *muurikka*, even though that's technically a brand name. The traditional model is round and comes in various sizes—the largest one measuring nearly four feet in diameter—and it's your perfect partner for outdoor cooking if you have a big family to feed or enjoy entertaining around the fire.

# 3. DUTCH OVEN

The Dutch oven is truly the Swiss Army knife of camp cook-ware—it can be used for soups, casseroles, lasagna, risotto, enchiladas, and even for baking bread and doughnuts. It's especially well suited for a backyard fire pit or car-camping trip, since it's a bit heavy to carry long distances. With a tripod you can regulate the heat under the Dutch oven more easily, but it's also possible to place it straight over the fire, especially if you make a platform fire (see page 177 for instructions). Use some rocks to make a U shape for the Dutch oven to stand on, so that you can keep feeding the fire through the opening of the U. Tip: To use the Dutch oven as an actual oven and distribute the heat evenly, simply put hot coals on top of it as well as underneath it.

# 4. CAMPING OR BACKPACKING STOVE

There is a jungle of camping and backpacking stoves on the market, ranging from super-lightweight single-burner stoves for ounce-chasing backpacking pros to large, professional-feeling camping stoves that are better suited for car camping. For the sake of minimizing gear, a backpacking stove takes up the least space and can get the job done in most situations. Backpacking stoves commonly run on alcohol or compressed gas; each kind comes with some pros and cons. Alcohol burners are simple to use, reliable even in cold conditions, and easy to maintain; but they have slower cooking times, since the heat output is limited, and the flame is sometimes hard to regulate. Camping stoves that use compressed gas are also easy to use, work well in windy conditions, and are fast. The drawbacks are that it can be hard to tell how much fuel you have left and that it may not work well in the cold.

# Easy-to-make recipes for the campfire

## *Basic Stick Bread*

If friluftsliv were a food, it would most likely be bread on a stick. In the Nordic countries, this simple comfort food is deeply associated with childhood, and for many, it's the first food they remember grilling over a fire. If you don't have much experience with cooking outside, stick bread is a great gateway dish, since it's extremely easy to make and a proven favorite snack for kids. I usually prepare the dough at home just before heading out, but you can also mix the dry ingredients at home and add the water later on-site. This basic recipe makes six to eight pieces of bread. The thinner you make them, the less time it will take to grill them.

Serves 4

### INGREDIENTS:

2 cups wheat flour or all-purpose gluten-free flour
2 teaspoons baking powder
½ teaspoon salt
¾ to 1 cup cold water
Butter, olive oil, honey, or jam, for serving

### DIRECTIONS:

Combine the flour, baking powder, and salt in a bowl. Add the water a little at a time, and knead until the dough is firm and smooth. Place the dough in a small plastic bag and bring it to the campsite or picnic site. Divide the dough into 6 to 8 pieces and roll them between the palms of your hands until they are long and thin (approximately 8 to 10 inches long). Pick some suitable sticks from the ground (according to the friluftsliv ethos, you should avoid breaking branches off live trees) and cut off any protruding twigs with a knife. Put one end of a dough piece at the end of a stick and push down to attach it, then twirl the dough around the stick; make sure that the dough is on properly before putting it over the fire. Grill the bread, turning it often so that it doesn't burn, until it's golden brown and baked on the inside. Gently remove it from the stick and add butter in the holes or dip it in some olive oil. To make it sweet, add honey or jam. Another option is to wrap it around a hot dog and use it in lieu of a bun.

*VARIATION:*

## Stick Bread with a Twist

The basic stick bread recipe can be modified in any number of ways
to suit your taste buds. Try jazzing it up by adding these ingredients to the dough for a zesty pizza flavor:

½ cup grated Parmesan or other sharp cheese
½ cup finely chopped sun-dried tomatoes
¼ cup finely chopped Kalamata olives
1 teaspoon thyme
2 teaspoons oregano

# Krabbelurer

*Krabbelurer* are small, puffy pancakes that are preferably made in a cast-iron pancake pan, frying pan, or campfire griddle. They're typically one of the first foods that Swedish Scouts learn to make over the fire, partly because they're easy to handle and partly because the sweet, simple flavor really appeals to children. Having said that, krabbelurer are an indulgent campfire treat that is just as appreciated by adults. This basic recipe makes about twelve krabbelurer and can be made gluten-free and/or vegan as needed.

Serves 2 to 4

## BATTER:

2 eggs or 8 tablespoons of aquafaba (canned chickpea liquid)
⅓ cup sugar
1 cup milk or plant-based alternative
2 cups wheat flour or all-purpose gluten-free flour
1 teaspoon vanilla powder
1 teaspoon baking powder
3 tablespoons butter or margarine, for frying

## DIP:

1 tablespoon sugar
½ tablespoon cinnamon
Whipped cream or whipped coconut cream, for serving

## DIRECTIONS:

To make the batter, whisk the egg or aquafaba with the sugar, then add the milk, flour, vanilla powder, and baking powder, and continue whisking until smooth. Heat a little bit of the butter in a cast-iron pan or muurikka over the fire and add the batter, making each pancake approximately the size of the palm of your hand. Fry until golden brown on both sides. To make the dip, mix the sugar and cinnamon together, then turn the pancake over in the mixture and serve with a dollop of whipped cream.

**TIP:** Make the batter at home ahead of time and pour it into in an empty and clean PET bottle for convenient storage and transportation to the campsite. The bottle also minimizes messes when you pour the batter into the pan, a boon if kids are involved in the process.

## Banana Boat

Healthy desserts are all fine and well, and rumor has it that grilled watermelon is the bomb, but in my book, campfires are a reason for decadence. In the United States, this comes in the form of s'mores; their Nordic equivalent is the banana boat. One banana boat per person will ensure that you end your campfire session in a state of utter and total chocolaty bliss.

Serves 1

### INGREDIENTS:

1 banana
1 ounce chocolate
Mini marshmallows, for sprinkling

### DIRECTIONS:

Make a deep cut along the inside curve of the banana, from the stem to the tip. Break up the chocolate in small pieces and stuff it, together with the mini marshmallows, in the slit of the banana. Wrap the banana in tinfoil and place it on some hot coals. When the banana is mushy and the chocolate and marshmallows have melted, it's done.

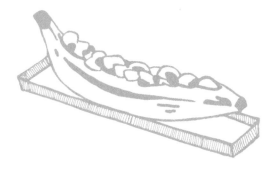

## Eating outside is better together

IF YOU'RE THE SOCIAL TYPE, the only thing that beats cooking and eating outside is doing it with other people. In the Nordic countries, gathering around a campfire with simple foods to grill is a common way to get together and enjoy nature. And in line with the tradition of open-air living, the dishes are often simple—hot dogs and burgers seem to be the universal outdoor go-to food. This Nordic penchant for cooking outdoors in a group came in handy in an unexpected way during the COVID-19 pandemic, when for long periods of time socializing outdoors was the only safe way to see family and friends. In keeping with government restrictions on avoiding indoor gatherings, people simply found creative ways to move birthdays, Christmas, New Year's Eve, and other celebrations outside. (As a sign of the times, hot dog sales at one of Sweden's biggest grocery chains increased by 24 percent in 2020 from the year before.) While this was most definitely a disruption of cherished traditions and the notion of what those types of celebrations should entail, people adapted. Some even found an upside with the new order. "You know, I have to admit that I kind of like it," my childhood friend Linda mused as we watched our kids burn their hot dogs to coal over a campfire in the woods on New Year's Eve. "When we saw our extended families over Christmas, we grilled hot dogs and burgers in the woods for three days straight. You'd think that it'd get old, but I liked not having the pressure of having my home in perfect shape for the holidays or stressing out over all the fancy food that we normally prepare. This year, everybody could just focus on being together, and I think we all really needed that."

COVID-19 brought outdoor cooking to new heights as people made a virtue out of necessity, but pandemic or not, there are good reasons to enjoy more meals with friends in the woods, by the beach, or at a park. Cooking and eating outside as a group is an easygoing and unassuming way to get together that doesn't put pressure on anybody to make their home presentable or prepare an exquisite three-course dinner. Keep it spontaneous or decide to meet up with friends at a predetermined place and time, for example once a month. Either everybody brings their own food to cook, or you take turns bringing the food. Another option is to decide what to cook in advance and divide the ingredients so that everybody contributes something (assuming that you go with a recipe a tad more ambitious than hot dogs). The latter is a great way to get everybody involved with the cooking and create a feeling of togetherness around the campfire. Want to take it one step further? Help build the outdoor community where you live by starting a public cooking group. That's what Mats Hellman of Tibro, Sweden, did when he was on paternity leave with his third child and suffered from a severe case of cabin fever. Since the regular indoor activities that were typically offered to parents with young children didn't appeal to him, he took matters into his own hands and created one that did.

"I never thought cooking inside with a bunch of kids was very enjoyable," said Hellman, who today is a father of five. "Outside, the cooking becomes an experience in itself, instead of being a chore. When you're outside, the kids can run around and be wild, and it's okay. It's a little more laid-back, and even though the food is simple, it usually tastes really good."

Hellman's idea was as simple as it was brilliant: Start a cooking group that would meet in the woods or one of the public parks around town and cook lunch together. Before each event he would post a map with a location and a recipe with a breakdown of the ingredients on a website, then anybody who wanted to join in could bring their share of the fixings and help put it all together. He presented his idea to the city council, which contributed funds for a tripod, a large pot, and reusable tableware.

One snowy Friday, the first parents, kids, and strollers rolled in. From then on, the parents gathered around the fire to cook every week, rain or shine, while the older kids played and the younger ones often napped in their strollers. Initially, none of the parents knew one another, but this soon changed. "Standing around the fire and adding the ingredients created a feeling of community," Hellman said. The recipes ranged from the basic to the eclectic: fish soup, risotto, chicken casserole, spaghetti Bolognese, taco soup, and more. The families soon noticed that cooking outside was not all that complicated, and that pretty much anything that you can cook inside also can be cooked over an open fire.

Now that his paternal leave is over, Hellman's job as a project manager keeps him inside all day. But the family still often eats outside together. "When you eat outside, it's easier to stay outside all day, and you know that it's good for you."

# START AN OUTDOOR COOKING GROUP IN FIVE SIMPLE STEPS

1. **Check who is in.** If you've already got a group of outdoorsy friends, they're probably game. But if you can't count on your closest friends to join in, you may need to reach out to a broader network. Social media is a good place to start gauging interest, both among your personal connections and in local interest groups.

2. **Work out the details.** If it's just you and your friends, you can definitely keep it as spontaneous and informal as you want it to be, but if scheduling your outdoor cooking sessions ahead of time is what it takes to make them happen, do it. If your cooking group will be public, you should probably be a little more organized. Will the group meet up for a set number of times or on an ongoing basis? At the same place every time or different places? Will you cook something together or bring your own food? You decide where to put the bar—and don't put it too high. Better a burned pancake in the forest than a lobster thermidor within four walls.

3. **Check the rules.** Make sure there aren't any fire restrictions in place at your location of choice. To minimize damage to the environment, always use existing campfire spots when you can. In particularly sensitive areas, it may be better to use a camp stove with a gas burner.

4. **Get the gear.** At a minimum, you'll need tableware and a large pot; a Dutch oven combined with a tripod usually does the trick. If your group is public, a community foundation might be willing to contribute money toward the purchase.

5. **Do a test run.** You'll feel much more in control if the first time you're meeting up is not also the first time you're starting a fire and using the equipment.

# How to take a crap in the wild

WHAT GOES IN EVENTUALLY MUST come out, and if you're eating in nature, chances are you may eventually feel the urge to do a number two. But how? This may not be the first question you ask somebody when you start planning for a camping or backpacking trip. Much like what happens in the bedroom usually stays in the bedroom, our bathroom habits are something we rarely feel comfortable airing with others. In this case it should be, however, because with the comforts of modern sanitation now readily available in our day-to-day life, the essential skill of going to the bathroom outdoors is about to become a lost art. To some people, even the thought of squatting over a cathole is enough to subconsciously induce multiday constipation, and that's definitely not good for your stomach.

In the Nordic countries, friluftsliv is often practiced in areas without any public bathroom facilities, so anybody planning to stay out for an extended period needs to know how to relieve themselves in the wild. If you haven't learned the proper way from your parents, Cajsa Rännar from the Swedish Outdoor Association is there to fill the void. To address the fact that more and more people are turning to the outdoors with questionable toileting skills, she even made a short instructional video about pooping in nature that got picked up by Swedish public service TV.

"We could print any number of brochures about this, but we know that the best way to learn is through socialization—that is, to do it with somebody else," said Rännar. "Whenever we share something about going to the bathroom, it blows up on social media. I'm sure part of the reason is that people think it's funny to share stuff about poop, but I also think it's something that a lot of people wonder about but are too embarrassed to ask about."

And when people don't know what to do, they tend to do it wrong. If you've ever stepped on somebody else's toileting mayhem while out in nature, you know exactly what I mean. This is not only gross, but it also presents a sanitary problem. To avoid this, here is a quick PSA on how to poop in nature in three simple steps:

1. **Choose a good location.** You want the hole to be at least 150 feet away from trails, campsites, and waterways that people might get their drinking water from.

2. **Dig a cathole.** A small garden trowel works great in most situations, but if you're backpacking, you may want to go with a lightweight trowel developed specifically for the purpose. The hole should be at least six to eight inches deep.

3. **Go to the bathroom.** Squat down over the hole and take aim. Wipe yourself, then cover up the hole. While toilet paper is biodegradable and usually can be buried along with the feces, it decomposes very slowly in barren mountain regions, so in these areas it's best to put it in a doggy bag and pack it out.

## Would you survive this?

IN 2018, WHEN THE SWEDISH Civil Contingencies Agency (MSB) sent out a brochure to all households in the country titled *If Crisis or War Comes*, it made international headlines, as it came out on the heels of escalating tension with Russia and was the first public awareness campaign of its kind since 1961. The purpose of the brochure was to help people prepare for emergencies that might prevent society from functioning normally, like a natural disaster, terror attack, global food shortage, cyberattack, collapse of the electrical grid, or even a military attack. Besides giving information about Sweden's military and civil defense, the brochure advised people how to prepare for the unexpected at home, for example by stocking up on nonperishable foods, making sure you have access to clean drinking water, and keeping warm by lighting candles and dressing in layers.

Survival techniques and what is today generally referred to as "prepping" used to be the domain of the military and rather small pockets of apocalyptic-minded civilians, and at first glance, a government pamphlet on how to prepare for the worst may not appear to have much overlap with open-air living. After all, how to behave in a crisis is probably not the first thing on your mind during an early-morning bird-watching session or a leisurely Sunday walk with friends. In reality, though, learning how to take care of your basic needs when you strip away modern conveniences has always been at the heart of the friluftsliv tradition. Looking at the list of home-preparedness tips and suggested equipment from MSB, it's easy to see that somebody who practices an open-air lifestyle by regularly going camping, for example, will have a leg up in the event of crisis. Fire steel or matches and a backpacking stove? Check. Woolen base layer and warm, all-weather outdoor clothing? Check. Alternative way of collecting, purifying, and storing clean drinking water? Check on that as well.

My personal interest in improving my survival skills through friluftsliv had very little to do with preparing for a potential Russian invasion, however, and more to do with the fact that I had created two tiny humans who were now in my care. If I wanted them to come with me into the backcountry (which I did), winging it was not an option. That, and my children joined the Scouts, an organization that seamlessly marries crisis preparation and open-air life. Their motto alone, "Be prepared," is the epitome of being mentally and physically ready for whatever challenges life throws at you. I was never a scout myself, but both Maya and Nora owe many of their practical outdoor skills to the Swedish Scout organization, and for some time, I helped lead their troop as well. Seeing them excelling at things like building shelters, tying knots, and handling an axe piqued my curiosity and made me want to learn too. Even though I was in my late thirties at that point, the beauty of friluftsliv is that it's never too late to learn new skills and that there is absolutely no shame in being a beginner. But after nearly two years as a Scout leader, the skill of starting a fire with a fire steel was still evading me and it was starting to bug me. To be fair, I had not practiced a whole lot, but when I did, I failed every time. Even though my backpacking trips with the girls were not extreme by comparison, we did sometimes venture pretty far into roadless country, where trails were poorly marked and cell phone coverage scarce. Add sketchy weather on top of that, and knowing how to start a fire without matches seemed like a good life insurance.

So I contacted Torbjörn Selin, a former officer in the Swedish Army with over twenty years of experience with prepping and survival training, who now educates regular mortals in a variety of friluftsliv skills, including the art of staying alive in all types of outdoor settings—the forest, the mountains, and by the ocean. Selin's signature class is a three-day survival course in the forest, but he also holds classes in wilderness first aid, hiking, outdoor cooking, fire, bushcraft, winter camping, and more. As an ever-present reminder to himself and others to always think ahead, he even has the motto of the Swedish Armed Forces Survival School, *Praeparatus Supervivet*, "the prepared one survives," tattooed on his upper right arm. If anybody could teach me how to master the fire steel, as well as some other survival tricks, I figured it was him.

I met up with Selin and his assistant instructor, Silvia Küller, at his base camp, in the quiet pine forests near Rydboholm, in southwestern Sweden. A thin plume of smoke was slowly dancing around the campfire as he threw on a couple of new logs to revive the flames. He sank down in the only camping chair available—one of the few luxuries that he treated himself to out here—and gestured for me to plant myself on one of the thick logs that were strewn on the ground.

Selin had just finished up an introductory course on fire making and noted that even in a country like Sweden, with a long tradition of friluftsliv, far from everybody masters the skill of making a fire with natural materials anymore. "Some people have lost touch with nature, some are even afraid of nature. I don't get it, but I suppose that you fear what you don't know," he said, somewhat disgruntled.

Selin poured himself a cup of coffee from a sooty stainless-steel coffee pan that was sitting on some rocks by the embers. I could tell he was in his right element here by the fire, and his clients felt it too. It was no coincidence that his corporate team-building events usually revolve around fire—starting it, cooking over it, sleeping around it, and keeping it going. "As soon as the fire is crackling, people feel calm. It's almost a trance-like feeling," Selin said. "Normally when you have a big conference, somebody always gets drunk before dinner, but you can't do that here. Everybody has to contribute. Sleeping around the fire is the best team building I know; even the skeptics like it, and many people think it's the best thing they've ever done."

Fire does have a unique standing not only when it comes to our well-being but also for our chances of survival in the wild. Being surprised by the weather or plunging through the ice are some of the reasons why people might end up in a survival situation, and at that point, avoiding hypothermia is crucial. Not only does fire give us necessary heat; it also provides a way to cook food, purify water, dry our clothes, and signal our whereabouts to others. It gives us light at night, and it's calming, a trait that should not be underestimated when your life may be at risk. Fire, in short, is the king of survival techniques.

As you might expect from an ex-military guy who has made a career out of crisis preparation, Selin has a commanding voice and a no-nonsense personality. Add in his heaping of social skills, and it's easy to see why Selin is the kind of person other people gravitate to and trust. That's probably a good thing, because his survival course is no picnic. It's seventy-two hours long and thoroughly tests the outer limits of the participants' resilience and willpower while they're navigating around the forest with the bare essentials for survival. Forget the sleeping bag—this is a survival course, not a camping trip. Food? "An element of starvation is included free of charge," Selin said and smirked. "It's pretty hard-core. I've had people come here who thought that they were going to have a cozy long weekend in the forest and then—*bam*—before they know it, they are lying under a pine tree in fetal position."

Now, Selin is no sadist. He is simply passionate about making people comfortable and prepared in nature. In his book, that includes anybody who participates in friluftsliv, not just the die-hard adventurers who purposely go far off the beaten track and may put themselves at greater risk than others. Even the casual dog walker benefits from having a plan B, for example if they were to fall and injure themselves badly, even if it just meant bringing a cell phone to use in emergencies. "It's always a good thing to think ahead and be aware of risks," he said. "Tell somebody where you're going, choose activities based on your abilities and knowledge, be aware of your surroundings, and bring a first aid kit. Those are the kind of things that make you a smart survivor, not that you know how to dig a bivouac or purify water using bark. Those skills are interesting and nice to have but are rarely applicable in real-life situations."

The people who sign up for Selin's survival courses come from all walks of life, and about half of them are women. All have an interest in friluftsliv, but their motives for wanting to learn new skills vary. Some are parents who want to be able to teach their children practical skills; others are people who want to feel safer in nature, or who don't want to be dependent on their more knowledgeable partner.

Küller, an outgoing mother of two who had taken several of Selin's courses before becoming one of his assistant instructors, said that she did it to feel more secure while venturing out in nature with her children. "My sense of direction is so poor I could get lost in my own backyard. Once I started taking my kids out in the woods, I got worried about what I'd do if we got into a bad situation or I lost my bearings, and I wanted to feel secure with them. That, and my husband has a tendency to hurt himself, so I wanted to learn first aid."

Although Küller got through the survival course with flying colors and said she even enjoyed it, Selin never knows in advance how the participants will react to the stress of spending three days and nights in the forest, unsure of their location and deprived of food. While some sleep quite well despite the circumstances, others anxiously lie awake all night. Hunger is bound to haunt you at some point, sometimes evolving into nausea. Whether you're able to make it through the full three days without giving up essentially comes down to one thing: how well you're able to handle discomfort. That cold, hard determination serves you well in a real-life survival situation as well.

"Imagine that you're surprised by bad weather or accidentally plunge into cold water on a dark fall night. The same situation could have two completely different outcomes depending on your mindset, knowledge, and preparation. Some people know that they need to move around to stay warm or seek shelter in nature. They know how to make fire and packed a little kit for that. Compare that with someone who is ignorant or naive. They might just give up and lie down. The person who gives up is toast. The one who soldiers on lives. You must have the mental strength to act when something happens."

## Always be prepared

KNOWING A FEW SURVIVAL TECHNIQUES is not as difficult or extreme as it may sound; they're simple, common-sense actions that will make you feel safer when you're out and about. As a bonus, learning how to handle risks in nature can boost your confidence and help you stay calm during other unexpected crises— minor as well as major. After all, whether you get lost in the woods or lose power at home after a storm, rational behavior founded on sound facts wins over panic every time. If you have kids, it's a good idea to involve them in the process too. It's never too soon to help children make smart choices in nature, and it may even save them from ending up in a survival situation to begin with.

These tips can help you stay safe while exploring outside:

- Always tell somebody where you're going and when you expect to be back, even if you're just taking the dog for a walk.

- Learn how to navigate with a map and compass—it's a good skill to have if you enjoy friluftsliv and a must if you plan to head out in the backcountry. Using the GPS in your cell phone is fine, but don't rely on technology alone, since it might run out of battery or lose service.

- Keep a basic first aid kit and fire-starting kit (see page 174 for tips on how to make one) in your backpack and know how to use them.

- Dress for the weather and be prepared for changing conditions.

- Have a plan B in case your original plan doesn't pan out. The greatest explorers know that there is no shame in turning around.

## HANDY FRILUFTSLIV HACK

Hand sanitizer can be good to have on hand outdoors for more than one reason. In a survival situation, hygiene is key, since getting sick can be life-threatening. Hand sanitizer is also flammable and can be used to start a fire, should no other suitable tinder be available.

FRILUFTSLIV IS INTIMATELY CONNECTED WITH the Nordic culture, landscape, history, and mindset, but our craving for nature is universal. Even the concept of friluftsliv was internationally inspired from the get-go, not the least by North American environmentalists like Henry David Thoreau, John Muir, and Aldo Leopold. It was the founding of Yellowstone National Park in 1872 that inspired the protection of wilderness areas in the Nordic countries, not the other way around. (In fact, it wasn't until 1909 that Sweden became the first country in Europe to catch up, by founding nine national parks in one go.) Nor was the Nordic form of outdoor recreation unique when it first came about—around the same time that friluftsliv began to gain momentum in the Nordic countries, a sizable back-to-nature movement flourished in North America, popularizing outdoor activities like birding, fishing, camping, and simple cabin life. Early American settlers even enjoyed the right to roam—and hunt—on private, unenclosed land, but this tradition fell by the wayside as states began to enact trespassing laws at the end of the nineteenth century. Since then, a series of Supreme Court decisions have strengthened landowners' rights to exclude others from their property even further.

Today, access to public green spaces is unevenly distributed in the United States. Even though an impressive 40 percent of the country consists of public land that is managed by federal, state, or local governments, the vast majority of it is located in remote areas out West, where it's effectively inaccessible to many Americans.

Open-air life hinges on the public being able to use green spaces close to home, and, without a Nordic-style right to roam, the United States needs other strategies to improve access to nature and provide safe places to walk, especially in underserved communities. As more and more people are clamoring for a life connected with nature and the future of all of us depends on our ability to combat global climate change, cities and states that have done their homework will have an upper hand. Take the twin cities of Minneapolis and St. Paul, for example. They were among the first to sign up for an initiative spearheaded by the Children and Nature Network and the National League of Cities to help cities increase equitable access to nature. And when the Trust for Public Land ranks metropolitan areas based on the availability to good parks and opportunities for outdoor recreation, Minneapolis and St. Paul have taken turns claiming the top two spots almost every year since 2015. There, almost everybody lives within a ten-minute walk of a public park and, as one *New York Times* article somewhat astoundingly noted, the residents seem to enjoy their green spaces, even during the unforgiving Minnesota winters. Considering Minnesota's history, this should come as no surprise. The state has the most descendants from the Nordic countries in the United States, with as much as one-third of the population claiming Scandinavian heritage. For an American take on open-air life, Minnesota may very well offer some clues.

Just like the concept of hygge has taken on a life of its own since it became popularized outside Denmark, friluftsliv will likely generate a plethora of local variations. This adaption is expected and necessary, since other countries have different climates, histories, geographies, and land availability than the Nordics. But whatever version of friluftsliv you run into, don't be fooled into thinking that friluftsliv is something that you can buy. Rather, it is, as Norwegian author Nils Faarlund so beautifully put it, a feeling of "'belonging' to the land" and a "living tradition for recreating nature-consonant lifestyles."

## Localizing friluftsliv—three stories

AUGUST CASSON, THE AMERICAN TEACHER who spent fifteen years living and working in Norway, is doing his part to emulate the Nordic outdoor culture that he became so attached to during his time overseas. Living north of Springfield, Illinois, is obviously a lot different, as he's no longer able to walk out his door and hike up a mountain, then ski down, like he used to in northern Norway. But he's embracing the idea of friluftsliv as something that can be localized. "People think that because it's flat in Illinois, there's nothing to do, but I can drive for thirty minutes and go hiking, paddleboarding, or riding on bike trails. I think there's stuff to do everywhere," Casson said. "Americans tend to think that bigger is always better, but it doesn't have to be Norway or the Colorado mountains or the Michigan Upper Peninsula. It could just be going to a local lake and renting a canoe."

Next, Casson is planning to gather a group from the community that will meet up once or twice per month to do things outdoors together and maybe try activities they haven't done before, like ice-skating and snowshoeing. Personally, he tries to get outside as much as possible with his two kids, mixing bike rides and walks with trail running, bouldering, and some gardening.

"When I realized what the concept of friluftsliv was, I wanted to instill it in my family," Casson said. "To me, friluftsliv is so much more than a word, it's a way of doing things, a way of living, and a part of the culture. It's not something you can touch—it's something you feel in your soul."

For Casson, the inspiration for open-air living came from direct experience with the culture in Norway, but for Tacy Quinn of suburban New Jersey, the turning point was the outbreak of COVID-19. Suddenly, she and her husband found themselves juggling working their full-time jobs from home and making sure their two tween boys keep up remote school. No longer able to travel to see family in Idaho and California like she used to, Quinn was struggling to stay positive in the day-to-day. Then came the lockdown in the summer of 2020. "Kids are resilient, but we needed something that we could do on a daily basis to just be in the moment. Since it was considered safer to be outside, we started doing more of that, and it was such a reprieve. It just felt great to be outside," she said.

That fall, Quinn came across an article about friluftsliv in *National Geographic* and had a proverbial aha moment. Quinn's ancestors emigrated from Norway to Iowa in the 1870s, and the idea of embracing open-air living all year round appealed to her on several levels, not the least because it gave her a way to honor her family heritage at a time when she was unable to see her parents in real life. "I started asking myself why I was dreading winter and thinking that I couldn't be outside in the cold. I really wanted to create some joy for my family during this heavy time and felt like this could be the answer."

Quinn knew going hiking every week would not fly with her kids, so instead she created what she called "15 Weeks of Friluftsliv," a weekly outdoor activity to do with her family and sometimes friends as well. Some weeks, it was as simple as having a picnic or creating nature art, other times they would go glamping or visit farmers markets. Among the most memorable moments was an outdoor progressive dinner that Quinn and her neighbors put on in the middle of winter, as well as a full-moon hike.

What started as a way to stave off cabin fever during a pandemic has left a permanent mark, not just on Quinn's family but on her local community and online followers as well. "I was surprised at how many families were interested in the ideas at first, but then again, I think we're all craving to reconnect with something powerful. Even before COVID, life was a little out of balance, and we were constantly on the move, without getting enough quality time together. That's what we needed."

Meanwhile in suburban Detroit, mother-of-five Ginny Yurich discovered open-air life when she felt like she was drowning in the day-to-day demands of parenting young children. After being invited on a picnic by a friend and seeing firsthand the positive effect that four hours of nature play had on the entire family, Yurich began to rearrange their schedule so they would be able to spend more time outside. She read up on the benefits of outdoor play for children and eventually came across the concept of friluftsliv. The Nordic ethos of going outside in any weather helped her reframe her mindset and enjoy being outside even in the dead of winter, something she used to dread. "What appealed to me about friluftsliv was also that it allows you to be outside without pressure to achieve. It's a simple concept that aims to fill your life with more outside moments. It really solved the puzzle for me."

Today, most people know Yurich as the founder of 1,000 Hours Outside, now a global movement that aims to roughly match the amount of time children spend in front of screens every year (a whopping 1,200 hours by some accounts) with outdoor time. While spending nearly three hours outside every day may seem like an impossible feat, Yurich believes having a goal can be a powerful motivator. "If you can't do one thousand hours, make your own numbers. But be intentional about it, and model it to your kids," she said. "Nature will exceed your expectations. Once you try it, you're hooked."

## Coming home

IBSEN, THE NORWEGIAN POET WHO coined the term *frilufts-liv*, escaped to the mountains when he thought the hoopla of society was too much to bear. Thoreau built a simple cabin in the woods to get away from what he regarded as over-civilization. As human activity has intensified exponentially since the nineteenth century, when Ibsen and Thoreau walked the earth, finding areas that are untouched by humans is increasingly difficult. At the same time, our need to take a break from the stressors of modern civilization is stronger than ever. Through open-air living, we can. Friluftsliv helps us to live happier, healthier lives right where we are, by being closely tuned into our local landscape and building the kinds of communities that we want to live in, not the kinds that we need to escape from. Cities with bike lanes and sidewalks, community gardens and neighborhood parks, urban woods and wildlife corridors, green roofs and clean waterways. Towns where there is room both for trees to grow old and for humans to flourish.

Just as the introduction of hygge made people swoon over candles, board games, and cozy family nights in front of the fireplace, my hope is that friluftsliv will trigger a similar craving for morning walks and fika in the forest. Because the journey toward an open-air life starts within ourselves, we just need to open the door for it. Literally.

When being in nature feels like coming home, you know you're living life the friluftsliv way. To get there, just keep this mantra as your guiding light:

LIVE SIMPLY.

GO OUTSIDE OFTEN.

BE KIND TO THE EARTH.

A FEW MONTHS AFTER I took my friend Jeanette backpacking for the very first time, she texted me out of the blue. "Guess what I did over the weekend! Number two! Outdoors!" I had suspected the toileting business had been a bit of a hang-up for Jeanette but didn't want to ask in case she felt like it was too private. Now her texts confirmed my gut feeling. "I used to feel resistant to it, but now I'm over it. Dug a cathole like you told me to. My stomach is feeling so much better!" I couldn't help cracking up at her excitement and pride over having mastered this great feat. Not only that: As it turned out, in the blink of an eye that is the Swedish summer, she had managed to put three more backpacking trips under her belt— two of them solo and the last one with her two daughters, a five-year-old and a seven-year-old. I was impressed but not surprised. Once you have experienced flow in nature, you know. The will to delve deeper into friluftsliv had been inside her all along. She had just needed a little nudging and somebody to show her how to properly use a water filter (and dig a cathole) to flourish. After our initial trip, she had gone all-in, hiking by herself for an entire week on the picturesque island of Gotland, just off Sweden's east coast. She chose a trail along the ocean to minimize the risk of getting lost and because she was longing to see the sun rise and set where the sky meets the water. The trip was all that she had dreamed of, and then some. "I'm so happy that I dared challenging myself to hike alone, with all that it entails. It was relaxing, lots of hard work, toughening, and absolutely fantastic," she told me over the phone from

Stockholm. "Being out there on my own reminded me that it's the simple things in life that count. You know, to discover and to explore. Those are the things that give you the most energy."

Jeanette had a challenge for me as well. With her signature unbridled enthusiasm, she suggested that we commit to sleeping outside at least one night per month for a year, together when possible but otherwise alone or with our children. I had always wanted to try winter camping, and this idea was all the nudging I needed. When I asked the kids if they wanted to come, Maya, the teen, gave me a blank stare that spoke louder than a thousand words. Nora, however, was game, and a few weeks later we took off on our first cold-weather camping trip. It was mid-November, with night temperatures hovering just above freezing, so in addition to our normal gear I packed an extra sleeping bag each and a couple of plastic bottles to use as hot-water bottles. To make it easy on ourselves, we chose a flat, three-mile-long trail that ended at a lean-to that I was familiar with, not too far from a historic mansion that was a popular summertime attraction. The lean-to was usually stocked with plenty of firewood, so we wouldn't need to carry our own in. Or at least so I thought. Cue our surprise when we got to our destination in the late afternoon and not only was there no firewood, but the lean-to had been torn down and replaced by a picnic shelter with benches and a huge table.

Nora's first reaction was to give in to the powers that be. "Let's just turn around and go home," she said, her voice brimming with disappointment. "Is that what a Scout would do?" I retorted. After ruminating on that thought for a while, the spark returned to her eyes, and we started to put together a plan B. We had a camping stove, so we would still be able to cook dinner as planned, but we really needed a fire to stay warm until bedtime. It would get dark by four o'clock and we only had an hour of good daylight left, so we had to find firewood fast. We checked the map and located a forested area a short walk from the picnic shelter where there would likely be some dead branches for us to pick. Channeling my inner MacGyver, I fashioned a firewood carrier out of some paracord and the rain cover for my backpack, and off we went.

After weeks of rain, all the firewood we could find was soaked. Using my ax, I cut the wet bark off the bigger pieces of wood to make them burn better, while Nora built a small pyramid using thin branches of fir. Then we placed the larger logs in a triangle around the kindling so that they would dry out once the thinner branches were burning. Preparing the fire was high-level teamwork, but when it was time to light it, Nora graciously bowed out. She knew I needed to face my very own personal kryptonite—the fire steel—head-on. I burned through almost every trick in our fire kit as I tried to get the fire going, but the wet kindling made it hard to sustain the fledgling flames. Finally, I was left with nothing but hope and a fluffed-up tampon. I struck the fire steel once, twice, thrice. On the fourth try, one of the sparks finally found fertile ground on the tampon-turned-tinder—and we rushed to feed the tiny flame with thin, dry pine branches. As the fire gradually gained strength, I could feel the warmth spreading from my fingertips to my core.

We cooked a pasta casserole over the fire and played some cards under the light of my headlamp. We talked about annoying boys at school, Nora's infatuation with Japanese anime films, and silly viral TikTok trends. Then we drifted off to sleep on the floor of the picnic shelter, deeply cocooned in our sleeping bags. We were so tired that we didn't even say goodnight.

—ACKNOWLEDGMENTS—

My name may be on the cover of this book, but many people had a part in making it what it is.

First of all, I'm grateful to my agent, Meg Thompson, who saw the potential in this book when it was still at the idea stage and patiently waited for me to bring my proposal to the finish line. Without you, this book may never have been written, and I'm forever grateful for your unwavering support. I'm also grateful that you introduced me to Sandy Hodgman, who is expertly helping me bring my books out into the world as my foreign rights agent. Additionally, my editor, Sara Carder at TarcherPerigee, has brought her invaluable experience, expertise, and editing magic to this project. Working with you, as well as the rest of your team, has been a real treat. Special thanks to my copyeditor, M. P. Klier, who helped me clean up mistakes I didn't even know I was making, down to the last misplaced comma and incomplete citation.

The illustrations in this book were created by my incredibly talented friend Heather Dent of Winterberry Studio. When we randomly met at a deserted county park in Illinois one cold winter day all those years ago, I had a feeling fate had something special in store for us. I'm delighted beyond words that we had the opportunity to collaborate on this project and hope there will be many more to come.

A heartfelt thank-you goes out to all the people who took time out of their busy lives to talk to me about friluftsliv. This book is so much richer thanks to your deep knowledge and valuable perspectives. As we say in Swedish, *Ingen nämnd, ingen glömd*. (Nobody mentioned, nobody forgotten.)

Most of all, I would like to thank my family for putting up with me during the intense phase of writing and editing this book. *Mamma*, *Pappa*, Susanne—your love and support have not gone unnoticed. Sverker, you understand my passion for the work I do better than anybody else and have given me the freedom to pursue my calling since the day we met. One day, we're going to ride around the country in a retrofitted camper van with no particular destination in mind, and it's going to be glorious. Molly and Lill-Nora, I love your unbridled enthusiasm for playing outdoors, and I'm happy to be able to call you my bonus daughters. Finally, Maya and Nora, you will always be my greatest inspiration and the reason why I embarked on this book-writing journey to begin with. Hopefully you will read my books one day and understand why I did it. I love you all. Now let's go camping.

*Unless otherwise noted, all translations are the author's own.*

**Epigraph. In the lonely seter-corner:** Henrik Ibsen, "On the Heights," quoted in Peter Reed and David Rothenberg, eds., *Wisdom in the Open Air: The Norwegian Roots of Deep Ecology* (Minneapolis: University of Minnesota Press, 1993), 12.

## Introduction

**xiv. "SOSOH"—stressed-out, survival-oriented humans:** Carla Hannaford, *Smart Moves* (Salt Lake City: Great River Books, 1995), 145.

**xiv. Almost 80 percent of the population:** "e-Handbook of Statistics 2021," United Nations Conference on Trade and Development, accessed April 13, 2022, https://stats .unctad.org/handbook/Population/Total.html.

**xiv. "restoring balance among living things":** "Friluftsliv Fact Sheet," VisitNorway .com, accessed March 4, 2022, https://thenoec.files.wordpress.com/2011/05/friluftsliv -fact-sheet-2.pdf.

**xv. "experience nature without pressure to achieve":** "Vad är friluftsliv?," Naturvårdsverket, accessed April 14, 2022, https://www.naturvardsverket.se /vagledning-och-stod/friluftsliv/kommunal-friluftslivsplanering.

**xv. "simple life":** Roger Isberg, *Simple Life: "Friluftsliv,"* trans. Sarah Isberg (Victoria, BC: Trafford Publishing, 2007).

## Friluftsliv for my thoughts

**xx. a goddess for skiing and snowshoeing:** "Skade—jättinnan som gifte sig med havsguden," Historiska.se, accessed November 29, 2021, https://historiska.se /nordisk-mytologi/skade.

**xxi. "Man is ruler and owner of nature":** Børge Dahle and Aage Jensen, eds., *Being in Nature: Experiential Learning and Teaching* (Nord-Trøndelag University College, 2009), 6, http://norwegianjournaloffriluftsliv.com/doc/being_in_nature.pdf.

**xxi. government campaign to implement friluftsliv:** Hans Gelter, "*Friluftsliv:* The Scandinavian Philosophy of Outdoor Life," *Canadian Journal of Environmental Education* 5, no. 1 (2000): 79, https://assets.website-files.com/5f30a62bbbdfa91806272 25f/5f30a62bbbdfa91720272742_Scandinavian%20Philosophy%20of%20Outdoor%20 Life.pdf.

**xxii. nature preserves were created:** Klas Sandell and Sverker Sörlin, *Friluftshistoria* (Stockholm: Carlsson Bokförlag, 2008).

**xxiv. "collision course with nature":** Nils Faarlund, "Touch the Earth," in *Wisdom in the Open Air: The Norwegian Roots of Deep Ecology*, ed. Peter Reed and David Rothenberg (Minneapolis: University of Minnesota Press, 1993), 173.

## Part I: Air

**1. In nature there is peace:** Sam Arsenius, *Boken om friluftslif: Upplysningar, råd och skildringar* (Stockholm: Silén, 1910).

**4. "enjoy the forest and hug the trees":** Rúnar Snær Reynisson, "Hvetja fólk til að fara út í skóg og knúsa tré," *RÚV*, August 4, 2020, https://www.ruv.is/frett/2020/04/08 /hvetja-folk-til-ad-fara-ut-i-skog-og-knusa-tre.

**4. company developed a free app:** Elisabeth Däljemar, "Ny promenad-app skapar nya möten i pandemin," *Norra Halland*, January 18, 2021, https://norrahalland.se /ny-promenad-app-skapar-nya-moten-i-pandemin.

**5. Christmas present of the year:** HUI Research AB, "Årets julklapp 2020," accesssed April 12, 2022, https://hui.se/arets-julklapp/2020.

**5. third most common coping strategy:** Fereshteh Ahmadi, *Undersökning om krishantering vid svåra livssituationer* (Högskolan i Gävle, 2019), https://www.hig.se /download/18.634237b5172176efd5d1ad9d/1590660876275/Krishantering.%20 Fereshteh.%20Ahmadi.pdf.

**5. cancer diagnosis:** Abigail Sykes, "Naturen har blivit svenskarnas kyrka," Forskning.se, May 28, 2020, https://www.forskning.se/2020/05/28/naturen-har-blivit -svenskarnas-kyrka/#.

**5. diffuse the spread of airborne particles:** Richard A. Hobday and John W. Cason, "The Open-Air Treatment of Pandemic Influenza," *American Journal of Public Health* 99, suppl. 2 (October 2009): S236–S242, https://doi.org/10.2105/AJPH.2008.134627.

**5. chances of contracting COVID-19:** Karin Brulliard and Lenny Bernstein, "A Year into the Pandemic, It's Even More Clear That It's Safer to Be Outside," *Washington Post*, April 13, 2021, https://www.washingtonpost.com/health/2021/04/13/covid -outside-safety.

**5. nineteen times greater:** Hiroshi Nishiura et al., "Closed Environments Facilitate Secondary Transmission of Coronavirus Disease 2019 (COVID-19)," preprint, April 16, 2020, https://doi.org/10.1101/2020.02.28.20029272.

**5. Chinese study:** Hua Qian et al., "Indoor Transmission of SARS-CoV-2," *Indoor Air* 31, no. 3 (May 2021): 639–45, https://doi.org/10.1111/ina.12766.

**6. complete physical, mental, and social well-being:** "Constitution," World Health Organization, accessed September 5, 2021, https://www.who.int/about/governance /constitution.

**7. British report *Walking Works*:** Walking for Health, *Walking Works*, 2014, the Ramblers and Macmillan Cancer Support, https://www.walkingforhealth.org.uk/sites /default/files/HCP_walkingworks_download.pdf.

**7. study of almost 140,000 people:** Stacy Simon, "Study: Even a Little Walking May Help You Live Longer," American Cancer Society, October 19, 2017, https://www.cancer.org/latest-news/study-even-a-little-walking-may-help-you -live-longer.html.

**7. "they walk every single day":** Aislinn Kotifani, "Research Says Walking This Much per Week Extends Your Life," Blue Zones, accessed September 10, 2021, https://www .bluezones.com/2018/07/research-says-walking-this-much-per-week-extends-your -life.

**8. 90 percent of Swedes walk:** Peter Fredman, Rosemarie Ankre, and Tatiana Chekalina, *Friluftsliv 2018*, Naturvårdsverket Rapport 6887, April 2019, https://www .naturvardsverket.se/Documents/publikationer6400/978-91-620-6887-5.pdf.

**8. close to 93 percent:** "Idrett og friluftsliv, levekårsundersokelsen," Statistisk Sentralbyrå, updated December 8, 2021, https://www.ssb.no/kultur-og-fritid/idrett -og-friluftsliv/statistikk/idrett-og-friluftsliv-levekarsundersokelsen.

**8. 50 percent of the adults:** Emily N. Ussery et al., "Transportation and Leisure Walking Among U.S. Adults: Trends in Reported Prevalence and Volume, National Health Interview Survey 2005–2015," *American Journal of Preventive Medicine* 55, no. 4 (October 2018): 533–40, https://doi.org/10.1016/j.amepre.2018.05.027.

**8. 19 percent say they go hiking:** *Outdoor Participation Report*, 2021, Outdoor Foundation, https://ipo06y1ji424m0641msgjlfy-wpengine.netdna-ssl.com/wp-content /uploads/2015/03/2021-Outdoor-Participation-Trends-Report.pdf.

**12. prevent seasonal affective disorder:** Pernilla Bloom, "Morgonljus minskar risken för depression," Doktorn, October 21, 2020, https://www.doktorn.com/artikel /328223.

**13. four to eight hours every day:** Åsa Frisk, "Promenera loss idéerna," *Kollega*, September 19, 2014, https://www.kollega.se/promenera-loss-ideerna.

**13. making us feel happy and positive:** Bum-Jin Park et al., "Relationship Between Psychological Responses and Physical Environments in Forest Settings," *Journal of Landscape and Urban Planning* 102, no. 1 (July 30, 2011): 24–32, https://doi.org /10.1016/j.landurbplan.2011.03.005.

**13. boosting the immune system:** "5 Surprising Benefits of Walking," Harvard Health Publishing, June 10, 2021, https://www.health.harvard.edu/staying-healthy /5-surprising-benefits-of-walking.

**15. documenting walk-and-talk meetings:** Frisk, "Promenera loss idéerna."

**15. top tips listed by 844 Swedish executives:** Calle Fleur, "Undersökning: Så motiverar svenska chefer," Chef.se, November 18, 2013, https://chef.se/sa-motiverar -svenska-chefer.

**16. reduce nervousness:** Cecilie Thøgersen-Ntoumani et al., "Changes in Work Affect in Response to Lunchtime Walking in Previously Physically Inactive

Employees: A Randomized Trial," *Scandinavian Journal of Medicine and Science in Sports* 25, no. 6 (2015): 778–87, https://doi.org/10.1111/sms.12398.

**16. the effect becomes even more pronounced:** Marc Berman et al., "The Cognitive Benefits of Interacting with Nature," *Psychological Science* 19, no. 12 (December 2008): 1207–12, https://doi.org/10.1111/j.1467-9280.2008.02225.x.

**18. decrease fatigue and anxiety while increasing the quality of life:** Heather Ray and Sonya Jakubec, "Nature-Based Experiences and Health of Cancer Survivors," *Complementary Therapies in Clinical Practice* 20, no. 4 (November 2014): 188–92, https://doi.org/10.1016/j.ctcp.2014.07.005.

**18. friends and family who help care:** Rebecca Lehto et al., "An Evaluation of Natural Environment Interventions for Informal Cancer Caregivers in the Community," *International Journal of Environmental Research and Public Health* 18, no. 21, 11124 (October 2021), https://doi.org/10.3390/ijerph182111124.

**19. placed in the top ten:** John F. Helliwell et al., eds., *World Happiness Report 2020* (New York: Sustainable Development Solutions Network, 2020), https://happiness-report.s3.amazonaws.com/2020/WHR20.pdf.

**19. appreciate their world-class education system:** "What Makes Finland the Happiest Country in the World for the Fourth Consecutive Year?," *Helsinki Times*, April 19, 2021, https://www.helsinkitimes.fi/lifestyle/19066-what-makes-finland-the-happiest-country-in-the-world-for-the-fourth-consecutive-year.html.

**20. "In the rush and crush of modern life":** "Finland Happiest in the World," Finland Convention Bureau, accessed April 26, 2022, https://www.visitfinland.com/fcb/fcb_newsletter/finland-happiest-in-the-world.

**21. number of health benefits:** "Benefits of Physical Activity," Centers for Disease Control and Prevention, accessed July 26, 2021, https://www.cdc.gov/physicalactivity/basics/pa-health/index.htm.

**27. a quarter of the population owns a hytte:** Cecilie Tvetenstrand, "Hyttelanddet Norge," *Nettavisen Økonomi*, September 20, 2020, https://www.nettavisen.no/okonomi/hyttelandet-norge/s/12-95-3424020518.

**27. sixty days per year at their cabin:** Helle Benedicte Berg, "Alla har stugfeber i Norge," *Scandinavian Traveler*, March 13, 2017, https://scandinaviantraveler.com/se/livsstil/alla-har-stugfeber-i-norge.

**27. four out of ten cabins in Norway:** Erik Waatland, "Ny undersøkelse: Tradisjonell TV er langt viktigere enn innlagt vann på nordmenns hytter," M24, April 10, 2017, https://m24.no/rikstv-tv/ny-undersokelse-tradisjonell-tv-er-langt-viktigere-enn-innlagt-vann-pa-nordmenns-hytter/154519.

**28. two hundred richest people in the world:** "#198 Olav Thon," *Forbes*, accessed September 15, 2021, https://www.forbes.com/profile/olav-thon/?sh=12a8dd7c2440.

**28. "a hytte with 15 bedrooms":** Leif Magne Flemmen, "Olav Thon langer ut mot vulgærrikingene:—Lev et mer allminnelig liv," *Hytteavisen*, December 9, 2008, https://www.hytteavisen.no/-lev-et-mer-allminnelig-liv.4533208-49617.html.

**29. come with more conveniences:** "Hytter og fritidsboliger," Statistisk Sentralbyrå, accessed September 15, 2021, https://www.ssb.no/bygg-bolig-og-eiendom/faktaside /hytter-og-ferieboliger.

**30. helped explain the inexplicable:** Robert de Vries and Arvid Dahlberg, "Fornnordisk religion och asatro," SO-rummet, updated January 21, 2022, https:// www.so-rummet.se/kategorier/religion/fornnordisk-religion-och-asatro#.

**31. gnome-like creature called *tomten*:** "Folktro och föreställningsvärldar," Institutet för Språk Och Folkminnen, updated June 1, 2021, https://www.isof.se /lar-dig-mer/kunskapsbanker/lar-dig-mer-om-vasen-i-folktron/folktro-och -forestallningsvarldar.

**31. Christianity struggled to take hold:** Sara E. Ellis Nilsson, "Nordens kristnande," SO-rummet, updated July 29, 2021, https://www.so-rummet.se/kategorier/religion /kristendomen/nordens-kristnande#.

**31. The Samis' relationship with nature:** Pia Sjögren, "Ett med naturen," Samer, April 28, 2015, https://www.samer.se/2177.

**31. the fastest-growing religion:** "11 Things to Know About the Present Day Practice of Ásatrú, the Ancient Religion of the Vikings," *Iceland Magazine*, January 22, 2019, https://icelandmag.is/article/11-things-know-about-present-day-practice-asatru -ancient-religion-vikings.

**32. Christians are four times more likely:** David Thurfjell, *Granskogsfolk* (Stockholm: Norstedts, 2020), audio ed.

**35. means of the spiritual experience:** Anna Davidsson Bremborg, "Creating Sacred Space by Walking in Silence: Pilgrimage in a Late Modern Lutheran Context," *Social Compass* 60, no. 4 (2013): 544–60, https://doi.org/10.1177/0037768613503092.

**37. can help ease anxiety:** Nicholas M. Hobson, David Bonk, and Michael Inzlicht, "Rituals Decrease the Neural Response to Performance Failure," *PeerJ* 5 (2017): e3363, https://doi.org/10.7717/peerj.3363.

**39. run on a twenty-four-hour cycle:** "Circadian Rhythms," National Institute of General Medical Science, accessed July 5, 2021, https://www.nigms.nih.gov/education /fact-sheets/pages/circadian-rhythms.aspx.

**40. a telltale symptom of depression:** David Nutt, "Sleep Disorders as Core Symptoms of Depression," *Dialogues in Clinical Neuroscience* 10, no. 3 (2008): 329–36, https://doi.org/10.31887/DCNS.2008.10.3/dnutt.

**40. camping can help:** Lisa Marshall, "Wilderness Camping Helps Reset, Rejuvenate Circadian Rhythm," Association of American Universities, February 1, 2017, https:// www.aau.edu/wilderness-camping-helps-reset-rejuvenate-circadian-rhythm.

**41. 69 percent of the effect:** Kenneth Wright, "Circadian Entrainment to the Natural Light-Dark Cycle Across Seasons and the Weekend," *Current Biology* 27, no. 4 (2017), https://doi.org/10.1016/j.cub.2016.12.041.

**57. disrupt entire ecosystems:** David Owen, "Is Noise Pollution the Next Big Public-Health Crisis?," *New Yorker*, May 6, 2019, https://www.newyorker.com /magazine/2019/05/13/is-noise-pollution-the-next-big-public-health-crisis.

57. **"Nature's voice is finely tuned":** Roger Isberg, *Simple Life: "Friluftsliv,"* trans. Sarah Isberg (Victoria, BC: Trafford Publishing, 2007), 30.

## Part II: Earth

62. **reduce feelings of anxiety, fatigue, and depression:** Chorong Song et al., "Psychological Benefits of Walking Through Forest Areas," *International Journal of Environmental Research and Public Health* 15, no. 12 (2018): 2804, https://doi.org/10.3390/ijerph15122804.

62. **extend our lives:** David Rojas-Rueda et al., "Green Spaces and Mortality: A Systematic Review and Meta-Analysis of Cohort Studies," *The Lancet* 3, no. 11 (2019): E469–77, https://doi.org/10.1016/S2542-5196(19)30215-3.

62. **make us happier:** "Garden Bacteria Can Combat Anxiety and Depression," RNZ, August 11, 2019, https://www.rnz.co.nz/national/programmes/sunday/audio/2018708175/garden-bacteria-can-combat-anxiety-and-depression.

62. **make our bodies heal faster:** R. S. Ulrich, "View Through a Window May Influence Recovery from Surgery," *Science* 224, no. 4647 (April 27, 1984): 420–21, https://doi.org/10.1126/science.6143402.

63. **don't want to hurt the things we love:** Thomas Harold Beery, "Nordic in Nature: Friluftsliv and Environmental Connectedness" (EdD dissertation, University of Minnesota, 2011), https://conservancy.umn.edu/bitstream/handle/11299/107691/Beery_umn_0130E_11804.pdf.

65. **anti-inflammatory effects on the brain:** Christopher Lowry, "Immunization with a Heat-Killed Preparation of the Environmental Bacterium *Mycobacterium vaccae* Promotes Stress Resilience in Mice," *Proceedings of the National Academy of Sciences* 13, no. 22 (2016), https://doi.org/10.1073/pnas.1600324113.

65. **make the brain more resilient:** Lisa Marshall, "Is an Immunization for Stress on the Horizon?," *CU Boulder Today*, June 6, 2018, https://www.colorado.edu/today/2018/06/06/immunization-stress-horizon.

66. **successful in getting people back to work:** "Forskning visar: Trädgårdsterapi effektivt mot utbrändhet," SVT Nyheter, November 25, 2018, https://www.svt.se/nyheter/inrikes/forskning-visar-tradgardsterapi-effektivt-mot-utbrandhet.

66. **nearly two-thirds of the people:** Patrik Grahn et al., "Longer Nature-Based Rehabilitation May Contribute to a Faster Return to Work in Patients with Reactions to Severe Stress and/or Depression," *International Journal of Environmental Research and Public Health* 14, no. 11 (2017), https://www.ncbi.nlm.nih.gov/pmc/articles/PMC5707949.

68. **held the caring tree in deep respect:** Martin Borg, "Vårdträdet—gårdens beskyddare," Släkthistoria.se, April 6, 2019, https://slakthistoria.se/livet-forr/vardtradet-gardens-beskyddare.

68. **Scientists studying forest bathing:** Yoshifumi Miyazaki, *The Japanese Art of Shinrin-Yoku* (Portland, OR: Timber Press, 2018), 34.

**69. The biophilia hypothesis:** Bjørn Grinde and Grete Grindal Patil, "Biophilia: Does Visual Contact with Nature Impact on Health and Well-Being?," *International Journal of Environmental Research and Public Health* 6, no. 9 (2009), https://doi.org /10.3390/ijerph6092332.

**69. Attention restoration theory:** Marie Pell, "Teorier om mental återhämtning— Kaplan, Ulrich och Grahn," Sveriges Lantbruksuniversitet, 2012, https://stud.epsilon .slu.se/4986/1/pell_m_121018.pdf.

**70. Psycho-evolutionary theory:** R. S. Ulrich et al., "Stress Recovery During Exposure to Natural and Urban Environments," *Journal of Environmental Psychology* 11 (1991): 201–30.

**70. Cultural learning theory:** Ebba Lisberg Jensen, "Gå ut min själ— forskningsöversikt om hälsoeffekter av utevistelser i närnatur," Statens folkhälsoinstitut (Stockholm: Strömberg, 2008), https://mau.diva-portal.org/smash /get/diva2:1410640/FULLTEXT01.pdf.

**71. Calm and connection theory:** Patrik Grahn, Johan Ottosson, and Kerstin Uvnäs-Moberg, "The Oxytocinergic System as a Mediator of Anti-stress and Instorative Effects Induced by Nature: The Calm and Connection Theory," *Frontiers in Psychology* 12, 617814 (July 2021), https://doi.org/10.3389/fpsyg.2021 .617814.

**72. beneficial to their health:** Patrik Grahn, "Att uppleva parken" (Alnarp: SLU Alnarp, 1989); and Patrik Grahn, "Om parkers betydelse" (Alnarp: SLU Alnarp, 1991).

**73. One of his most cited studies:** P. Grahn, F. Mårtensson, B. Lindblad, and P. Nilsson, "Ute på dagis" (Alnarp: SLU Alnarp, 1997); and Patrik Grahn, "Wild Nature Makes Children Healthy," Swedish Building Research 4 (1996): 16–18.

**73. the more stressed they were:** Patrik Grahn and U. A. Stigsdotter, "Landscape Planning and Stress," *Urban Forestry and Urban Greening* 2 (2003): 1–18.

**73. less satisfied with their home and neighborhood:** J. Björk et al., "Recreational Values of the Natural Environment in Relation to Neighbourhood Satisfaction, Physical Activity, Obesity and Wellbeing," *Journal of Epidemiology and Community Health* 62, no. 4 (2008): e2.

**73. stimulating the production of endorphins:** M. Annerstedt et al., "Green Qualities in the Neighbourhood and Mental Health—Results from a Longitudinal Cohort Study in Southern Sweden," *BMC Public Health* 12, no. 1 (2012): 1–13.

**74. three hundred meters:** P. Grahn and J. Stoltz, "Urbana grönområden— indikatorer för hälsa och välbefinnande Movium," *Sveriges Lantbruksuniversitet* 3 (2021).

**74. open area with a view:** J. Stoltz and P. Grahn, "Perceived Sensory Dimensions: An Evidence-Based Approach to Greenspace Aesthetics," *Urban Forestry and Urban Greening* 59 (2021): 126989.

**74. serenity, space, and natural elements:** Patrik Grahn and U. K. Stigsdotter, "The Relation Between Perceived Sensory Dimensions of Urban Green Space and Stress

Restoration," *Landscape and Urban Planning* 94, no. 3–4 (2010): 264–75, https://www.academia.edu/24020275/the_relation_between_perceived_sensory_dimensions_of_urban_green_space_and_stress_restoration.

75. **a vast majority of the population:** "e-Handbook of Statistics 2021," United Nations Conference on Trade and Development, accessed April 13, 2022, https://stats.unctad.org/handbook/Population/Total.html.

75. **less restorative from a stress perspective:** Grahn and Stigsdotter, "Relation Between Perceived Sensory Dimensions."

76. **nearly four hundred thousand people:** "Fågelsångsnatten del ½," Sveriges Radio P1, May 3, 2020, https://sverigesradio.se/avsnitt/1488533.

76. **"the greatest cultural event of the year":** Jan Gradvall, "Fågelsångsnatten blir en global symfoni," Dagens Industri, April 29, 2020, https://www.di.se/weekend/fagelsangsnatten-blir-en-global-symfoni.

77. **nearly five hundred thousand people:** "Nytt rekord för Fågelsångsnatten—nära en halv miljon lyssnare," SVT Nyheter, June 4, 2021, https://www.svt.se/kultur/nytt-rekord-for-fagelsangsnatten-nara-en-halv-miljon-lyssnare.

77. **Academy Awards and the Emmy Awards:** Sarah Whitten, "Audiences for Award Shows Are in Steep Decline," May 2, 2021, https://www.cnbc.com/2021/05/02/oscars-2021-nielsen-data-shows-viewers-have-lost-interest-in-award-shows.html.

77. **approximately five hundred hours:** "Den stora älgvandringen," SVT, updated September 20, 2021, https://kontakt.svt.se/guide/den-stora-algvandringen.

78. **"Most Innovative Show":** "Den stora älgvandringen vann kristallen som årets förnyare," SVT, August 30, 2019, https://www.svt.se/nyheter/lokalt/vasterbotten/den-stora-algvandringen-vann-kristallen.

79. **When the flowers appear:** August Strindberg, "Göken" (1883), translated as "The Cuckoo" by John Irons (2019), first two verses.

80. **cuckoos held special powers:** Jonas Sandström, "Gökotta en folkrörelsetradition," Folkrörelsearkivet för Uppsala Län, May 2, 2017, http://www.fauppsala.se/gokotta-en-folkrorelsetradition.

80. **the number of cuckoos:** Håkan Steen, "Guide: Gökottans ABC—så håller du liv i mysiga traditionen," Tidningen Land, May 18, 2020, https://www.land.se/djur-natur/gokotta.

81. **birds can boost our well-being:** Ulla Ahlgren, "Sångfåglar lyft för stadsmiljön," SLU:s kunskapsbank, updated May 18, 2021, https://www.slu.se/forskning/kunskapsbank/2017/sangfaglar-lyft-for-stadsmiljon.

82. **the more notable the effect:** Elin Viksten, "Sångfåglar får oss att trivas i staden," SLU:s kunskapsbank, April 11, 2017, https://www.extrakt.se/sangfaglar-far-oss-att-trivas-i-staden.

85. **releases endorphins:** "Live Whole Health: Self-Care Blog Episode #19—Acupressure," US Department of Veterans Affairs, May 13, 2020, https://blogs.va.gov/VAntage/74776/live-whole-health-self-care-blog-episode-19-acupressure.

**85. improve balance and reduce blood pressure:** Li Fuzhong, K. John Fisher, and Peter Harmer, "Improving Physical Function and Blood Pressure in Older Adults Through Cobblestone Mat Walking: A Randomized Trial," *Journal of American Geriatrics Society* 58, no. 8 (August 2005): 1305–12, https://doi.org/10.1111/j.1532-5415 .2005.53407.x.

**85. result in stronger feet:** Karsten Hollander et al., "The Effects of Being Habitually Barefoot on Foot Mechanics and Motor Performance in Children and Adolescents Aged 6–18 Years: Study Protocol for a Multicenter Cross-Sectional Study," *Journal of Foot and Ankle Research* 9, no. 1 (2016): 36, https://doi.org/10.1186/s13047-016-0166-1.

**85. prevention of common injuries:** Samantha Olson, "Walking Barefoot Helps You Avoid Foot Injuries; Also Improves Posture, Balance, and Stability," Medical Daily, November 18, 2015, https://www.medicaldaily.com/walking-barefoot-helps-you-avoid -foot-injuries-also-improves-posture-balance-and-362164.

**88. The video was a clever PR stunt:** Visit Sweden, "Sweden on Airbnb," May 2, 2017, YouTube video, https://www.youtube.com/watch?v=C6671CL5fFg.

**88. a right for all people to enjoy nature:** "Land of the Free," Visit Sweden, updated November 19, 2020, https://visitsweden.com/what-to-do/nature-outdoors/nature /sustainable-and-rural-tourism/land-of-the-free.

**88. Norwegian law as late as 1957:** "Allemansretten—Friluftsloven," Norskt Friluftsli, accessed March 4, 2022, https://norskfriluftsliv.no/temaer/allemannsretten /friluftsloven.

**88. local laws from medieval times:** Hanna Stenmyr, "Från nytta till nöje— allemansrätten i den svenska skogen" (Alnarp: SLU Alnarp, 2010), https://stud .epsilon.slu.se/1396/1/stenmyr_h_100617.pdf.

**89. "a human right to be in nature":** Errol Meidinger, Kim Diana Connolly, and Ezra Zubrow, *The Big Thaw: Policy, Governance, and Climate Change in the Circumpolar North* (Albany: State University of New York Press, 2019).

**89. Landowners have rights too:** "Allemansrätten," Institutet för språk och folkminnen, accessed November 25, 2021, https://www.isof.se/lar-dig-mer /kunskapsbanker/levande-traditioner/forslag/2018-01-17-allemansratten.

**90. new rights-of-way legislation in 2000:** Countryside and Rights of Way (CROW) Act, Department for Environment Food and Rural Affairs, accessed November 25, 2021, http://adlib.everysite.co.uk/adlib/defra/content.aspx?doc =18302&id=18304.

**90. for the rest of the UK to follow:** "The Right to Roam Is the Right to Connect," accessed November 25, 2021, https://www.righttoroam.org.uk.

**91. "every person's right":** Ken Ilgunas, "This Is Our Country. Let's Walk It," *New York Times*, April 23, 2016, https://www.nytimes.com/2016/04/24/opinion/sunday /this-is-our-country-lets-walk-it.html.

**92. "reminiscent of those at Disneyland":** "How Crowded Are America's National Parks? See for Yourself," *New York Times*, July 8, 2021, https://www.nytimes.com/2021 /07/08/travel/crowded-national-parks.html.

**96. ten thousand species of fungi:** Svampguiden, accessed August 20, 2021, http://svampguiden.com.

**96. nearly half of all Swedes:** Peter Fredman, Rosemarie Ankre, and Tatiana Chekalina, *Friluftsliv 2018*, Naturvårdsverket Rapport 6887, April 2019, https://www.naturvardsverket.se/Documents/publikationer6400/978-91-620-6887-5.pdf.

**97. their main motivation:** Peter Fredman, Marie Stenseke, and Klas Sandell, *Friluftsliv i förändring: Studier från svenska upplevelselandskap* (Stockholm: Carlsson Bokförlag, 2014).

**98. ten thousand to fifteen thousand years ago:** "Evidence That Northern Hunter Gatherers Ate Mushrooms," University of Cape Town, July 28, 2015, https://www.news.uct.ac.za/article/-2015-07-28-evidence-that-northern-hunter-gatherers-ate-mushrooms.

**98. "Food of the Gods":** María Elena Valverde et al., "Edible Mushrooms: Improving Human Health and Promoting Quality Life," *International Journal of Microbiology* 2015, article ID 376387, https://doi.org/10.1155/2015/376387.

**100. retains about 30 percent of the sugar:** B. Holewinski, "Underground Networking: The Amazing Connections Beneath Your Feet," National Forest Foundation, accessed November 7, 2021, https://www.nationalforests.org/blog/underground-mycorrhizal-network.

**101. "what we do not love":** Robert Macfarlane, *The Lost Words* (website), accessed April 12, 2022, https://www.thelostwords.org/lostwordsbook/#:~:text=Robert%20explains%3A%20%22We've,love%20we%20will%20not%20save.%E2%80%9D.

**106. one of fourteen wild edibles:** Försvarsmakten, *Handbok överlevnad* (Stockhom: Försvarsmakten, 1988).

**106. Dandelions are also rich in antioxidants:** Paula Martinac, "The Health Benefits of Eating Dandelion Greens," updated December 2, 2018, SFGate, https://healthyeating.sfgate.com/health-benefits-eating-dandelion-greens-4433.html.

**107. Plantain does in fact contain bioactive compounds:** Muhammed Zumair et al., "Kloka gummorna hade rätt—groblad kan läka sår!," LTJ-fakultetens faktablad 9 (Alnarp: SLU Alnarp, 2012), https://pub.epsilon.slu.se/8702/7/zubair_et_al_120411.pdf.

**109. But it is not only young people:** Sam Arsenius, *Boken om friluftslif: Upplysningar, råd och skildringar* (Stockholm: Silén, 1910).

**111. Sleep quality and cognition can improve:** Angela Ko and Jenna Williams, "Impact of Garden Spaces on Dementia Residents: Translating Evidence-Based Research into Clinical Practice," *School of Occupational Master's Capstone Projects* 11 (2016), http://soundideas.pugetsound.edu/ot_capstone/11.

**111. the park has many distinct spaces, or "rooms":** *Sinnenas och minnenas park*, 2008, accessed September 14, 2021, https://www.hellefors.se/download/18.680983e5147f9a93525141d4/1448581179280/Sinnenas-+och+minnenas+park.pdf.

**112. "residents can re-create a relationship with nature":** Thomas Lerner, "Parken ett lyft för äldrevården," September 15, 2008, https://www.dn.se/insidan/parken-ett-lyft-for-aldrevarden.

# Part III: Water

**116. 75 percent of Earth's surface:** "The Water Planet," NASA, April 22, 2011, https://www.nasa.gov/multimedia/imagegallery/image_feature_1925.html.

**116. almost as much of our own bodies:** "The Water in You: Water and the Human Body," US Geological Survey, accessed December 30, 2020, https://www.usgs.gov/special-topic/water-science-school/science/water-you-water-and-human-body?qt-science_center_objects=0#qt-science_center_objects.

**116. source of healing throughout history:** Gregory Tsoucalas et al., "Hydrotherapy: Historical Landmarks of a Cure All Remedy," *History of Medicine* 50 (2015): 430–32, https://www.researchgate.net/publication/316062869_hydrotherapy_historical_landmarks_of_a_cure_all_remedy.

**117. within a kilometer from the coast:** Joanne K. Garrett et al., "Coastal Proximity and Mental Health Among Urban Adults in England: The Moderating Effect of Household Income," *Health & Place* 59 (2019), https://doi.org/10.1016/j.healthplace.2019.102200.

**117. people are happier in general:** George MacKerron and Susana Mourato, "Happiness Is Greater in Natural Environments," *Global Environmental Change* 23, no. 5 (2013): 11, https://doi.org/10.1016/j.gloenvcha.2013.03.010, https://eprints.lse.ac.uk/49376/1/Mourato_Happiness_greater_natural_2013.pdf.

**117. especially happy when they are near water:** Mathew P. White et al., "Feelings of Restoration from Recent Nature Visits," *Journal of Environmental Psychology* 35 (2013): 40–51, https://doi.org/10.1016/j.jenvp.2013.04.002.

**117. valued 21 to 33 percent higher:** "Så mycket är sjöglimten värd," *Privata Affärer*, June 25, 2012, https://www.privataaffarer.se/articles/2012/06/25/sa-mycket-ar-sjoglimten-vard.

**119. a stress-induced condition:** A. Adamsson and S. Bernhardsson, "Symptoms That May Be Stress-Related and Lead to Exhaustion Disorder: A Retrospective Medical Chart Review in Swedish Primary Care," *BMC Family Practice* 19, no. 172 (2018), https://doi.org/10.1186/s12875-018-0858-7.

**120. triggers the production of noradrenaline:** B. E. Leonard, "The Role of Noradrenaline in Depression: A Review," *Journal of Psychopharmacology* 11, 4 suppl. (1997): S39–47, https://pubmed.ncbi.nlm.nih.gov/9438232.

**120. symptoms of depression gradually decreased:** B. Knechtle et al., "Cold Water Swimming—Benefits and Risks: A Narrative Review," *International Journal of Environmental Research and Public Health* 17, no. 23 (December 2020): 8984, https://doi.org/10.3390/ijerph17238984.

**120. improve your mood, memory, and general well-being:** P. Huttunen, "Winter Swimming Improves General Well-Being," *International Journal of Circumpolar Health* 63, no. 2 (May 2004): 140–44, https://doi.org/10.3402/ijch.v63i2.17700.

**120. rheumatism, fibromyalgia, and asthma:** Knechtle et al., "Cold Water Swimming."

**127. disturb aquatic life and impair water quality:** Timothy Asplund, "The Effects of Motorized Watercraft on Aquatic Ecosystems," Wisconsin Department of Natural Resources, 2000, https://dnr.wi.gov/lakes/publications/documents/lakes.pdf.

**127. increasing by 12 percent in 2020:** "U.S. Boat Sales Reached 13-Year High in 2020, Recreational Boating Boom to Continue Through 2021," National Marine Manufacturers Association, January 6, 2021, https://www.nmma.org/press/article/23527.

**127. grew by 19 percent in Finland:** "Coronaåret ökade efterfrågan på speciellt små motorbåtar," Finnboat, February 12, 2021, https://www.sttinfo.fi/tiedote/coronaaret-okade-efterfragan-pa-speciellt-sma-motorbatar?publisherId=46330459&releaseId=69900734.

**128. "speed has become the icon of our time":** Hans Gelter, "*Friluftsliv* as Slow Experiences in a Post-modern 'Experience' Society," in *Nature First: Outdoor Life the Friluftsliv Way*, ed. Bob Henderson and Nils Vikander (Toronto: Natural Heritage Books, 2007).

**129. call it "flow":** Roger Isberg, *Simple Life: "Friluftsliv,"* trans. Sarah Isberg (Victoria, BC: Trafford Publishing, 2007), 46.

**131. six hundred million years ago:** "Välkommen till Vättern," Vätternvårdsförbundet, accessed May 31, 2022, http://www.vattern.org/wp-content/uploads/2017/05/212646-valkommen_till_vattern_sv-1.pdf.

**131. a giant once rode his horse across the ice:** "Rödgavels grotta," Visit Ödeshög, updated March 15, 2021, https://www.visitodeshog.se/visitodeshog/uppleva/artiklar/rodgavelsgrotta.5.4096a1e8175d74d083daa93.html.

**133. "international leisure activity culture":** Børge Dahle, "Norwegian 'Friluftsliv'—'Environmental Education' as a Lifelong Communal Process," USDA Forest Service Proceedings RMRS-P-27, 2003, https://www.fs.fed.us/rm/pubs/rmrs_p027/rmrs_p027_247_252.pdf.

**134. one thousand to one hundred thousand:** Soo Kim, "Norway's Natural Wonders 'Threatened by Ill-Prepared Tourists,'" *Telegraph*, October 20, 2021, https://www.telegraph.co.uk/travel/destinations/europe/norway/articles/norway-nature-group-calls-for-limits-to-its-most-iconic-spots.

**137. cleaning the air of pollutants:** Jennifer Chu, "Can Rain Clean the Atmosphere?," MIT News, August 28, 2015, https://news.mit.edu/2015/rain-drops-attract-aerosols-clean-air-0828.

**138. greater happiness:** Aljawharh Ibrahim Alsukah, "The Relative Contribution of Mindfulness and Gratitude in Predicting Happiness Among University Students," *Journal of Educational and Social Research* 11, no. 4 (July 2021), https://doi.org/10.36941/jesr-2021-0097.

**138. aromatic molecules and bacteria:** Daisy Yuhas, "Storm Scents: It's True, You

Can Smell Oncoming Summer Rain," *Scientific American*, July 18, 2012, https://www
.scientificamerican.com/article/storm-scents-smell-rain.

**138. perfume ingredient:** M. Halton, "Petrichor: Why Does Rain Smell So Good?,"
BBC News, July 27, 2018, https://www.bbc.com/news/science-environment-44904298.

**141. eight drops of 6 percent bleach:** "Emergency Disinfection of Drinking Water,"
US Environmental Protection Agency, accessed March 14, 2022, https://www.epa.gov
/ground-water-and-drinking-water/emergency-disinfection-drinking-water.

**147. lose more heat through our head:** Katharine Gammon, "Do We Really Lose
Half Our Body Heat from Our Heads?," Livescience.com, February 1, 2013, https://
www.livescience.com/34411-body-heat-loss-head.html.

**151. crucial to the national defense:** Klas Sandell and Sverker Sörlin, *Friluftshistoria*
(Stockholm: Carlsson Bokförlag, 2008), 35.

**154. self-efficacy scores increased:** Michael Mutz and Johannes Müller, "Mental
Health Benefits of Outdoor Adventures: Results from Two Pilot Studies," *Journal of
Adolescence* 49 (June 2016): 105–14, https://doi.org/10.1016/j.adolescence.2016.03.009.

**158. "Then they fell in":** "Drunknade när de skulle filma vinterlandskapet," Sveriges
Radio, January 24, 2019, https://sverigesradio.se/sida/artikel.aspx?programid=114
&artikel=7141532.

**158. They had been on a video call:** SVT Nyheter, "Polisen om dödsolyckan: 'Var i
videosamtal med bekanta,'" January 25, 2021, https://www.svt.se/nyheter/lokalt
/uppsala/polisen-dodsolyckan-live-sandes.

**159. nearly 80 percent of the people:** "68% of the World Population Projected to
Live in Urban Areas by 2050, Says UN," United Nations, May 16, 2018, https://www
.un.org/development/desa/en/news/population/2018-revision-of-world-urbanization
-prospects.html.

**159. The strongest ice:** "Ice Safety Tips," Michigan State University, accessed
March 4, 2022, https://www.canr.msu.edu/news/ice_safety_tips_selden18.

**162. worse health outcomes than ethnic Swedes:** Bita Latifi Damavandi, "Faktorer
som påverkar invandrares hälsa och ohälsa" (diss., Högskolan i Borås, 2015), https://
www.diva-portal.org/smash/get/diva2:840563/FULLTEXT01.pdf.

**163. improve public health and the quality of life:** Yusra Moshtat, "Med andra
ögon: Naturmöten med invandrare" (Stockholm: Naturvårdsverket, 2007), http://
naturvardsverket.diva-portal.org/smash/record.jsf?pid=diva2%3A1623212&dswid
=-4406.

**163. those who don't know how to swim:** Lisa Röstlund, "8 000 femteklassare kan
inte simma," *Aftonbladet*, August 30, 2012, https://www.aftonbladet.se/nyheter/a
/G1jvzx/8-000-femteklassare-kan-inte-simma.

**164. positive impact on their physical and mental health:** "Nature-Based
Integration," Nordic Council of Ministers, 2016, https://norden.diva-portal.org
/smash/get/diva2:1099117/FULLTEXT01.pdf.

**166. "lying in Mother Earth's womb":** Jonna Jinton, *Jonna Jinton Sweden* (blog),
accessed April 13, 2022, https://jonnajintonsweden.com/blog.

**166. When Jinton posted her second ice video:** Jonna Jinton, "Did You Know That Ice Can Sing?—Ice Sounds—Singing Ice," November 10, 2019, YouTube video, https://www.youtube.com/watch?v=chxn2szgEAg.

**167. Snow is porous and absorbs sound:** Whitney Harder, "The Science Behind Snow's Serenity," University of Kentucky, January 21, 2016, http://uknow.uky.edu/campus-news/science-behind-snows-serenity.

**167. makes a creaking sound:** "Varför knarrar snön när man går på den?," Forskning och Framsteg, December 1, 2004, https://fof.se/tidning/2004/8/artikel/varfor-knarrar-snon-nar-man-gar-pa-den.

**167. loses its sound-absorbing qualities:** "Snö dämpar ljudet," SVT Nyheter, January 22, 2020, https://www.svt.se/vader/fragor_och_svar/sno-dampar-ljudet.

## Part IV: Fire

**169. The small sparks:** Meik Wiking, "The Sound of Hygge," in *The Little Book of Hygge* (New York: HarperCollins, 2017), 198.

**170. a million years ago:** Jennie Cohen, "Human Ancestors Tamed Fire Earlier Than Thought," History.com, updated August 22, 2018, https://www.history.com/news/human-ancestors-tamed-fire-earlier-than-thought.

**170. contributed to expanding our brains:** Jerry Adler, "Why Fire Makes Us Human," *Smithsonian Magazine*, June 2013, https://www.smithsonianmag.com/science-nature/why-fire-makes-us-human-72989884.

**170. greatest discovery of humanity:** J. A. J. Gowlett, "The Discovery of Fire by Humans: A Long and Convoluted Process," *Philosophical Transactions of the Royal Society B* 371, no. 1696 (2016), https://doi.org/10.1098/rstb.2015.0164.

**170. helped the development of language:** Andrew C. Scott, "When Did Humans Discover Fire? The Answer Depends on What You Mean By 'Discover,'" *Time*, June 1, 2018, https://time.com/5295907/discover-fire.

**181. the solstice was filled with magic:** Tommy Kuusela, "Midsommarnattens magi," Institutet för Språk och Folkminnen, August 31, 2020, https://www.isof.se/lar-dig-mer/bloggar/folkminnesbloggen/inlagg/2020-08-31-midsommarnattens-magi.

**181. celebrate the longest day:** Emma Gillies, "How to Celebrate the Summer Solstice in the Nordics," *Nordic Visitor Blog*, updated July 6, 2021, https://www.nordicvisitor.com/blog/celebrating-the-solstice-midsummer-in-the-nordics.

**183. several hours for your vision:** Christopher Baird, "How Long Does It Take Our Eyes to Fully Adapt to Darkness?," Science Questions with Surprising Answers, August 9, 2013, https://www.wtamu.edu/~cbaird/sq/2013/08/09/how-long-does-it-take-our-eyes-to-fully-adapt-to-darkness.

**184. marked the first day of spring:** "Vårdagjämningen," Institutet för Språk och Folkminnen, accessed October 25, 2021, https://www.isof.se/lar-dig-mer

/kunskapsbanker/lar-dig-mer-om-arets-namn-och-handelser/handelser
/vardagjamningen.

**184. run barefoot around the farm:** "Vårfrudagen (Våffeldagen)," Nordiska Museet, accessed October 24, 2021, https://www.nordiskamuseet.se/aretsdagar/varfrudagen
-vaffeldagen.

**185. twenty-four hours that go:** "Words and Sayings in Icelandic That Don't Exist in English," *Iceland Magazine*, June 16, 2015, https://icelandmag.is/article/words-and
-sayings-icelandic-dont-exist-english-chapter-2.

**185. "the energy of life":** Yngve Ryd, *Eld: Flammor och glöd—samisk eldkonst* (Stockholm: Natur & Kultur, 2005), 23–25.

**186. development of another uniquely human trait:** Gowlett, "The Discovery of Fire by Humans."

**186. research involving the Ju/'hoan:** Polly W. Wiessner, "Embers of Society: Firelight Talk Among the Ju/'hoansi Bushmen," *PNAS* 111, no. 39 (2014), https://doi
.org/10.1073/pnas.1404212111.

**186. "fireside chats":** "The Fireside Chats," History.com, April 23, 2010, updated June 7, 2019, https://www.history.com/topics/great-depression/fireside-chats.

**191. fear of missing out:** "FOMO," Mindler.se, updated July 1, 2021, https://mindler
.se/fomo.

**191. excessive social media use:** Noor Bloemen and David De Coninck, "Social Media and Fear of Missing Out in Adolescents: The Role of Family Characteristics," *Social Media and Society* 6, no. 4 (2021), https://doi.org/10.1177/2056305120965517.

**191. "emotionally intelligent antidote to FOMO":** Kristen Fuller, "JOMO: The Joy of Missing Out," *Psychology Today*, July 26, 2018, https://www.psychologytoday.com
/us/blog/happiness-is-state-mind/201807/jomo-the-joy-missing-out.

**195. sensory input in combination with the context:** Julie R. Thomson, "Psychologists Explain Why Food Memories Can Feel So Powerful," *HuffPost*, May 10, 2017, https://www.huffpost.com/entry/power-of-food-memories_n_5908b1d7e
4b02655f8413610.

**195. Taste is a powerful sense:** Donald B. Katz and Brian F. Sadacca, "Neurobiology of Sensation and Reward," chapter 6, in *Neurobiology of Sensation and Reward*, ed. J. A. Gottfried (Boca Raton, FL: CRC Press/Taylor and Francis, 2011), accessed July 10, 2019, https://www.ncbi.nlm.nih.gov/books/NBK92789.

**197. Invented in the 1970s in Finland:** Muurikka official website, "Finnish Classic— the Muurikka Griddle Pan," accessed September 30, 2021, https://opamuurikka.fi
/in-english.

**203. increased by 24 percent in 2020:** "Coronaviruset ökar försäljningen av korv," SVT Nyheter, December 10, 2020, https://www.svt.se/nyheter/inrikes/coonaviruset
-okat-forsaljning-av-korv-och-grillkol.

**208. international headlines:** Laignee Barron, "Sweden Advises Its Citizens to Prepare Wet Wipes and Tinned Hummus in the Event of War," *Time Magazine*, May 22, 2021, https://time.com/5286505/sweden-war-preparation-pamphlet.

**209. help people prepare for emergencies:** Swedish Civil Contingencies Agency (MSB), *If Crisis or War Comes*, 2018, https://rib.msb.se/filer/pdf/28706.pdf.

## Friluftsliv for all

**216. founding nine national parks:** "Från 1800-talet in i framtiden," Sveriges Nationalparker, accessed September 11, 2021, https://www.sverigesnationalparker.se/om-sveriges-nationalparker/historia.

**216. back-to-nature movement flourished:** Klas Sandell and Sverker Sörlin, *Friluftshistoria* (Stockholm: Carlsson Bokförlag, 2008), 27.

**216. even enjoyed the right to roam:** Ken Ilgunas, "This Is Our Country. Let's Walk It," *New York Times*, April 23, 2016, https://www.nytimes.com/2016/04/24/opinion/sunday/this-is-our-country-lets-walk-it.html.

**216. 40 percent of the country:** Ray Rasker, "Public Land Ownership in the United States," Headwaters Economics, June 2019, https://headwaterseconomics.org/public-lands/protected-lands/public-land-ownership-in-the-us.

**217. seem to enjoy their green spaces:** Jane Brody, "The Secret to Good Health May Be a Walk in the Park," *New York Times*, December 3, 2018, https://www.nytimes.com/2018/12/03/well/move/the-secret-to-good-health-may-be-a-walk-in-the-park.html.

**217. claiming Scandinavian heritage:** David Nikel, "The Scandinavian American Story," Life in Norway, October 28, 2021, https://www.lifeinnorway.net/scandinavian-american.

**218. "nature-consonant lifestyles":** Nils Faarlund, "A Way Home," in *Wisdom in the Open Air: The Norwegian Roots of Deep Ecology*, ed. Peter Reed and David Rothenberg (Minneapolis: University of Minnesota Press, 1993), 164.

## ABOUT THE AUTHOR

**LINDA ÅKESON MCGURK** is a Swedish American journalist and author who believes life is better outside. Her first book, the parenting memoir *There's No Such Thing as Bad Weather: A Scandinavian Mom's Secrets for Raising Healthy, Resilient, and Confident Kids (from* Friluftsliv *to* Hygge), was published in 2017 to critical acclaim, receiving mentions in *The Wall Street Journal* as well as *The New York Times*. Since then, the book has become an Amazon bestseller and been translated into five languages. *The Open-Air Life: Discover the Nordic Art of Friluftsliv and Embrace Nature Every Day* is her second book. McGurk's writing about Scandinavian culture and the Nordic outdoor tradition friluftsliv has appeared in many national and international publications, including *Time*, *Parents*, *Green Child Magazine*, and others. She frequently shares her passion for outdoor living on TV shows, podcasts, and her own blog, *Rain or Shine Mamma*, to inspire people to get outside every day, regardless of the weather. When McGurk does not work, she is typically found sitting around a campfire or sleeping under a tarp in the pine forests of southern Sweden, where she lives with her family.